Price Waterhouse is a leading worldwide professional organization of tax practitioners, auditors, and management consultants. Operating from over 400 offices in more than 100 countries and territories, Price Waterhouse firms provide a variety of services to businesses, individuals, government entities, and nonprofit organizations.

The Price Waterhouse U.S. firm frequently consults with the Treasury Department and the Internal Revenue Service on tax issues. The firm also offers seminars and publishes a variety of periodicals and booklets on tax and personal financial planning subjects.

Through its more than 100 U.S. offices and its legislative monitoring service in Washington, D.C., Price Waterhouse advises businesses and individuals nationwide on the planning and compliance implications of the tax law.

THE PRICE WATERHOUSE

PERSONAL TAX ADVISER

1990-1991 EDITION

New York   London   Toronto   Sydney   Tokyo   Singapore

POCKET BOOKS, a division of Simon & Schuster, Inc. 1230 Avenue of the Americas, New York, N.Y. 10020.

Copyright © 1990 by Price Waterhouse and Donna S. Carpenter.

ISBN: 0-671-72879-2

First Pocket Books printing October, 1990

10 9 8 7 6 5 4 3 2 1

POCKET and colophon are registered trademarks of Simon & Schuster, Inc.

Printed in the U.S.A.

Contents

As We Went To Press . . .

Congress and the Administration were discussing various options to be included in a deficit reduction package. Although no one can say for certain what the final outcome will be, the chances of reaching an agreement were greatly increased after President Bush stated that tax revenue increases would be a necessary part of the deficit reduction package. Most of the ideas have been put forth as a way of raising additional revenue because of the substantial pressure to meet deficit reduction targets for 1991, although a few of them may provide for or extend certain tax breaks.

Since a number of these proposals could impact your tax position, we thought it would be helpful to summarize some of the major items.

- **Capital gains tax reduction.** At present, capital gains (long term) and ordinary income are taxed at the same rate. President Bush has been a proponent of lowering the capital gains tax rate for individuals to encourage capital investment. However, it appears that if such a tax reduction is implemented, it may be accompanied by an individual marginal tax rate increase.

☞ **CAUTION** At this time, neither the effective date of any reduction in the capital gains tax rate, nor the form such a reduction might take, is known. You should make sure that, if such a reduction in rates is passed and you attempt to take advantage of the reduction, your sale of a capital asset falls within the effective dates for a lower capital gains tax.

- **Stocks and bonds excise tax.** To raise revenue, an excise tax on the purchase or sale of stocks and bonds is being considered. This could lower the net proceeds received from the sale of securities or increase the cost to purchase such securities.

- **Other excise taxes.** To raise additional revenue, further excise taxes are being considered including a new broad based energy tax, an increase in alcohol and tobacco excise taxes, and an extension of the expiring 3% telephone excise tax. Any or all of these or other excise taxes may be included in a deficit reduction package.

- **Expiring tax provisions.** Certain tax provisions are currently set to expire in the near future. These include the deduction of 25% of health insurance premiums paid by self-employed persons and the exclusion from employee's income of certain tuition reimbursements made by employers. Due to the broad based support for these items, they may be further extended.

There are a great number of other options currently included in the deficit reduction discussions. Included in these are incentive savings plan proposals, limitations on state and local tax deductions and further limitations on interest expense deductions.

However, keep in mind that, if they are enacted into law, they may affect your tax strategy. As a result, you should consult with your tax advisor to determine how any of the proposals may affect you.

1

Why Tax Planning?

The best way—in fact, the only way—to be absolutely sure that you pay no more in taxes than you should is to devise and use effective tax strategies.

This book will help you plan strategies to use for the remainder of 1990 and throughout 1991. It's not a line-by-line guide to preparing your tax return. Instead, it will help you ensure that when preparation time does roll around, the number that winds up on the tax-due line of your Form 1040 is as small as it legally can be.

Before we get started, though, let's run through the tax law changes already enacted by Congress that will affect your 1990 and 1991 returns.

For starters, tax rates are slated to remain the same but the amount of your income subject to lower rates is going up, thanks to indexing or adjustments for inflation.

Say, for example, that you're married and file a joint return. You paid a tax of 15 percent on your income up to $30,950 in 1989. In 1990, Uncle Sam gives you a small break. He requires you to pay a 15 percent tax on your first $32,450 in income, instead of $30,950. (See Chapter 2 for the tax tables that apply to you.)

What else is changing?

- The standard deduction is going up, thanks to the magic of indexing. For 1990, it's $3,250 for a single person, $4,750 for a head of household, $5,450 for a married couple filing jointly, and $2,725 for a married person filing separately. (See Chapter 4.)

- The personal exemption amount you may claim on your tax return is also rising. It's $2,050 in 1990. (See Chapter 3.)

- The maximum pre-tax contribution you may make to a 401(k) plan is jumping to $7,979 from $7,627—again, thanks to indexing. (See Chapter 22.)

- Congress repealed the Medicare surtax, a supplemental premium of up to $800 paid by everyone eligible for Medicare.

Are more tax law changes in the offing?

As we mentioned earlier, no one can say for certain what Congress and the Administration will do, but as we go to press, our lawmakers are scrambling to find ways to raise new revenues to meet deficit reduction targets slated for 1991.

Congress is also considering several proposals for the restoration of preferential treatment for long-term capital gains (at least on a temporary basis), and this is one idea President Bush has endorsed. (In fact, it was one of his campaign promises.)

One possibility is to index capital gains for inflation similar to other tax provisions mentioned above. Another possibility is to cap the capital gains rate at 28 percent, but only if ordinary rates rise.

Now you know what tax law changes affect your 1990 and 1991 returns. But how do you go about trimming your personal tax liability?

For starters, most people won't benefit from the strategy of accelerating income, at least not in 1990. It's quite likely that the top federal marginal tax rate in 1991 will be about the same as in 1990—28 percent, except possibly for certain high-income taxpayers, who pay 33 percent. (See Chapter 2.)

Also, the time value of money, meaning the benefit you gain by keeping your money in your pocket longer, will help offset any increase in 1991 rates.

What about deferring income and accelerating deductions? Most people will still benefit from these traditional year-end tax planning strategies. (For more information on these strategies, see Chapter 2.) But "most people" doesn't include everyone.

Say that your 1990 taxable income is abnormally low. For you, the opposite tactic—accelerating income and deferring deductions—might work best depending on your anticipated top federal tax rate for 1990 and 1991. You should also be sure to consider your alternative minimum tax (AMT) situation. (See Chapter 20 for more on the AMT.)

For 1991, it's too early to tell whether accelerating income or deferring deductions will be beneficial. Once you know if and how much 1992 federal tax rates will rise, you can determine which is more valuable, the time value of money or the value of lower tax rates. Then you can choose the strategies that will benefit you most.

How about capital gains? The best tax strategy for many is to wait as late as possible in 1990 to make your decision to sell appreciated property in 1990 or 1991.

By that time, both rates may be more certain. You should also know that most of the capital gains proposals don't cover collectibles, such as art.

Keep in mind that when it comes to capital assets, the economic aspects of selling or holding should be your primary concern. If the economics make sense, then you should develop a tax strategy to enhance your gain. Now, on to Chapter 2.

2

How the Tax Rates Affect Your Bottom Line

Do you know how our two-rate system works? In this chapter, we'll help you understand our two-rate tax structure and its impact on your bottom line.

Before we start, though, a couple of definitions will be useful, because we use these terms frequently in this and other chapters.

Your *taxable income** is, logically enough, the amount of income on which you actually pay taxes. You calculate this amount by adding up your income from all sources and subtracting all of the deductions the tax laws allow you to claim.

As we'll see in the following chapters, allowable deductions include adjustments to income (a Keogh contribution, for example); itemized deductions or the standard deduction; and the deductions you claim for personal exemptions.

Your *marginal tax rate* is the rate of tax you pay on your last dollar of earnings. Take, for the sake of illustration, a purely imaginary tax system with two rates. Income up to $10,000 is taxed at 5 percent; income that tops $10,000 is taxed at 10 percent.

If you earned $12,000 in salary and pocketed a $1,000 bonus, your

---

*Terms that appear in bold italic are defined in the Glossary.

marginal tax rate on the bonus is 10 percent—that is, the rate on the last dollar you received.

You also use your marginal tax rate to determine the tax benefit of a deduction. If your marginal tax rate is 10 percent, a $1,000 deduction saves you $100 in income taxes.

Effective tax rate, on the other hand, is the average rate at which your income is taxed. Assume the same simple two-rate system and an income of $15,000.

The tax on your first $10,000 in income is $500 ($10,000 times 5 percent), and on income of more than $10,000, the tax is $500 ($5,000 times 10 percent).

So your total tax comes to $1,000 ($500 plus $500). Your top marginal tax rate is 10 percent, but your effective tax rate is only 6.7 percent ($1,000 divided by $15,000).

HOW IT WORKS

The law contains only two regular tax brackets, 15 percent and 28 percent, but a 5 percent surcharge applies to some higher levels of income. That means some of your income may be taxed at a 33 percent rate. The following tax rate schedules illustrate these rates.

1990 TAX RATE SCHEDULE

Taxable Income	Rate
SINGLE	
$ 0 to $19,450	15%
19,451 to 47,050	28
47,051 to 97,620	33
97,621 or more	28
HEAD OF HOUSEHOLD	
$ 0 to $26,050	15%
26,051 to 67,200	28
67,201 to 134,930	33
134,931 or more	28

Taxable Income	Rate
MARRIED FILING JOINTLY AND SURVIVING SPOUSE	
$ 0 to $32,450	15%
32,451 to 78,400	28
78,401 to 162,770	33
162,771 or more	28
MARRIED FILING SEPARATELY	
$ 0 to $16,225	15%
16,226 to 39,200	28
39,201 to 123,570	33
123,571 or more	28

The 15 percent rate applies to taxable income up to the following limits: $19,450 for single people; $26,050 for heads of households; $32,450 for married individuals filing joint returns and surviving spouses; and $16,225 for married individuals who file separate returns.

Income that tops these amounts is taxed at 28 percent. However, the income levels at which the higher rate takes effect will be adjusted annually for inflation. So the examples we're about to give may not be precisely accurate after this year. The principles involved, however, remain the same. Let's see how the two-rate tax system works.

Say you're married, file a joint return, and your 1990 taxable income comes to $50,000. Your federal income taxes for the year add up to $9,782.

Here's how we arrived at that figure. Your first $32,450 in income is taxed at 15 percent. That comes to $4,868. The remaining $17,550 of your income falls in the 28 percent bracket, generating a tax of $4,914. The total ($4,868 plus $4,914) comes to $9,782.

What could be simpler? For taxpayers with modest incomes, the two-rate system is simple. It isn't so simple, though, when your taxable income rises beyond certain levels: $47,050 for single filers; $67,200 for heads of households; $78,400 for married joint filers and surviving spouses; and $39,200 for married individuals filing separately.

Beyond these points the tax law begins to phase out the benefit of the lower 15 percent bracket until, eventually, all income is subject to a flat 28 percent tax rate. In effect, beyond certain income levels your effective tax rate and your marginal tax rate become the same: 28 percent.

The sneaky device that makes this flattening out happen is called a phase-out *surtax*. How does it work? The law, as we noted earlier, imposes an additional 5 percent tax on taxable income that falls within certain ranges.

On this income, you pay a 33 percent marginal tax rate—the normal 28 percent rate plus the 5 percent phase-out surtax. These ranges of taxable income vary with inflation adjustments made in 1990 and later. In 1990 they run from:

- $47,051 to $97,620 for single individuals

- $67,201 to $134,930 for heads of household

- $78,401 to $162,770 for married individuals filing joint returns and surviving spouses

- $39,201 to $123,570 for married individuals filing separate returns.

Congress didn't want married couples who file separate returns to enjoy a tax break not available to married couples who file joint returns.

So if you're married and file separate returns, the benefit of the 15 percent tax rate is subject to the phase-out surtax not once but twice.

That means the maximum effective tax rate paid by a married person filing separately reaches 29.7 percent when his or her income adds up to $123,570. Why 29.7 percent? That's because the 33 percent rate remains in effect for the equivalent of two 15 percent tax brackets. (For income in excess of $123,570 the marginal tax rate is 28 percent, which will reduce the effective tax rate to below 29.7 percent as taxable income increases. However, an actual effective tax rate of 28 percent won't be achieved.)

Now, let's run through a simple example that shows you how a two-rate system turns into a flat tax. Suppose that in 1990 you and your spouse report taxable income of $162,770. The first $32,450 is subject to tax at 15 percent. The tax comes to $4,868.

Between $32,450 and $78,400, your income is taxed at the 28 percent rate. The tax comes to $12,866 ($78,400 minus $32,450 times 28 percent).

Between $78,400 and $162,770, your tax rate is 33 percent—28 percent plus the 5 percent surtax. The tax comes to $27,842 ($162,770 minus $78,400 times 33 percent).

So your total tax is $45,576, and look what has happened to your effective tax rate. Divide $45,576 by $162,770 (taxable income), and you get 28 percent. The surtax effectively wipes out the lower 15 percent bracket for you and other higher-income taxpayers.

☞ CAUTION   The surtax comes into play again when you claim personal exemptions for yourself and your dependents. We'll show you how in Chapter 3.

QUESTIONS AND ANSWERS

QUESTION: *In the past, I've heard my accountant say that the best tax strategy is to defer income and accelerate deductions. Does this advice apply to 1990?*

In any year, making the decision to defer income and accelerate deductions (we'll get to deductions in Chapter 4) involves some fortune-telling.

You have to project your income and deductions for 1990 and 1991 and decide whether you'll save tax dollars by deferring income or accelerating deductions.

In short, you have to run the numbers as best you can.

But you should be aware that 1990 is a special year, from a tax point of view anyway. Rates are as low as they've been in many years.

So it's more important than ever to estimate your income and deductions for both 1990 and 1991. And you probably will want to enlist your tax adviser to help you early on in the process. Keep in mind, too, that most tax experts think that 1990's low rates won't last forever.

It may make better sense for you, then, to reverse the traditional wisdom by accelerating income into 1990 and deferring deductions until 1991.

That way you'll take maximum advantage of 1990's low rates. You should know, though, that taking advantage of the lower rates also requires you to pay your tax sooner. The best strategy for you depends on your personal financial circumstances.

Some items you and your accountant should pay close attention to are the impact of the alternative minimum tax; passive losses and passive income; the phase-out surtax; and deductions (miscellaneous deductions, for example) that are subject to a so-called threshold amount.

We'll discuss all of these tax issues in the chapters that follow and we'll present some savvy strategies for dealing with them.

QUESTION: *I've run the numbers and think it makes sense for me to postpone receiving some of my income until 1991. Do you have any ideas for doing so?*

First, a word of caution: Whatever good reason you may have to defer income, you should keep in mind these other considerations.

One key to whether it makes sense for you to postpone income is, can you afford to go without a portion of your earnings? And how long can you do without this money?

Another key for employees is the interest rate your company pays you on your deferred money. For starters, find out if your company will pay you any interest on your deferred earnings. If it does, see if it will pay a competitive interest rate.

Also, weigh the risks. When you defer compensation, you become a creditor of your company. And if it goes belly up, you stand to lose the amount owed you.

Now here are some ways you can defer income. If you're self-employed and keep your books on the cash basis, you can easily defer income by postponing the billing of clients or customers until near the end of the year. That way, you receive payment after December 31.

QUESTION: *What other types of transactions give you some leeway when it comes to deferring or accelerating income?*

Try to time the following transactions to best suit your tax needs, keeping in mind, of course, relevant nontax considerations:

- Selling stock that may generate gains or losses (see Chapter 14 for more information)

- Exercising taxable stock options (see Chapter 21)

- Collecting pension and profit sharing payouts (see Chapter 23)

- Paying off bills for itemized deductions—a big medical bill, for example (see Chapter 7)

- Timing the purchase and renewals of certificates of deposit and Treasury bills with maturities of one year or less.

If you own a business, you should decide whether to elect the special $10,000 write-off for equipment purchases in 1990. And you should choose the most favorable depreciation method for your equipment purchases. (See Chapter 18 for the lowdown on depreciation.)

QUESTION: *I understand that Congress adopted legislation in 1988 to levy a Medicare surtax on older Americans and others who are eligible for Medicare. I think I may be subject to the surtax. Would you provide the details, please?*

Good news: Congress repealed the Medicare surtax.

3

Making the Most of Your Personal Exemptions

Rarely does anyone give you credit for just making it through another year, but that's what Congress does with the *personal exemption*. Every taxpayer gets to deduct $2,050 (or more in 1991 and beyond, depending on the inflation rate) from his or her taxable income.

And you get to deduct this amount just for being alive. You can also claim a personal exemption for your spouse, if you file a joint return, as well as for each *dependent* you claim. But there are rules and qualifications, of course.

In this chapter, we'll run through them and show you how to make the best use of the personal exemptions that are due you.

QUALIFYING AS A DEPENDENT

Uncle Sam says that you may claim a personal exemption for yourself as long as you're not listed as a dependent on someone else's return. If you're married and file jointly, you're entitled to take two exemptions, one for yourself and one for your spouse.

You may also claim a personal exemption for each of your dependents. But to qualify as a dependent, a person must meet five tests.

He or she must

- Receive more than half of his or her support from you

- Live full-time in your household or be a relative

- Receive less than $2,050 a year in gross income unless he or she is your child younger than age 19 or a full-time student who hasn't attained 24 years of age

- Be a U.S. citizen or resident of Canada or Mexico

- Not file a joint return with someone else

Let's run through the particulars of each of these tests.

Support Test

If you provide more than half of a person's total support during the tax year, you meet this test. Here's how you calculate how much support you provide.

First, you add up the amount you contribute toward the support of your prospective dependent. Then you compare this sum to the entire amount of support this person receives from other sources. This figure includes the individual's own funds if he or she uses them for support.

The figure will also include any tax-exempt income—such as Social Security or interest on tax-exempt municipal bonds—that the individual receives.

You may add into the total the amounts you spend for necessities—that is, food, lodging, clothing, education, medical and dental care, recreation, and transportation.

But you may not include in your contribution any part of the support that your dependent pays with his or her own wages, even if you're the one forking over the wages.

Say, for example, that you pay your mother $100 a week to stuff envelopes. Under the law, you may not claim the amount you pay her in wages as support payments.

Another point: Money that a person receives isn't support unless the funds are actually spent on items Uncle Sam classifies as support.

What does this rule mean to you? Say, for example, that your father receives $2,400 in Social Security benefits and $300 in interest on his savings. He pays $2,000 for lodging, $400 for recreation, and $300 for life insurance premiums.

Even though your father received a total of $2,700, he spent, in Uncle Sam's eyes, only $2,400 for his own support. The reason?

Life insurance premiums aren't considered a support item. So, assuming that your father receives no support from any other sources, you provided more than half your father's support if you spent more than $2,400 to support him.

Here's one other wrinkle to consider: It matters to the IRS whether you're supporting one parent or two. Why? Assume that both of your parents spent a total of $14,000 on their own support and that you contributed $7,500. That's more than half, isn't it? Not the way the IRS counts.

The tax agency would say that you gave each parent $3,750. That amount plus half of $14,000 comes to $10,750, and this, the IRS says, is the amount of each parent's individual support. Your contribution of $3,750 falls short of being half.

But if you were contributing all of your support to just one parent, and you could back that claim up with, say, canceled checks, then your $7,500 would be more than half of that parent's total support. And he or she could qualify as your dependent.

Member of Household or Relationship Test

The law defines a dependent as either a relative or someone who lives with you in your principal residence on a full-time basis. So a person who's related to you passes this test even if he or she isn't a member of your household.

But who qualifies as a relative?

Your natural or legally adopted children or stepchildren qualify. And so do your brothers, sisters, half brothers, half sisters, stepbrothers, stepsisters, parents, grandparents, stepfathers, stepmothers, uncles, aunts, nieces, and nephews—but not your cousins.

In the eyes of the IRS your father-in-law, mother-in-law, brother-in-law, and sister-in-law are relatives, too. And their status as relatives doesn't change with death or divorce.

A stillborn child doesn't qualify as a dependent for the year, but a baby who lives even a short time does. On the other hand, someone who's simply a friend may qualify as a dependent if he or she meets all of the other qualifying tests.

As we've seen, a person who isn't related to you for tax purposes qualifies as a dependent only if he or she lives with you at your principal residence. So if you allow a cousin to live in, say, a beach house on which you pay the rent, he or she doesn't qualify as a dependent.

Another important rule: A nonrelative who's temporarily absent from your home—at school, for example—may still meet the member of household test. The absence is considered temporary even if your dependent is in a nursing home for an indefinite period.

Gross Income Test

First, a word about how Uncle Sam defines gross income for this test. It's income—in the form of money, property, and services—that's not exempt from tax. So tax-exempt income, such as income from tax-exempt municipal bonds and some Social Security payments, isn't included in the definition. It *does*, however, count as income in the support tests mentioned above.

The law says that the person you're claiming as a dependent must not report gross income that equals or exceeds the amount of the personal exemption.

But there are exceptions to this rule. If the person is your child and under age 19 or a full-time student under the age of 24, the test doesn't apply.

To meet the student exemption, your dependent must be enrolled for at least five months of the year in an institution in which education is the primary purpose.

For example, a hospital providing programs for interns and residents doesn't qualify. Those programs fall into the category of on-the-job training or other employee training programs. The law doesn't consider them to be qualifying educational programs. However, if your dependent is studying in a part of the hospital where the main purpose is teaching—a student nursing program, for example—he or she will qualify.

Why the gross income exception for full-time students? It's Uncle Sam's way of encouraging young scholars to work their way through school without jeopardizing the parent's dependency deduction. But keep in mind that you still must continue to provide over half of the student's support to collect your deduction.

Another point you should keep in mind: The exception for children doesn't extend to a son-in-law or daughter-in-law.

Here's an example of how the gross income test works.

Say your father retired five years ago, and he now receives more than half of his support from you. Your father is a partner in a real estate partnership, and his share of its gross rental income is $2,100 a year before expenses. After expenses, his share of net rental income comes to $200.

May you claim your father as a dependent? The answer is no. His share of the partnership's gross rental income exceeds the amount of the personal exemption.

Citizenship Test

This test requires that a dependent be a U.S. citizen, resident, or national, or a resident of Canada or Mexico for some part of the tax year.

Let's say you're a U.S. citizen married to a French citizen. The two of you and your son make your home in the United States, and you file a joint return.

You may claim your child as a dependent regardless of your citizenship or your spouse's citizenship because he's a U.S. resident.

TIP A special rule applies to adopted children of U.S. taxpayers who live abroad. In such cases you may claim the child as a dependent, even if he or she isn't a U.S. citizen or resident, as long as the child lives with you.

Joint Return Test

Even if the other tests are met, you're not allowed to claim an exemption for a dependent if he or she files a joint return. Here's an example.

Say you supported your daughter for the entire year while her husband served in the armed forces. The couple files a joint return. You may not claim a dependency exemption for her because she files a joint return with her husband. Uncle Sam does carve out an exception to this rule.

You may claim an exemption for a dependent if neither the dependent nor the dependent's spouse is *required* to file a return, but they file a joint return to claim a refund.

PECULIAR CIRCUMSTANCES

Occasionally, especially in the case of children supporting aging parents or other relatives, no one provides more than half of the support of a person.

Instead, two or more people, each of whom would be entitled to take the exemption if it weren't for the support test, together provide more than half of the dependent's support.

In these cases of multiple support, the law says, you may agree that any one of you—but only one—who individually provides more than 10 percent of the person's support may claim an exemption for that person. You may not split the personal exemption among you.

Each of the others must sign a written statement (Form 2120, "Multiple Support Declaration") agreeing not to claim the exemption for that year. The statements must be filed with the income tax return of the person who claims the exemption.

Here's an example.

Say you, your sister, and two brothers support your mother. You provide 45 percent of her support; your sister, 35 percent; and your two brothers, 10 percent each.

Either you or your sister may claim an exemption for your mother. The other must sign a Form 2120 or a written statement agreeing not to claim an exemption for her.

Because neither of your brothers provides more than 10 percent of your mother's support, neither of them may claim the exemption. And they don't have to sign a Form 2120 or the statement.

You should consider taking advantage of this planning opportunity by allowing the person who would benefit most from the personal exemption to claim it, even if that person doesn't contribute the most support.

FAMILY MATTERS

Uncle Sam imposes special rules for a child of separated or divorced parents or parents who've lived apart from each other for the last six months of the year.

In the case of separated parents, the parent who has custody of the child for the greater part of the year may claim the child as a dependent. And it doesn't matter whether that parent actually provided any support, as long as both parents together provide at least half of the child's support and the child is in the custody of one or both parents for more than half of the year.

In the case of divorced parents, custody is usually determined either by the terms of your most recent divorce decree or separate maintenance agreement or a later custody decree.

What happens if neither a decree nor an agreement establishes custody? Then the law considers the parent who has physical custody of the child for the greater part of the year to have custody.

This rule also applies if the validity of a decree or agreement that awards custody is uncertain because of legal proceedings that may still be pending on the last day of the calendar year.

PERSONAL CONSIDERATIONS

If your taxable income is high, you begin to lose the benefits of any personal exemptions. In 1990, as your income rises beyond designated levels, you get hit with an extra 5 percent tax. And this tax continues to apply until all of the tax savings of the personal exemption are wiped out.

Here are the triggering levels of taxable income for this *surtax*. (Uncle Sam adjusts these income levels annually for inflation.)

- $162,770 for married individuals filing joint returns and surviving spouses

- $134,930 for heads of households

- $97,620 for single individuals

- $123,570 for married individuals filing separate returns

The surtax starts at the trigger point and stays with you until it recaptures all of the tax saving you gained by claiming one or more personal deductions.

Up to what amount must you pay it?

The range of income over which the personal exemption surtax applies depends on how many personal exemptions you claim. It's easy to calculate.

One personal exemption in 1990 reduces your taxable income by $2,050. That's a tax saving of $574, or 28 percent (the maximum tax rate) times $2,050.

To recover the full $574 with a 5 percent surtax, the IRS must apply that tax to $11,480 of income ($11,480 times 5 percent equals $574).

So if you claim one personal exemption, you pay the surtax on the first $11,480 you earn over your trigger point. If you claim two personal exemptions, you pay the tax on the first $22,960 (two increments of $11,480) in income over the trigger point, and so on. Still confused? Let's look at an example.

Say you're married with two children. You file jointly and claim four personal exemptions. You pay this 5 percent surtax on taxable income between $162,770 (the trigger point for joint returns) and $208,690 ($162,770 plus 4 times $11,480). The surtax equals $2,296 (5 percent times $45,920).

TIP You say your income is near the top of the surtax range? Here's a strategy for your family to consider: Fail to meet the dependency tests for a child who's a full-time student and between the ages of 18 and 24. That way, the child may claim an exemption for himself or herself and enjoy the benefit of a personal exemption even though you can't.

CAUTION You should know that married couples are penalized if they file separate returns. You're charged a surtax on your personal exemption plus a surtax on an exemption for your spouse. This surtax is imposed even though you didn't claim an exemption for your spouse. This rule applies to both spouses.

Another important point: Blind and elderly taxpayers no longer get the extra personal exemptions that they used to claim. But they do get other benefits, such as a larger standard deduction. (For more information on the standard deduction, see Chapter 4.)

QUESTIONS AND ANSWERS

QUESTION: *My child was born in November of this year. May we claim him as a dependent for part of the year?*

You're in luck.

You may claim a full dependency exemption for your child in the year he or she is born. And this rule holds true even if your child's birthday is December 31.

QUESTION: *I claim my mother as a dependent. She passed away in early 1990. Am I still entitled to a personal exemption?*

You are. The IRS says that a person who died during the year but was a dependent until death meets the test, even if that person passed away on January 1.

4

Adding Up Your Deductions

Deductions, for many taxpayers, are a significant tax-saving device, and no one understands that better than Uncle Sam. Nearly every taxpayer has *some* deductible expenses.

The law recognizes this fact by giving you the option of claiming a **standard deduction** without requiring you to list the specifics. Should you claim the standard deduction? Or should you *itemize*? We show you how to make that decision.

If you decide not to take the standard deduction and itemize your write-offs instead—that is, reduce your taxable income by claiming specific deductible expenses—you want to make sure that you can back up your claims. In the event of an audit, this is one part of your tax form that the IRS will scrutinize carefully. And the auditor will ask for proof.

Don't be alarmed, however. This cautionary note isn't meant to discourage anyone from claiming legitimate deductions. On the contrary, we encourage you to deduct every dollar you legally can from your taxable income. In this chapter, we'll show you which expenses qualify for a write-off. We'll also suggest several ways you can maximize the tax-saving value of your deductible expenses.

YOUR STANDARD DEDUCTION

As we noted, when it comes time to file your tax return, Uncle Sam gives you two options. You may claim the standard deduction, or you may itemize your deductions.

Here, arranged by filing status, are the latest standard deductions. The law requires the IRS to adjust these figures each year to reflect inflation.

YOUR STANDARD DEDUCTION

Filing Status	1990
Married, filing jointly	$5,450
Surviving spouse	5,450
Married, filing separately	2,725
Head of household	4,750
Single	3,250

It's your situation on the last day of the tax year that determines your filing status, with this large exception: If your spouse died during the year, you're considered to have been married for the entire tax year, not just part of it.

What does this rule mean to you? If you would have qualified to file a joint return if your spouse had lived, you may still do so for the year he or she died. And, the law says, you may use the standard deduction and rate tables for joint returns for the next two years as well.

That means you may file a joint return for the year your spouse died, plus the equivalent of a joint return for two additional years. You may not, however, claim an exemption for your spouse in the years following his or her death.

The only catch, when it comes to filing as a surviving spouse, is that you must meet certain conditions, as follows: You were eligible to file a joint return in the year your spouse died; you don't remarry; you have a child, stepchild, adopted child, or foster child who qualifies as a dependent; and you paid more than half of the cost of maintaining a home for the child.

By "single" the IRS means that you're unmarried or separated from your spouse either by divorce or by a court-approved separate maintenance decree and that you don't qualify as a head of household. If you and your spouse are living apart but not legally separated, or if your divorce decree isn't yet final, the two of you may file jointly.

You may file a tax return jointly with your common-law spouse. The federal tax law recognizes common-law marriages as long as the state you live in, or the state in which the common-law marriage began, also recognizes its legality.

You qualify as "head of household" if at the end of the year you're unmarried and pay more than half of the cost of keeping a home for yourself and at least one dependent.

TIP Here's a break for people who are 65 or older. If you're single, the law allows you to add $800 to your standard deduction. If you're married, the law says you may add $650 for each spouse who's aged 65 or older.

You may also claim these same amounts if you're blind. Uncle Sam classifies you as blind if your vision is 20/200 or worse in the better of your two eyes while you're wearing glasses or contact lenses, or your field of vision is no more than 20 degrees.

Say you're single and aged 65 or older. Your standard deduction for 1990 adds up to $4,050; that is, you claim the 1990 standard deduction of $3,250, and you add $800 to that amount.

Now let's assume you're married and file a joint return.

You add $650 to your 1990 standard deduction, $5,450, if you or your spouse is 65 or older. If you're both in the 65-or-older category, you add $1,300.

TIP You may claim *all* of the deductions to which you're entitled, not just the largest one for which you qualify.

In other words, a single taxpayer who's both blind and 65 or older may add $1,600 to the standard deduction. A married taxpayer may add $1,300 ($2,600 if you and your spouse are both blind, 65 or older, and file a joint return).

CAUTION Say you claim your father as a dependent, and he's both blind and age 65 or older. May you claim a deduction for his blindness and advanced age?

Unfortunately, the rules say that you may not claim a deduction for the blindness or old age of a dependent. This break is available only to people who file their own 1040s.

However, your father may claim his own standard deduction for blindness and old age on his own return, even if you claim him as a dependent.

☞ CAUTION   Children and other dependents who file their own returns aren't always entitled to claim a full standard deduction. (For the details, see Chapter 24.)

FINE LINE

Before we go further, two key definitions: "above the line" and "below the line." The "line" refers to your adjusted gross income (AGI).

Uncle Sam used to allow you to deduct "above the line"—that is, as part of your AGI calculation—such items as moving expenses and employee business expenses.

Now, you must subtract these items "below the line." That is, they're itemized deductions that no longer figure in your AGI calculation.

What difference does this change make?

Consider this example. Say that the year is 1985, and your only income is your salary, a hefty $100,000. From this amount, you subtracted moving expenses of $2,000.

The result—$98,000—was your AGI.

Once you calculated your AGI, you then deducted your itemized expenses or claimed the standard deduction, whichever was greater.

Now, say the year is 1990. Once again your only income is your salary of $100,000, and you report moving expenses of $2,000. This time, though, you may not subtract your moving expenses above the line—that is, to arrive at your AGI.

You must add your moving expenses to all of your other itemized deductions—mortgage interest, property taxes, and so on—below the line. If these itemized write-offs top the standard deduction, you're entitled to itemize. If not, you take the standard deduction.

The bottom line? If you claim deductions above the line, you're guaranteed to receive a benefit. If you claim deductions below the line, you benefit only if you itemize.

STANDARD PROCEDURE

To itemize or not?

The answer: If you may itemize, do so. You always come out ahead. How do you know if you may itemize? You add up your deductible expenses to see whether they're more or less than the standard deduction. If they're more, itemize; if not, take the standard deduction.

In the chapters that follow, we'll take a look at those items that are deductible from your adjusted gross income. We'll also examine itemized deductions that don't kick in until they exceed a percentage of your adjusted gross income.

QUESTIONS AND ANSWERS

QUESTION: *I can't itemize this year because my deductible expenses are less than the standard deduction. Does that mean I totally lose the benefit of these deductions?*

You will, unless you take steps now.

Say you've run your numbers for 1990, and you know you can't itemize. What should you do? Put off paying some deductible expenses until 1991. That way, you increase the amount of your deductions for 1991, and, with luck, you can write off the costs in that year.

In short, you should always try to bunch your deductions in one year, by either accelerating or deferring payments. In doing so, you may exceed the standard deduction—and itemize—at least every other year.

For instance, say you normally receive your bill for real estate taxes on December 20. And you paid last year's bill when it was due: January 15, 1990.

By accelerating your payment of the current bill to December 31, you pay two years' worth of property taxes in one year and increase your deductions for that year.

QUESTION: *I'm trying to boost my deductions for the year. I* *know I'm going to owe my dentist more than $5,000 for the recon-struction work he will be doing. Can I pay him now, before he works on my mouth, and increase my medical expense deduction this year?*

Sorry, but Uncle Sam won't allow you to deduct payments for services not yet rendered. But say the dentist has already begun the reconstruction work, and you've agreed to pay him a flat fee when he's done. In this case, you may claim the deduction this year.

QUESTION: *What about my mortgage interest payments and state income taxes? May I prepay and deduct these amounts?*

The IRS says you may not write off mortgage interest payments in advance. (See Chapter 5 for more information on interest deductions).

But you may prepay—and deduct—your state income taxes, as long as your payments are based on a reasonable estimate of your final tax bill at the time you make your payment. (For more information on prepaying state and local income taxes, see Chapter 8.)

5

Those Late, Great Interest Deductions

Let's face it. Interest deductions aren't what they used to be. In the old days, you could write off all of the interest you paid on personal loans and credit cards.

But no more. This interest is only 10 percent deductible in 1990. In 1991 this write-off disappears entirely.

The tax laws cover many types of interest, not just interest on consumer debt. But there are only five kinds most of us need to worry about: *mortgage interest*, *business interest*, *personal interest*, *investment interest*, and *passive activity interest*.

Mortgage interest is, as the name suggests, the interest you pay on a loan that is secured by your residence.

Business interest is interest on money you borrow to pay salaries or other operational costs of your business or to purchase assets for it. You may write off business interest only if you are involved with operations on a regular, continuous, and substantial basis.

Uncle Sam defines personal interest as interest on loans you take out to buy personal items—an automobile, say, or furniture for your house.

And he says that investment interest is interest you pay on a loan you have taken out to make an investment, such as buying stock.

Finally, Uncle Sam defines passive activity interest as interest on money borrowed to invest in a business that you don't operate or manage.

In this chapter, we tell you what you need to know about the tax rules governing each of these kinds of interest.

Understanding these rules isn't a job for accountants and lawyers alone. If you learn these rules, complicated as they are, you can alter your borrowing habits to make the most of the interest deductions available to you.

MORTGAGE INTEREST

Uncle Sam treats home ownership favorably.

The reason is the long-standing philosophy of the federal government that says people who buy homes deserve some sort of tax benefit.

One tax break homeowners receive is the right to deduct all or a portion of their mortgage interest on their tax returns. The interest on any *mortgage* loan signed on or before October 13, 1987, is fully deductible on your return.

And this rule holds true regardless of whether the debt is a first or *second mortgage,* a *home-equity loan,* or refinanced mortgage. But special rules apply to mortgage loans entered into after that date and to people who own three or more homes.

We'll look at those rules one at a time.

You purchased a new home, refinanced an existing mortgage, or incurred additional mortgage debt after October 13, 1987. If you fall into this category, Uncle Sam divides your deductible mortgage debt into two categories: *acquisition debt* and *home-equity debt.*

How does he define these two terms?

Acquisition debt is a loan that's secured by your primary or second home and is incurred when you buy, build, or substantially improve your home. Acquisition debt is limited to $1 million ($500,000 if you're married and file separate returns).

What if you refinance an existing mortgage?

In that case acquisition debt includes only the debt that's outstanding at the time of the refinancing and only up to the ceiling of $1 million.

Home-equity debt is a loan that's also secured by your primary or second home. But in contrast to acquisition debt, you don't use the proceeds to buy, build, or substantially improve your primary or secondary residence. The maximum amount of home equity debt you may have is limited to $100,000 ($50,000 if you're married and file separate returns), depending upon the fair market value of your home and the amount of acquisition debt you have outstanding.

Here's something else you should know: A mortgage loan can include both acquisition debt and home-equity debt. How?

Suppose you refinance your mortgage, using part of the proceeds to pay off your original mortgage and the rest to pay off some personal debts—a car loan, for example.

The interest on a home-equity loan or on the home-equity portion of a mortgage loan is fully deductible as long as the debt doesn't exceed the lesser of the following:

- The *fair market value* of your home minus the total acquisition debt or

- $100,000 ($50,000 if you're married and file separate returns).

What if you own two homes? It makes no difference. The cap on your home-equity debt, whether on one or two residences, still may not exceed a total of $100,000.

TIP The best idea—for tax purposes, at least—is to lock in the largest possible amount of acquisition debt when you purchase or substantially improve your home. That way, if you need more money later on, you won't eat away at your $100,000 home-equity debt ceiling.

☞ **CAUTION** In the case of home-equity loans a caveat applies. Whether you're borrowing to buy a boat or a bond, putting your home up as collateral is serious business. You should think through all of the pros and cons before making that decision.

Your mortgage debts total more than $1 million. As noted earlier, Uncle Sam says that you may deduct mortgage interest only on acquisition debt of up to $1 million—$500,000 if you are married and file separate returns.

But he provides a break to taxpayers who incurred their mortgage debt before October 14, 1987. This debt isn't subject to the $1-million ceiling. But—and here is the kicker—any new debt they assume over $1 million is automatically home-equity debt.

Say your acquisition debt tops $1 million, and you took out your mortgage loan before October 14, 1987. Say, too, you borrow money after that date—to improve your kitchen, for instance. This new debt is home-equity debt, not acquisition debt.

The reason? Your acquisition debt already tops $1 million.

☞ **CAUTION** Here's another point homeowners should consider. Even if you may write off all of the interest on a refinanced mortgage loan for regular tax purposes, you may not be able to do so when you compute your alternative minimum tax (AMT).

The AMT is a flat tax of 21 percent. Who pays it? Taxpayers whose legitimate deductions reduce the regular tax they owe substantially below the amount their incomes suggest they ought to be paying. (Chapter 20 explains the AMT rules in detail.)

Here's an example to illustrate how you would compute the deductibility of a refinanced mortgage for AMT purposes. Say that your house costs $80,000. The outstanding balance on your old mortgage is $70,000. Now you refinance, and the bank lends you $125,000.

What's the maximum amount of interest on this new loan that you may write off when computing your AMT? You subtract your old mortgage balance—$70,000—from the amount of the new loan—$125,000. The result is $55,000. And the interest on this amount isn't deductible for AMT purposes.

An easy way to calculate how much interest you may deduct is to divide your old mortgage balance ($70,000) by the amount of your new loan ($125,000). That's the amount (56 percent) of the interest on your refinanced mortgage loan that you may write off when you figure your AMT.

Under the AMT rules you may also deduct interest on amounts you borrow to substantially improve your home, just as you take a regular tax deduction for mortgage interest. The big difference is that home-equity debt isn't deductible for AMT purposes.

You own three or more homes. Uncle Sam classifies the mortgage interest on your third (or more) home(s) based on how you use the properties and the loan proceeds.

Say, for example, that you use your third house—a ski chalet in the Colorado mountains—solely as a weekend retreat for you and your family.

Since you use the chalet for personal purposes only, interest on the loan you take out to purchase the property is treated for tax purposes as personal interest. That is, it's 10 percent deductible in 1990 and not deductible at all in 1991 and beyond.

Here is another example. Say you borrow money on your chalet and use it to purchase stock in a high-technology company. The rules allow you to write off the interest on such a loan but only according to how you spent the money you received.

In this case, you deduct the interest not as mortgage or personal interest but as investment interest, because that's how you used the cash.

For more information on mortgage interest, ask the IRS to send you a free copy of Publication 936, "Limits on Home Mortgage Interest Deduction."

BUSINESS INTEREST

The rules governing business interest are simple. Whether you own Consolidated Worldwide Corp. or Wilbur's Window Washing, the interest you pay on loans you take out to operate your business or buy assets for it is completely deductible.

PERSONAL INTEREST

Before Congress adopted the 1986 Tax Reform Act, interest you paid on personal loans—the money you borrowed to take a vacation, say, or the interest you paid on your charge cards—was fully deductible. After 1990, the law says, personal interest will not be deductible at all.

For the interim, Congress enacted a gradual phase-out period. In 1990 only 10 percent of your personal interest expense is deductible. As you can see, you receive little or no benefit from personal interest deductions now and in the years ahead.

So, you ask, what are your options?

TIP Actually, you have four.

First, you can go on borrowing as in the past, knowing that you are gaining no tax benefit from the interest you pay. Or you might reduce your borrowing by delaying purchases, for example, until you accumulate all or even some of the cash required.

A third alternative is to convert personal interest into another category—mortgage interest, for instance—that's still deductible.

What types of personal interest might you convert to deductible interest? The answer is any interest that you pay on personal loans for a car, a boat, or even a vacation.

Many people, in fact, are using their homes to finance some of their borrowing. You can too, but you should exercise caution if you go this route.

The fourth way to minimize your nondeductible interest is, in the case of cars, by *leasing*. For some people the savings can be substantial. The only way to know if you should lease or buy is to run the numbers yourself. In either case you will make a monthly payment.

Although the payments required to purchase a car will be higher than lease payments, eventually you'll own the car you buy, and the payments will stop. If you lease, on the other hand, the payments continue as long as you have the car.

Is the car worth the extra money you must shell out? That's a question you must answer for yourself. And as you perform your calculations, keep these points in mind.

There are many different types of leases; some even require you to put down money up front. Always read the lease carefully before you sign on the dotted line.

TIP A key variable in determining whether to buy or lease is whether you use the car for employee business purposes. The interest on a car you buy to use for employee business purposes is considered personal interest, thus only 10% is deductible in 1990.

But when you lease a car, you may deduct the portion of the lease payment attributable to employee business use. (One word of caution, though: You may not get the full benefit of your deduction, depending on the value of your car. We discuss these rules in Chapter 13.)

Our advice is to compare the total after-tax costs of leasing and buying *before* you go the leasing route. It's the only way to know for sure if leasing is right for you.

INVESTMENT INTEREST

Investment interest is the interest you pay on your *stock margin account* or on any other loan you take out to purchase an investment. Different rules apply to interest on so-called *passive activities*, a subject we get to shortly.

As a general rule, you may deduct investment interest only up to the amount of your investment income. If you earn $5,000 from various investments and pay your broker $1,000 interest on a margin account, you may deduct the entire $1,000.

But if your investment earnings had totaled a mere $50, that's also the maximum amount of investment interest you could deduct.

On the other hand, what you may *not* deduct in one year you may carry forward into future years. In our previous example you had $950 in unclaimed investment interest.

The law allows you to carry that amount forward indefinitely until you generate enough investment income to write it off.

☞ **CAUTION** In one recent case, the Tax Court ruled that a taxpayer couldn't carry forward any more in investment interest than his taxable income for the year.

What does this rule mean to you?

Say, for example, that your taxable income from 1991 adds up to $10,000. And your investment interest comes to $15,000, and you aren't able to deduct any of it.

Under the rules, you may carry forward only $10,000 of investment interest to future years. You lose the right to write off $5,000 of your investment interest.

And keep in mind that investment income includes both periodic earnings from your investments—stock dividends, for example, and your gain from the sale of those investments.

The specific rules governing investment interest are just a bit more complicated, at least for 1990.

First, you may recall that before 1986 you could write off from your regular income investment interest that was as much as $10,000 more than your investment income for the year. This $10,000 allowance is phased out through 1990 at the same rates as personal interest.

In 1990, you may deduct only 10 percent of excess interest up to $10,000. That means that the maximum amount of interest that you may deduct under this rule is $1,000—$10,000 times 10 percent.

Suppose that your investment interest in 1990 adds up to $4,000, but your investment income comes to just $1,000. That means that you may write off only $1,300—$1,000 plus 10 percent of the balance, or $300 (which is $3,000 times 10 percent).

After 1990 the investment interest you may deduct is limited to the investment income you earn.

Another wrinkle: Any passive losses you claim in 1990 under the phase-out rules—10 percent in 1990—reduce the investment income against which you may deduct investment interest. (We cover passive investment losses in Chapter 19.)

TIP As with personal interest, you may convert investment interest to deductible home-equity interest by borrowing against your first or second home. Doing so will make the interest totally deductible—as long as your borrowings do not top $100,000.

Again, consider all the pros and cons before using your home as collateral for an investment loan.

PASSIVE ACTIVITY INTEREST

In 1986 Congress created a new category of interest expense: interest from passive activities. We'll get to the definition of this term in a minute. First, though, you should know that the tax code treats this interest much like investment interest.

For instance, just as you may deduct investment interest only against investment income, you may write off **passive activity** interest only against passive activity income. If you report no passive activity income, you claim no deduction.

Also, like investment interest, you may carry passive activity interest expense forward indefinitely. That is, you may use the interest you carry forward—the interest you are unable to claim—to offset passive income in future years.

But there's one difference. In the year you dispose of a passive investment the law lets you deduct the passive activity interest that you hadn't been able to deduct in previous years. This break does not apply to investment interest.

But what in the world is a passive activity?

The tax code says that it's any business in which you do not "materially participate." So you must be involved in the operation of a business on a "regular, continuous, and substantial basis." If you aren't, the business qualifies as a passive activity for you.

And if it's a passive activity, you may deduct any interest expense you incur only against income that you also derive from a passive activity. In other words, you may not deduct this interest from wages, investment or business income.

TIP Say you want to buy a new car and invest in a passive activity. You've got the cash to buy one or the other but not both. Our advice?

Pay cash for the car, then borrow to invest in the passive activity.

That way, the interest is passive activity interest and is deductible against passive activity income, or can be carried forward to future years if you don't have enough passive income in the year the interest is incurred.

If you borrow to buy the car, the interest is personal interest which is only 10 percent deductible in 1990 and not deductible at all thereafter, and you can't carry forward any of the interest you're not able to deduct.

Limited partnerships are, in the eyes of the law, almost always passive activities. Most rental activities also fall into the category of passive activities. (See Chapter 19 for more information on passive activities.)

QUESTIONS AND ANSWERS

QUESTION: *May I boost my mortgage interest deductions by making my mortgage payments in advance?*

The law won't allow you to claim a deduction for prepaid interest, no matter what category that interest falls into.

TIP But most people actually pay their mortgage in arrears. That is, the interest portion of the payment you must make on January 1 is for interest that accrued in December. So if you make this January 1 payment on December 31, the amount isn't prepaid, and you may deduct it in the year paid.

TIP Banks and other lending institutions send out statements of interest paid on Form 1098. But lenders often omit from these statements the interest on the payment you made in December. Check the statements to make sure the interest listed is the actual interest you paid during the year.

TIP Also, when you buy a home or refinance your mortgage, make sure you pick up interest you paid from the date of closing to the end of the month in which you buy or refinance. This amount is seldom reported on statements issued by lending institutions.

Similarly, when you sell a house, the interest you paid at closing for the portion of the month up to the date of sale is usually not included in the Form 1098 you receive from the bank or other lending institution.

So make sure you account for all of the interest you paid, including amounts that appear only on the settlement papers.

QUESTION: *Are points still deductible?*

Points, the additional amount of interest you pay when a loan is closed, are deductible in the year you buy your home and pay the points. (One point equals 1 percent of the amount of your loan.)

But a word of warning: You may not deduct points *currently* if you pay them with money you borrowed from the same bank that holds your mortgage.

TIP Our advice is to write a separate check to your lender for points attributable to any borrowings secured by your home. Also, when it comes time to prepare your tax return, make sure you pick up the amount of points you paid from your settlement sheet. The bank probably will not include them on the Form 1098 it sends you at the end of the year.

CAUTION The IRS maintains—not without controversy—that you may not take a deduction in the current tax year for points that you pay as part of a refinancing.

Instead, it wants you to write off the points paid on a refinancing over the life of the loan—usually 15 years or more. What happens if you sell your home before you write off all of the points you paid? Uncle Sam says that you may deduct any remaining points in the year of sale.

TIP The Tax Court has ruled in favor of the IRS on this issue concerning refinancing of a short term loan, while side-stepping whether points paid on a bridge or construction loan fall under this rule. In fact, a circuit of the U.S. Court of Appeals recently overturned this decision in at least one instance and allowed a current year deduction for points paid on refinancing a short-term loan.

The bottom line? If the loan you refinance falls into the category of a bridge, construction or other short-term loan, or some other unusual category, check with your tax adviser.

QUESTION: *How can a loan I make to my kids to purchase a home qualify as acquisition indebtedness?*

Make sure that the home secures the debt by filing the appropriate papers. Otherwise, the interest is personal interest and only 10 percent deductible by the kids in 1990.

QUESTION: *We bought our house ten years ago for $75,000. Its fair market value went up to more than $120,000. So in January 1987 we refinanced our original mortgage and obtained a new loan. We used the money for personal purposes. Is the interest on our refinanced mortgage deductible?*

Good news: The interest is fully deductible because the mortgage is secured by your home and was incurred before October 14, 1987. In the eyes of the IRS your mortgage is acquisition debt, even though it tops the cost of your home.

QUESTION: *I want to turn the equity in our house into cash. What's the best way?*

You have three ways to get at your accumulated *equity*. You can refinance your house. You can take out a second mortgage loan. Or you can apply for a home-equity line of credit. When you refinance, you apply for an entirely new mortgage loan. Doing so is usually costly. What is more, it takes time.

Second mortgages and home-equity loans are, in many respects, one and the same. Both allow you to borrow against a portion of the difference between the balance due on your existing mortgage and the current value of your home.

With a second mortgage loan, you usually get a single check for the full amount of the loan. Home-equity lines of credit, on the other hand, usually allow you to take the money as often as you need it by writing a check or using a credit card.

Although second mortgage loans usually run for 5 to 15 years, home-equity lines of credit can run years longer or can even be completely open-ended.

☞ CAUTION More and more people are using one of these three devices to tap the equity in their homes in order to finance other purchases. It can be smart, provided you understand the limitations and are aware of the pitfalls of borrowing.

The pitfalls, however, are sometimes subtle.

First, there's the expense. Banks frequently charge *loan*

origination fees, or points, of 2 or 3 percent on second mortgages and home-equity credit lines. And there are closing costs that can add up to hundreds or even thousands of dollars.

You pay all of these fees up front—that is, the bank subtracts these amounts from the money you borrow before it gives you the rest of the cash.

Less obvious—and more significant—is the risk you assume when you use your house as collateral. Suddenly you have tens of thousands of dollars available to you.

Feeling flush, you succumb to buying the boat you've dreamed of for years. But the payments and maintenance costs turn out to be more than you can handle.

You fall way behind. With a standard loan you lose the boat, but with a home-equity loan it's your house the bank comes after.

Here's another example.

Say that you buy a new car. A standard auto loan requires you to pay off the principal over a specified period, typically three to five years.

Now what if you buy the same car but pay for it with a home-equity line of credit? Your home-equity line of credit requires you to pay interest only. Without self-discipline, at the end of five years you could easily have an old, unpaid-for automobile.

Another risk of the home-equity line of credit is rising interest rates. Because the rate on most home-equity lines of credit floats with the market, you may start out with an easy payment. But if interest rates rise, you could wind up with a monthly payment you can no longer afford.

We aren't advising you to avoid tapping the equity in your home, but we're urging caution. Also, if you do opt to refinance or sign up for a home-equity line of credit, shop around. The rates and terms of these loans vary enormously from institution to institution.

QUESTION: *I'm in the process of purchasing a cooperative apartment. May I deduct my mortgage interest?*

As you probably know, you may deduct mortgage interest only as long as the loan is secured by your residence. But as the owner of a *co-op*, you do not actually own your apartment. Rather, you own stock in a cooperative that entitles you to occupy your residence.

But Uncle Sam gives you a break. He considers indebtedness that's secured by stock you hold as a tenant-stockholder in a cooperative housing corporation as also secured by the house or apartment that you're entitled to occupy.

In other words, he allows you to deduct the interest on debt secured by your stock, just as if the loan were secured by your residence.

What if your co-op agreement won't allow you to use the stock or the apartment as security? Uncle Sam still allows you to deduct the interest as mortgage interest.

QUESTION: *Not all of my mortgage interest is deductible. What do I do with the rest?*

You would write it off as personal interest.

Although personal interest is only 10 percent deductible in 1990, a partial deduction is better than no deduction at all.

QUESTION: *My son fell onto hard times, and I made three mortgage payments for him. May I deduct the interest?*

Sorry, but you may write off interest only on debts for which you're legally liable. You aren't entitled to a write-off unless you are a signatory to your son's mortgage.

QUESTION: *I ran up a big balance on my credit cards over the last few months, and I owe a bundle in interest. Unfortunately, I do not have the money to pay it. I know if I wait until next year to pay off the interest, I won't even get the 10 percent deduction for the interest. Is there anything I can do?*

The answer is yes. As you point out, you must pay the interest this year in order to deduct 10 percent. But there's nothing preventing you from borrowing money at a lower rate—a personal loan from a bank, say—to pay the interest and principal on your credit card.

One word of warning, however. Uncle Sam won't let you take a deduction if you borrow the money from the same bank or institution to which you owe the interest. So borrow the money you need from a different source, pay off your credit card, and claim the deduction.

QUESTION: *Is it still worthwhile to check my credit card statements for personal interest I paid during the year?*

It certainly is. And the same applies to other personal interest, such as the interest you pay on personal loans, charge accounts, and college education loans.

Because the interest deduction is so small, though, it's all the more worthwhile to periodically shop around to see whether you're paying a competitive interest rate on your credit cards.

Some banks charge much lower rates than others. Also, some banks do not charge an annual fee for the privilege of having their credit card. (This annual fee, incidentally, doesn't qualify as interest, personal or otherwise, and isn't deductible.)

You should know, too, that some banks charge interest from the date you make your purchase, whereas others charge you no interest as long as you pay in full each month.

The bottom line: It may well be worth your while to take your credit-card business elsewhere if you can get a better deal.

QUESTION: *May I deduct interest I pay the IRS?*

It may not seem fair, but any interest that you pay as a result of your income taxes—both interest you shell out to the IRS, say, and interest on loans you take out to pay your tax bill—is only partially deductible as personal interest. But any interest the IRS pays you is fully taxable.

TIP What if you're locked in a dispute with the IRS and don't think you'll reach a settlement in 1990? You may want to make an interest-only payment to the IRS.

That way, you may get a deduction equal to 10 percent of the amount you pay. Your tax adviser will know if this strategy makes sense in your situation.

QUESTION: *How do I know whether interest is personal interest or investment interest?*

You trace how you use the money you borrowed. And you trace it from the day the money is in your hands until the day you repay the loan.

Say you take out a loan, and you use the money to buy a new car for the family. The car is a personal asset, so the interest on the loan is personal interest.

Simple, you say. But wait a minute. Let's suppose you borrow $25,000 and deposit the money in your checking account. Later in the year you use the money to purchase some stock, a car for your son, and a word processor for your business.

In the eyes of the IRS, this single loan generates three types of interest: investment interest on the stock purchase, personal interest on the car, and business interest on the word processor. And different rules govern the deductibility of these different types of interest.

Usually, when you borrow money, you either use it immediately for a particular purpose or deposit it in your checking or savings account until you are ready to buy.

What happens if you deposit the money in an account that contains other funds? Uncle Sam says the interest on the loan is investment interest. And it remains investment interest until you take the money out of your account and use it.

What's more, you must spend the money you borrow within 30 days before or after the debt proceeds are actually deposited into an account if you want interest on the loan classified according to how you use the money.

And if you wait longer than 30 days? The IRS bases the interest deduction on the first purchase you make from your account.

Here's how the 30-day rule works.

Say you borrow $1,000 on September 1 to purchase some stock. You put the money in your checking account, which already has a balance of $1,000.

On October 3, your washer goes on the blink. So you buy a new one for $600 and write a check for that amount. On October 9, 39 days after you took out the loan, you purchase the stock. You fork over $1,000 for 100 shares of ABC Co. What are the tax consequences?

The IRS treats the interest on the entire $1,000 as investment interest until October 3, when you purchased the washer.

Then it classifies the interest on $600—the amount you paid for the washer—as personal interest. The remaining $400 is investment interest.

 TIP How do you avoid this paperwork nightmare? Do not mingle borrowed funds with other monies.

Also, maintain separate accounts for funds you borrow for personal, business, investment, and passive-investment purposes. That way, you will not be tripped up by the tracing rules. The tax benefits outweigh any additional bank fees for segregating accounts.

If you do not go this route—that is, if you put your borrowed funds and personal stash in one account—observe the 30-day rule.

Otherwise, you should be prepared to wade through the IRS debt allocation and tracing rules. And there is more than paperwork hassles involved. You could wind up with more nondeductible interest expense than you bargained for.

Also, make sure you can trace debts you rack up for investments. For example, ask your lender to make the loan amount payable not to you but to a third party—your stockbroker, for example.

QUESTION: *A friend tells me that there is a 90-day rule governing mortgage interest deductions. True?*

The answer is yes.

You are given 90 days from the time you purchase your house to secure a mortgage. If you wait longer, you are entitled to write off your mortgage interest as acquisition debt only if you can prove, under the tracing rules, that you spent borrowed money to acquire or improve your home.

QUESTION: *We are building a new home. Does our construction loan qualify as acquisition debt?*

The answer is a qualified yes. You may count as acquisition debt the amount of money you spent up to the time construction was completed and up to 24 months before you took out the loan.

QUESTION: *I borrowed money to invest in tax-exempt bonds. Is the interest on my loan investment interest?*

This interest indeed falls into the category of investment interest, but you may not claim a write-off. The reason is simple.

The rules do not allow you to deduct interest on money you borrow to invest in instruments, such as municipal bonds, that do not produce taxable income.

QUESTION: *I have $6,000 in my personal savings account, and I borrowed money to buy an interest-bearing bond. Six months later I sold the bond and used the sales proceeds to repay my credit cards. How does the IRS treat the interest on the money I borrowed?*

Uncle Sam treats your interest as investment interest for six months because you used the loan to buy an investment. He then reallocates the interest to the personal category, because you used the money to pay off your credit cards.

TIP You could have kept the deduction as an investment deduction, and you would have been able to deduct the interest in full against your investment income, if you had used your savings account money to pay off your credit cards instead.

QUESTION: *I lent my daughter $15,000. I'm not charging her interest. What are the tax implications of the loan?*

Even though your daughter is paying you no interest, the law requires you to "impute," or assume, interest income. The interest equals the lesser of the following:

- The amount of the outstanding loan times the applicable federal rate (based on a rate the federal government pays on its borrowing).

- The net investment income of the borrower if it exceeds $1,000.

- Zero if the net investment income of the borrower is less than $1,000.

Say, for example, that your daughter reports $200 of investment income for the year. There's no imputed interest to you because her net investment income, $200, is less than $1,000.

But say she reports $10,000 in net investment income. In this case you must impute interest income on the loan—that is, $15,000 times the applicable federal rate (say, 8 percent, or $1,200)—and declare this amount as income on your return. And this imputed interest, in addition to your being required to report it as income on your return, would also be treated as a gift from you to your daughter.

The law *does* make an exception to the imputed interest rules for so-called *de minimis loans* of $10,000 or less. If you make personal loans that total $10,000 or less, you don't have to impute interest income at all. But this exception doesn't apply if the loan is used to buy income-producing assets, such as rental property.

Another wrinkle: If the primary purpose of the loan was to avoid paying income tax—for example, you lent your daughter money to make an investment so that the investment income would be reported on her return instead of yours—the net investment income limitation does not apply. You must impute interest based on the applicable federal rate.

Depending on how your daughter used the money, she may be entitled to a deduction for the imputed interest even though she never actually paid that amount to you.

TIP The rules governing imputed interest are lengthy and complex. If you've borrowed or lent money at no interest or at a rate below the applicable federal rate, see your tax adviser.

QUESTION: *I own a business and a house, and I want to make the most of my interest deductions. Do you have any suggestions for me?*

If you must borrow, borrow for business purposes because business interest is 100 percent deductible. Alternatively, borrow on your home; mortgage interest is also deductible although certain limits do apply. But avoid using borrowed money for personal expenses, because deductions for personal interest are severely limited in 1990 and not deductible at all thereafter.

QUESTION: *How can I tell what a partnership or S corporation in which I've invested is spending its borrowed money on?*

Partnerships and *S corporations* are supposed to provide you with this information on the Schedule K-1 that they're required to send you. If you don't get the information, you or your tax adviser will have to obtain it directly.

QUESTION: *I'm a shareholder in an S corporation that operates a retail clothing store, and I don't participate in the management of the company. The corporation purchased some stock on margin. Is this interest passive interest or investment interest?*

Your S corporation owes interest on an investment that had nothing to do with selling clothing, its trade or business. So Uncle Sam considers the interest to be investment interest, not passive interest.

Your share of this interest passes through the S corporation to you. And you may deduct the expense if you have investment income. Otherwise, as we saw earlier in the chapter, you must carry the amount forward to future years.

Similarly, income from dividends, annuities, or royalties earned by the S corporation are also passed through to you as investment income, which may be used to allow a deduction for investment interest expense.

QUESTION: *Should I pay this year the interest that has accrued on my life insurance policy loan?*

The interest that accrues on policy loans is payable at any time. And if you have many years of interest due, it would probably make sense to pay up this year. After all, in 1990 personal interest is still 10 percent deductible.

Be careful though. If you used your loan for an investment or for a passive activity, the interest is deductible only under the rules that apply to these categories.

Another caveat: Though interest you pay on a loan against the cash surrender value of your life insurance policy is usually deductible, there are exceptions to this rule. For example, if the insurance company deducted the interest in advance from the amount of the loan, it is not deductible. Neither is the interest deductible if you used the loan to buy a single-premium life insurance policy, an endowment, or an annuity contract.

Finally, you may not deduct interest on your life insurance if you plan to systematically borrow part or all of the increases in the cash value of the policy.

QUESTION: *I took out a loan to purchase an interest in a partnership. How is the interest I pay on this loan treated under the tracing rules?*

The IRS has issued some temporary guidelines to address this question. (These rules also cover interest on a loan you take out to purchase shares in an S corporation.)

The rules generally require you to allocate debt among the partnership's assets. Or if your purchase was from the entity itself, you must trace the use of the money by the entity. You should consult your tax adviser to see how these rules apply to your own situation.

6

The Right Way to Write Off Charitable Contributions

We are not suggesting that the main reason most people donate to charity is to reduce their tax bills. But if you are going to make the contribution anyway, it is nice that Uncle Sam may reward an act of generosity with a tax deduction.

Nonitemizers don't get to deduct *charitable contributions*. For them, the issue is simply whether they want to give and how much.

People who itemize deductions on Schedule A, however, have other questions they have to ask about their acts of charity. In this chapter we will tell you the questions and show you how to figure the answers. Let's start with a few general rules.

The IRS defines a charitable contribution as a contribution or gift "to, or for the use of, a *qualified organization*." But do not let the jargon confuse you.

A qualified organization is simply a nonprofit charitable, religious, or educational group that meets government guidelines. In fact, an organization can (and undoubtedly will) tell you whether your contribution to it is tax deductible.

Moreover, the tax law requires organizations to state clearly that donations are not deductible when that is the case. One note of caution, however: You are responsible for any additional tax if you are misled by an organization.

As a rule of thumb, your contribution is probably deductible if an organization is operated solely for charitable, religious, scientific, literary, or educational purposes, and you have no power to earmark a specific individual as the recipient of your generosity. But if the organization you favor tries to influence legislation substantially or gets involved in political campaigns, you are out of luck.

Note, too, that the law even permits you to write off contributions to federal, state, and local governments. The only requirement: The governmental body must use your gift solely for public purposes—to build a park or a playground, say.

Furthermore, the law allows you to deduct 80 percent of your donation to a school if, in exchange for that donation, you receive the right to buy seating in its athletic stadium. If instead of the right to buy tickets you receive the tickets themselves, the contribution is not deductible. Neither, of course, may you deduct the cost of any tickets that you purchase in exercising this right.

GIVING ITEMS OF VALUE

Something else you should know: The law allows you to contribute either money or property to a charity. If you donate money, you write off the amount of your gift. If you donate property, you deduct an amount equal to the *fair market value* of the property at the time you make the donation.

The government defines fair market value as "the price at which the property would change hands between a willing buyer and a willing seller, neither being under any compulsion to buy or to sell and both having reasonable knowledge of relevant facts," which means only the amount the property would bring if you sold it on the open market.

Fair market value isn't always easy to determine, however. One acceptable indication: a sale or purchase of similar property close to the date of your contribution.

So if you donate a Winslow Homer painting, say, to your local museum and a comparable Homer just sold at auction for $1 million, you may be fairly confident that you'll be able to write off a full million.

The opinion of an appraiser is valid, too. In fact, appraisals are required if you donate property with a total value of more than $5,000. For example, if you donate two automobiles, valued at $3,000 each, to an area vocational school, you would be required to get an appraisal because the value of the two cars tops the $5,000 limit.

Additionally, the IRS requires you to attach to your income tax return a complete copy of a signed appraisal to support charitable donations of works of art with a total value of $20,000 or more. A color photograph must also be provided upon request.

As far as appraisals go, the tax law does carve out an exception for publicly traded securities. No appraisals are required for them. Appraisals are required, however, if you donate nonpublicly traded securities with a value of more than $10,000. As we have seen, if you make more than one gift, the value of your donations is added together to see if you exceeded the $5,000 and $10,000 limits.

☞ CAUTION   Make sure you get an accurate appraisal of property you donate. You may find yourself liable for a special penalty if you overstate your gift's value.

When does the penalty apply? Here are the two conditions: first, the value you claim on your personal return is 200 percent or more of the correct fair market value; second, you underpaid your tax by at least $5,000 because of the overstatement.

The penalty isn't insignificant. It adds up to 20 percent of the underpaid tax that the IRS attributes to the overvaluation. And there's also a gross valuation overstatement penalty to pay if the value you claimed on your return is 400% or more of the correct fair market value. It amounts to a hefty 40 percent.

☞ CAUTION   Here's another rule to keep in mind. The IRS wants to make sure that an appraisal is not made by someone with a stake in overstating your gift's value.

So appraisals may not be made by you, the organization receiving the gift, the party from whom you acquired it, or any *related entity*— that is, a member of your family or a corporation that is controlled by any of the above individuals or organizations. For the same reason, the appraiser must not base his or her fees on the gift's appraised value.

And note: You may deduct the cost of an appraisal but only as a miscellaneous deduction, not as a charitable contribution. And miscellaneous deductions are subject to a 2 percent floor. (See Chapter 9 for more information on the 2 percent rule.)

Another rule to keep in mind: Using a trust, you may donate a partial interest in property, such as stocks or bonds, to a charitable organization and still collect a tax deduction. Under this arrangement, you or another beneficiary continue to get the annual income from the trust. When you die, however, the property passes to the charity.

You get your deduction, which equals the present value of the gift, the year you create the trust. If your gift consists of securities that have risen in value since you purchased them, you also avoid paying the capital gains tax on that appreciation.

Also, be aware that if you make noncash gifts of more than $500, you must file Form 8283, "Noncash Charitable Contributions," with your personal tax return. Form 8283 requires that you state when and how you acquired the property and the amount you paid for it.

For more information on how to value donated property, ask your local IRS office for a free copy of IRS Publication 561, "Determining the Value of Donated Property."

☞ CAUTION If the value of the property you contribute has appreciated considerably, you may be subject to the alternative minimum tax. See Chapter 20 for the details.

💰 TIP It makes no sense (from a tax perspective, that is) to make a donation of business or investment property that has dropped in value since you acquired it.

Although you may claim a deduction for the value of the property at the time you donate it, you may not claim a deductible loss on property when you make the gift.

So unless the charitable organization actually needs the property itself, you are better off selling it, then donating the proceeds to charity. That way, you may take a loss on the property and also claim the value of the charitable contribution.

Here is an example to illustrate what we mean. Let's assume that you own securities that cost $20,000 several years ago.

Today those securities are worth $5,000. If you donate the securities, you may take a $5,000 charitable deduction. By selling the securities, however, you may claim a $15,000 capital loss as well as the $5,000 donation.

☞ CAUTION You may not use this strategy when you donate personal assets, such as clothing or an automobile, to a charity, since the law doesn't allow you to write off losses on personal assets.

TIP The law also allows you to write off as charitable contributions expenses you run up when you provide volunteer services.

Say you work as a volunteer at a local nonprofit hospital. The hospital requires you to wear a bright yellow smock while you are on duty, and you purchase one from the hospital for $20. Feel free to deduct the cost and cleaning of your garment.

The reason: It is not suitable for everyday use, and you are required to wear it while you perform services for a charitable organization.

Or say that every Tuesday you drive 24 miles from your home to a nonprofit child-care center, where you donate three hours of your time. The law permits you to write off your actual out-of-pocket automobile expenses—that is, gas and oil—or claim a deduction at the standard rate of 12 cents a mile. You may also write off the cost of tolls and parking.

But as a practical matter, you may find that it's more trouble than it's worth to keep track of your actual car costs. So our advice is to opt for the standard rate of 12 cents a mile unless you log substantial mileage each year.

Finally, let's say you serve on the board of a nonprofit group. You are asked to attend a two-day training session in your state capital.

The law says you may deduct your travel expenses—in this case, the cost of your meals and lodging during these two days—under one condition. Your trip must not include any "significant element of personal pleasure, recreation, or vacation."

☞ CAUTION Remember, however, that the cost of meals you eat during these trips might fall under the 80 percent rule. This is the same rule that limits the deduction you claim for business meals to 80 percent of the cost. Unless the IRS changes its mind, this same limit on deductions will apply to meals eaten during charitable travel. Check with the IRS or your tax adviser at tax time.

You should know, too, that the rule about significant personal pleasure does not mean that you must get no enjoyment out of your charitable activity. You are free to have a dandy time if, say, you volunteer to take your daughter's Sunday school or kindergarten class on a field trip to a local zoo.

You will pocket the write-off as long as you're genuinely on duty throughout the trip.

☞ **CAUTION** You may not write off the value of your time in connection with any charitable volunteer services you perform.

And you may not claim deductions for entertainment or for personal expenses, such as the cost of bringing your spouse or child along on the trip.

What if your charity pays you a per diem amount to cover the cost of meals and lodging while you are away from home?

If the per diem amount exceeds your actual costs, you must report the extra cash as income on your personal tax return. But if the amount adds up to less than your actual expenses, you may write off the deficit as a charitable contribution.

Charitable groups often hold or sponsor events in order to raise money. You may write off the cost of tickets to these charitable events. But the amount shown on the ticket is not necessarily the amount of your gift. You may deduct only the amount of your actual contribution.

Say, for example, that you pay $50 to attend a special showing of a movie for the benefit of a charitable organization.

Printed on the ticket is "Contribution—$50." If the regular price for the movie is $4, you made a contribution of $46. If the "regular price" is not indicated on the ticket or anywhere else, just note the normal price for similar events or activities in your area and reduce your donation by that amount.

☞ **CAUTION** If you purchase a ticket for a charitable event and the amount of the deductible contribution is not specified, Uncle Sam will assume that the total amount paid is for your personal benefit. That means you could lose your entire write-off unless the charity shows the deductible portion of the ticket price or you can prove that the amount you claim is a bona fide charitable donation.

However, the IRS has recently established "safe harbor" rules under which certain benefits received by donors will be considered insignificant or insubstantial. If these rules apply to your contribution, the entire amount will be deductible. Check with your tax adviser to determine if these safe harbor rules may apply.

TIP   You may deduct the entire cost of a benefit ticket if you donate it back to the organization for resale or to another charitable group.

WHEN YOU MAY DEDUCT YOUR CONTRIBUTION

The law says that you may deduct charitable contributions in the year you make them. But it really means the year that you mail them.

Let's say the date is December 31, 1990, and you mail a check for $200 to your church. The church receives your donation on January 2, 1991. Under the rules, you are entitled to write off the contribution on your 1990 return, because you mailed your check in 1990.

What if you charge your contribution to your bank credit card? You deduct these donations in the year you charge them.

If your gift is in the form of a stock, you claim a deduction in the year in which a properly endorsed stock certificate is mailed or delivered to the charity.

But let's say you give a stock certificate to your agent or to the issuing corporation—IBM, say—for transfer to your favorite charity. Your gift does not count for tax purposes until the date the stock is actually transferred on the books of the corporation.

CHARITABLE DEDUCTION LIMITS

Under a complicated set of rules, Uncle Sam limits your total yearly deductions for charitable contributions. If your contributions for the year total 20 percent or less of your adjusted gross income (AGI), you have little to worry about.

Say, for example, that your AGI adds up to $50,000 in 1990. You should feel free to deduct up to $10,000 in charitable donations.

But let's say you are an exceptionally generous soul, and you contribute 30 percent or even 50 percent of your AGI to charity. In this case, the amount you may write off depends on what you contributed and to whom you contributed it.

Our advice: If your charitable contributions top 20 percent of your adjusted gross income, you should consult your tax adviser.

QUESTIONS AND ANSWERS

QUESTION: *My country club operates as a nonprofit organization. Are my annual dues deductible as a charitable contribution?*

Sorry, but the answer is a resounding no.

The law will not allow you to deduct as charitable contributions dues, fees, or bills you pay to country clubs, business or civic leagues, social clubs, or other similar groups—even if they are nonprofit organizations. Also, contributions to fraternal orders or lodges are not deductible unless the organization is using the contribution solely for charitable, religious, or educational purposes.

Also forbidden: the cost of raffle, bingo, or lottery tickets, tuition expenses, the value of your time or services, the value of blood given to a blood bank, donations to homeowners associations, and gifts to individuals.

QUESTION: *I want to make a donation to a day-care center. May I deduct this amount as a charitable contribution?*

Donations to nonprofit day-care centers are deductible only if certain conditions are met. Specifically, the center must provide care primarily to children whose parents are gainfully employed. Also, the center must make its services available to the public, and the contribution cannot be a substitute for tuition or other enrollment fees.

QUESTION: *Am I entitled to a deduction for the clothes I give to charity?*

Many people donate used clothing to charities, then forget to claim a deduction. So be sure to write off the fair market value of these items on your tax return.

 TIP The IRS says the fair market value of used clothes is the amount people would pay for these items in thrift shops and used clothing stores. So check with stores in your area to find out the value of articles you donate.

QUESTION: *We donated our old couch to a local shelter for the homeless. Do we get a tax deduction?*

The same rules that apply to gifts of used clothes apply to donations of used furniture and other household goods. Claim a deduction on your return equal to the fair market value of these items. Keep a detailed list of every item, and write down the value of each item separately.

QUESTION: *My spouse and I care for a foster child. Are any of our costs deductible?*

You are entitled to tax deductions if a foster child is placed in your home by a charitable organization, as long as you provide the child with food, clothing, and general care.

Also, you must not have a profit motive. For example, it does not count if you are paid for your time or services as a foster parent.

You may deduct the excess of your out-of-pocket expenses over the amount you are reimbursed by the charitable organization. Even the cost of the child's tickets to attend sporting events and movies qualifies for the deduction.

QUESTION: *An exchange student from Sweden is living with our family this school year. Are we entitled to any tax breaks?*

Uncle Sam knows it costs you money when an exchange student comes to live in your home. So part of the cost of housing an exchange student, whether from the United States or another country, is deductible as long as the student is not related to you and is not your dependent. Uncle Sam allows you to write off as much as $50 a month of these costs.

Here are the details: The student, enrolled in grade 12 or lower, must be a member of your household under a written agreement between you and a qualified nonprofit charitable organization. And the purpose of the exchange must be to provide educational opportunities for the student.

You may take your $50 deduction for each full calendar month the student lives with you. But the youngster must attend a U.S. school at least 15 days a month.

If, however, the organization reimburses you for your exchange student's costs, you may not take a deduction. In fact, Uncle Sam says you may not take a write-off if you receive any reimbursement, in the form of either money or gifts, to help defray your expenses. This even includes, for instance, a series of food packages from your student's parents.

Reimbursement for extraordinary or one-time expenses, such as a hospital bill or vacation trip, however, will not deprive you of your deduction provided you paid the cost at the request of the student's parents or the sponsoring organization.

And keep this fact in mind: You may not deduct the costs of a foreign student living in your home if the arrangement is part of a mutual exchange program that also allows your child to live with a family in a foreign country.

QUESTION: *Last year, I donated a week's use of my family's vacation home to a charity auction. We used the home ourselves for 14 days during the year and rented it for 80 days. Am I entitled to a deduction for the week of use we donated?*

In a word, the answer is no. Furthermore, the IRS holds that your donation of a week's stay in your vacation home constitutes personal, not business, use of the house and is not deductible. (For more information on this topic, see Chapter 17.)

7

How to Write Off Your Medical and Dental Expenses

In theory, Uncle Sam allows you to write off almost any medical or dental expense. But, in practice, it's now almost impossible for a person with health insurance to claim an actual write-off for medical and dental expenses on his or her tax return.

The reason is simple enough.

The law says you may write off only those medical expenses that exceed 7.5 percent of your adjusted gross income (AGI). In other words, someone whose AGI totals $50,000 would have to have medical expenses of $3,750 before he or she could claim a cent.

Timing, then, is an important tactic when it comes to writing off medical and dental expenses. If you expect to incur $3,500 in additional medical expenses in each of the next two years, try to arrange to pay the entire amount during one year. In that way, at least part of your medical expenses would be deductible.

In this chapter, we provide a checklist of deductible medical and dental expenses. We start, though, with the general rules for these write-offs.

Uncle Sam defines *medical expenses* as amounts you pay for the diagnosis, treatment, or prevention of disease or for treatment affecting any part or function of the body.

Included in these expenses are the costs of medical and dental insurance and transportation for needed medical and dental care.

You may write off medical and dental expenses if you itemize your deductions on Schedule A of your Form 1040. But as we have seen, you may deduct only those expenses that top 7.5 percent of your AGI. And you must write off these expenses only in the year you pay them.

What happens if you mail a check to your doctor on December 31? The law allows you to claim the expense in the year you mail the check.

The same rule holds true for medical and dental expenses you charge to a credit card. You may deduct the expense in the year you make the charge.

You may also claim a deduction for medical expenses you pay for your dependents. (See Chapter 3 for more on who qualifies as a dependent.)

In addition to dependents, you may also claim medical and dental expenses you incur on your children's behalf—even if you are divorced and your ex-spouse is entitled to claim the kids as dependents.

Also, you may ignore the gross income test for dependents when claiming medical expense deductions. If, in other words, your aging father would qualify as your dependent except for the fact that his income is too high, he would still qualify for purposes of any medical payments you made on his behalf.

Our advice: If you are chipping in to cover your parents' living costs, pay for their medical and dental bills—not their cable television.

WHAT IS DEDUCTIBLE?

Now, here is our alphabetical checklist of deductible medical and dental expenses. Before we begin, though, one quick word to the wise.

You should know that the same restriction that applies to business meals—their cost is only 80 percent deductible—may also apply to meals that are medically related. And medically related meals include those you consume while you are in the hospital.

Our advice is to check with your tax preparer or the IRS before you claim such expenses.

Alcohol and Drug Abuse Treatment

The law allows you to deduct the cost of treatment at a center for substance abusers. You may write off charges for therapy and medical care. You may also write off the amount you pay the center for lodging and meals provided during your treatment.

Care for the Handicapped

Uncle Sam says you may deduct as a medical expense the cost of sending a mentally or physically handicapped person to a special school. There is just one catch: The primary purpose of the special school must be to treat the student's medical problem.

TIP You may deduct payments you make in advance for the lifetime care of a handicapped person as long as the prepayments are not refundable and are not for medical insurance premiums.

Fees for Hospital Services

You may deduct the cost of hospital services, including ambulances and fees for laboratory, surgical, obstetrical, and diagnostic services. You may also write off the expense of private nurses, including the cost of meals you provide for them.

Fees for Medical Services

Uncle Sam says you may write off fees you pay to any doctor, surgeon, or other qualified practitioner. Who qualifies? The list includes dentists, ophthalmologists, osteopaths, optometrists, acupuncturists, chiropractors, podiatrists, psychiatrists, and psychologists.

Home Alterations to Accommodate a Handicap

If you install ramps or railings, widen hallways or doors, lower kitchen cabinets, or adjust electrical outlets and fixtures to accommodate a physical handicap, you may write off the full cost of these home alterations as medical expenses, because Uncle Sam assumes that these alterations don't increase the value of your home.

Home Alterations to Accommodate a Medical Condition

The amount you deduct depends on how much the equipment you install or the improvement you make increases the value of your home. Here is an example.

Say you suffer from heart disease, and you are unable to climb the stairs in your home. Your doctor suggests you install an elevator. And you do—at a cost of $2,000.

Next, you ask an appraiser to tell you how much the installation of the elevator increases the value of your home. The answer: $1,400.

You may deduct $600 as a medical expense—that is, the difference between the cost of the improvement ($2,000) and the value it adds to your home ($1,400).

What if the improvement does not increase the value of your home? You may write off the entire amount you pay—in this case, $2,000.

TIP Under special circumstances the rules allow you to write off as a medical expense the cost of removing lead-based paints from your walls and woodwork.

What are the conditions? You must perform the work to prevent a child who has or has had lead poisoning from eating the paint. And the walls and woodwork from which you remove the lead-based paint must be in poor repair and within the child's reach.

CAUTION If the IRS audits your return, it may ask you to provide a written statement from the doctor who recommended you make your improvement. Our advice is to secure a statement from your physician before you undertake the work.

The IRS may also ask you to prove how much the value of your property was or was not increased by your improvement. So you should obtain a reliable written appraisal of the improvement from a qualified real estate appraiser or a valuation expert.

Meals and Lodging

The law says you may deduct as a medical expense the cost of meals while you are away from home for medical treatment under one condition: The meals must be provided as part of your stay at an inpatient hospital or similar facility—for example, an alcohol or drug treatment center.

As for lodging outside a hospital, the rules say you may deduct $50 per person per night for the cost of a room. So if you travel with your sick child for out-of-town medical care, you may write off $100 per night for lodging expenses.

TIP You may also write off the cost of trips you take on doctor's orders—to a warmer or drier climate, say. But the purpose of your trip must be to alleviate a specific ailment. You get no deduction if you travel for general health reasons.

Here is an example. Say you suffer from a respiratory disease, and each winter you travel from your home in northern Ohio to Arizona. And you take the trip on the advice of your physician.

You may write off as a medical expense your transportation costs between your home and your residence in Arizona. You may also write off lodging expenses and the meal costs that you incur when you travel from Ohio to Arizona. But you may not deduct meals and lodging once you arrive at your destination.

Medical and Hospital Insurance Premiums

The cost of health and hospitalization insurance premiums are allowable deductions. And this includes Medicare premiums and the premium cost for contracts to repair or replace lost or damaged glasses or contact lenses.

When Congress adopted the 1986 Tax Reform Act, it provided an extra tax break for sole proprietors, partners, and owners of S corporations who pay for their own and their family's health insurance. For insurance coverage paid for and applicable to periods before October 1, 1990, they may deduct 25 percent of the cost of this insurance "above the line" (directly from their gross incomes). Congress is expected to extend this tax break.

The other 75 percent of the insurance bill is lumped together with other medical expenses. So it's deductible to the extent that it, when added to these other medical costs, totals more than 7.5 percent of your adjusted gross income.

You may not take the deduction for health insurance premiums if the cost tops your earned income from your business. Here's an example.

Say that you report a $6,000 loss from your sole proprietorship. Your health insurance bill for the year adds up to $1,600.

You aren't entitled to claim an above-the-line deduction of $400 (25 percent of your premiums), because doing so would simply allow you to claim a larger loss.

☞ **CAUTION** The rules say that you qualify for the 25 percent write-off only if you are not eligible to participate in the health insurance plan of another employer—including your spouse's employer.

Medicines

You may deduct the cost of prescribed drugs and insulin.

You may also write off the cost of birth control devices if they are prescribed by your doctor and are not available for purchase over the counter.

Drugs that you buy without a prescription—aspirin, for instance—are not deductible even if a physician recommends their use.

Mental Health Services

You may deduct as a medical expense amounts you pay for mental health services, including counseling and therapy.

Nursing Home Services

Uncle Sam allows you to write off the cost of nursing home services provided to you or one of your dependents—as long as the service is needed for medical reasons.

So if you have no medical problems and are perfectly able to care for yourself but just happen to live in a retirement or nursing home, you pocket no deduction.

Nursing Services

Amounts you pay for nursing services are deductible. And you may write off these costs even if the services are not performed by a registered nurse.

The only requirement: The services must be similar to those provided by licensed nurses—for example, dispensing medicine, changing dressings, and bathing the patient.

You may claim as medical expenses the cost of nurses' salaries, any Social Security taxes paid on their wages, and the cost of any meals you provide them.

Special Equipment

The tax law allows you to deduct the cost of purchasing special medical equipment, including motorized wheelchairs.

Also, you may write off the expense of installing special equipment, such as hand controls in your automobile. And you may deduct repairs or other operating costs of this equipment as long as the equipment helps you compensate for a specific disability.

But you are not allowed to deduct operating costs that are ordinarily considered a personal expense. For instance, you may not write off the cost of oil or gasoline for a specially equipped automobile.

Special Items

Included in this catchall category: false teeth, artificial limbs, eyeglasses, contact lenses, hearing aids, cosmetic surgery, hair implants or transplants, guide dogs, and crutches. The category also includes the cost of oxygen equipment and oxygen to relieve breathing problems caused by a medical condition.

Transportation

You may write off the cost of transportation to and from needed medical care. Transportation expenses include automobile (including tolls and parking), taxi, train, and plane fares, as well as ambulance service fees.

TIP Calculate your automobile expenses either by using nine cents a mile (the amount the IRS allows) or your actual out-of-pocket costs. Actual costs include expenses for gas and oil, but they do not include interest on a car loan, insurance, depreciation, and so forth.

QUESTIONS AND ANSWERS

QUESTION: *I know what is deductible as a medical expense. What isn't deductible?*

For starters, you may not write off the cost of bottled water, disability insurance, funeral, burial, or cremation expenses, health club dues, household help, illegal operations or treatments, and insurance that pays your ordinary living expenses if you are ill.

Nor may you deduct the cost of life insurance, diaper services, maternity clothes, nursing care for a healthy baby, toothpaste, toiletries, and cosmetics. And you may not write off the cost of piercing your ears or veterinarian fees for pets.

QUESTION: *What about the cost of stop-smoking and weight-loss programs? May I deduct these expenses?*

You may deduct the cost of programs designed to help you lose weight or stop smoking only if the program is prescribed by a doctor to alleviate a specific ailment.

For instance, if you're told to stop smoking because of your emphysema, the cost is deductible. If you enroll in a program just to improve your general health, however, the cost is entirely yours to shoulder.

QUESTION: *I ran up $5,000 in medical bills in December of 1990. But my insurance carrier did not reimburse me until January of 1991. How do I handle these amounts on my tax return?*

Uncle Sam requires you to write off medical expenses in the year you pay them. So you must deduct your $5,000 medical bill on your 1990 return. Then you report the amount you received from your insurance carrier as income on your 1991 return to the extent attributable to the earlier deduction.

Say you rack up $5,000 in medical expenses, but you deduct only $3,000—that is, the amount of your medical expenses that exceed 7.5 percent of your AGI. The rules require you to report as income only the amounts you receive from your insurance carrier that are equal to or less than your medical expense deduction.

You received $5,000 from your insurance company but wrote off only $3,000. That means you do not have to claim $2,000 of your reimbursement as income on your 1991 return.

QUESTION: *I pay a nurse to look after my physically handicapped child so I can work. May I claim her salary as a medical deduction?*

You may claim all or part of the nurse's wages as a *credit* for a dependent-care expense (see Chapter 24 for details on this credit) or as a deduction for a medical expense.

The most beneficial treatment will depend on your marginal tax bracket. Your tax adviser can help you determine the best method.

If you claim the dependent-care credit on these wages, and these wages add up to more than the maximum allowable for the credit, you may write off the remainder of the wages as a medical expense— subject, of course, to the 7.5 percent floor.

QUESTION: *My spouse and I are expecting our first child. May we claim a deduction for the cost of the childbirth classes we are attending?*

When it comes to writing off the cost of childbirth classes, Uncle Sam is strict. He says you may deduct only the cost of courses that prepare you for your "active role in the process of childbirth." What, you ask, does this phrase mean?

You may write off as a medical expense that portion of your program that consists of instruction in Lamaze breathing and relaxation techniques, stages and phases of labor, labor and delivery processes, birthing positions, and cesarean delivery.

But you may not deduct the cost of sessions that are not related to the labor process. For example, you may not write off the cost of classes on fetal or child development.

As the IRS writes in a recent ruling, "Attendance at classes or participation in programs on health-related topics are excluded from the definition of medical care if they are merely beneficial to the general health of the individual and are not related to a specific condition."

Also, you may not deduct the cost of classes that your husband attends. Say, for example, that you pay $300 for you and him to attend Lamaze-type classes.

Two-thirds of the course time is devoted to preparing you for actual childbirth. The other third is devoted to instruction on child-care topics.

To calculate your deduction, you multiply two-thirds times $300 and get $200. But you may deduct only your portion—not your husband's—so your write-off is $100.

8

Claiming Deductions for Taxes

When the income tax was first enacted back in 1913, your grandfather was allowed to deduct from his income virtually every other tax he paid.

This practice was grounded in the belief that taxes are involuntary expenditures and that people should not be taxed on income used to pay taxes.

But that was then, and this is now. And in the past seventy-seven years the practice—if not the belief—has changed. Today you may deduct only a few taxes from your federal taxable income. Which ones, to what extent, and how? That is what this chapter is all about.

Let's start, though, with a few general rules. If you itemize deductions on your Schedule A of Form 1040, you may write off some or all of the following:

- State and local income taxes

- State and local *real property* taxes

- State and local *personal property* taxes

We say that you *may* write some or all of these taxes off because there are qualifications and exceptions. We cover these later. But by and large, the deductibility of state and local income and property taxes is determined by a few general rules.

The tax must be imposed on you, not on someone else. If, for instance, you pay the property taxes on your mother's house, you may not deduct those taxes on your return. And you must actually pay the tax in the calendar year for which you are filing.

If you pay your taxes by check, the IRS considers the day you mail or deliver the check as the date of payment. If you use a pay-by-phone account, the date of payment is the payment date reported on the statement of the financial institution with which you have the account.

INCOME TAXES

Every state except Alaska, Florida, Nevada, South Dakota, Texas, Washington, and Wyoming imposes some kind of personal income tax. Some cities—New York, Cincinnati, and Philadelphia, for instance—impose their own income taxes as well.

The law allows itemizers to deduct these state and local income taxes on Schedule A of Form 1040. Specifically, you may write off the income taxes that are withheld from your paycheck. You also may deduct *estimated tax* payments that you are required to make and any state and local taxes that you pay when you file your state tax return.

REAL ESTATE TAXES

If you itemize, you may also deduct nonbusiness state and local real estate taxes on Schedule A of your Form 1040 in the year that you pay them. Remember, though, that you may deduct only those real estate taxes that you actually pay.

Say, for example, that you and your spouse own your home jointly but file separate returns. Each of you may write off only the taxes that you respectively pay.

The one exception to this rule are taxpayers in community property states: Arizona, California, Idaho, Louisiana, Nevada, New Mexico, Texas, and Washington. The IRS considers that taxes paid from community funds are paid on a fifty-fifty basis.

TIP In some cases, you may want to transfer property to another family member who could make better use of the property tax deduction than you can.

Just keep in mind that there is a serious drawback to this strategy. When you transfer property to another person, you lose control of it. Also, you may be liable for gift taxes on the transfer.

One other note: You may not deduct real estate taxes placed in *escrow*—that is, in the care of a third party—until they are actually paid. This issue crops up most often with a home mortgage.

If your monthly mortgage payment includes an amount placed in escrow for real estate taxes, you may not write off the total of those escrow payments. You may deduct only the amount of the tax that the lender actually paid to the taxing authority, such as a city or county.

TIP Most lenders pay taxes out of escrow accounts on the tax due date. But if the due date is shortly after the end of the calendar year, you may want to ask your lender to accelerate the payment so that you can claim the deduction a year earlier.

You may also deduct taxes on properties that produce rent or royalty income, such as apartments. (You claim these deductions on Schedule E of your Form 1040.)

CAUTION It's a little-known fact, but trash and garbage service fees that are listed separately on your real estate tax bill for your home aren't deductible.

What if the municipality where you live provides these services but does not break out their separate costs on your real estate tax bill?

You may continue to write off the entire amount.

CAUTION You should know that if you buy or sell real estate during the tax year, whether it is a home or income-producing property, you must divide real estate taxes between yourself and the buyer. You split the taxes that each of you may deduct based on the number of days each of you owned the property.

So, if you're the seller, you pay and deduct the taxes up to the date of the sale. The buyer pays and deducts the taxes after the sale.

(See Chapter 15 for more information on this topic.)

PERSONAL PROPERTY TAXES

Uncle Sam allows you to write off personal property taxes on your return. But to qualify for the deduction, a personal property tax must meet the following three tests.

The tax is based on the value of your property. Say your state imposes an annual motor vehicle registration tax of 1 percent of the value of your car plus 75 cents per hundred pounds of weight. You pay a tax of $84 based on your automobile's value ($6,000) and its weight (3,200 pounds).

You may deduct $60 (the part of the tax that is based on your car's value) as a personal property tax. The remaining $24 (based on the car's weight) is not deductible.

The tax is imposed annually. Your county mails you a personal property tax bill once a year. But it gives you the option of paying the tax quarterly. The tax qualifies as personal property tax—no matter when you pay it—because it is actually imposed annually.

The tax is imposed on personal property. Here is a break. Uncle Sam considers the tax imposed on personal property even if it is for the "exercise of a privilege."

What does this cryptic rule mean? Say, for example, that your city imposes a yearly tax on your car based on its value.

But it defines this tax as a registration fee for the privilege of registering your car or driving it on the highways. As long as the fee is based on your car's value, however, the tax law looks upon it as a tax on personal property.

OTHER TAXES

The law permits you to deduct taxes if they are "ordinary and necessary expenses of producing income." For example, if you are self-employed, you may deduct on Schedule C any tax you incurred as a cost of doing business. Examples include:

- Social Security taxes you pay on your employees' wages.

- Beginning in 1990, 50 percent of the self-employment tax paid on your net self-employment earnings

- Excise taxes you pay on merchandise you sell in your business.

- 80 percent of the sales tax you pay on a deductible business meal.

STATE
LOCAL

- Sales taxes on nondepreciable business property (if the property is depreciable, you add the tax to the cost of the property).

The law carves out an exception to this rule, though, for state transfer taxes on sales of securities, such as stocks and bonds.

The law won't allow you to deduct transfer taxes on your return, but you may subtract them when it comes time to calculate your gain or loss from the sale of securities.

Usually, foreign income and real property taxes are deductible. However, you may not deduct the foreign tax if you paid it on income that was excluded from your federal tax return. Further, you may choose to take a *credit* for foreign taxes instead of claiming an itemized deduction.

As you remember, a credit reduces your tax by the amount of the foreign tax paid. A deduction reduces only the amount of your income subject to tax. If you paid foreign taxes, we suggest that you consult with your tax adviser.

WHAT ISN'T DEDUCTIBLE?

Which federal, state, and local government taxes and other fees may you not write off on your personal return? Here's an alphabetical checklist of many of those *non*deductible taxes.

- Car inspection fees.

- Cigarette, tobacco, liquor, beer, and wine taxes.

- Dog tags and hunting licenses.

- Driver's license fees.

- Estate taxes.

- Federal excise taxes on telephone service.

- Federal gasoline taxes.

- Federal income taxes.[4]

- Fines—for parking or speeding, for example.

- Gift taxes.

- Inheritance, legacy, or succession taxes.

- Marriage licenses.

- Mortgage recording taxes.

- Occupancy taxes, such as taxes on hotel rooms.

- Parking meter fees.

- Passport fees.

- Penalties assessed as taxes.

- Sales taxes.

- Social Security taxes.

- Stamp taxes.

- Tolls for bridges and roads.

- Transfer taxes.

- Utility taxes.

- Water bills, sewer, and other service charges.

TIP Some of the above taxes may be deductible if incurred in a trade or business or for the production of income. Check with your tax adviser.

CAUTION Don't make the mistake some taxpayers do and deduct Social Security and other employment taxes you pay on the wages of a household worker. The law will not allow you to write off these amounts.

However, any Social Security taxes you pay for baby-sitters can qualify for a tax credit as "child and dependent care" expenditures. (See Chapter 24 for details.)

QUESTIONS AND ANSWERS

QUESTION: *I make estimated payments of my state income taxes. My last payment for 1990 is due in January 1991. Do I deduct this amount in 1990 or 1991?*

You write off a January 1991 payment of 1990 state income taxes on your 1991 return. But here is a way to claim the deduction in 1990.

TIP Make your last quarterly estimated payment in December 1990. If you speed up your payment by a few weeks, you accelerate your deduction by a full year.

☞ **CAUTION** We have seen IRS auditors deny deductions to taxpayers who wrote off state estimated payments that substantially exceeded their state tax liability.

The only way you can guarantee yourself a deduction is to prove that your payments were based on a reasonable estimate of your final tax bill at the time you made your payment. (If circumstances change later on, your deduction is still safe in Uncle Sam's eyes.)

Say that you paid $3,000 in estimated state income taxes last year. But the payment you made was far beyond what you estimated you would actually owe. In fact, at tax time, you discover you are entitled to a refund of the full amount you paid in.

The result: The IRS—on audit—may disallow the $3,000 in estimated payments you deducted from your income, because you were not required to pay this $3,000.

In any case, the amount the IRS may disallow is the difference between what a reasonable estimate would have been—meaning an estimate that was based on facts at the time the payment was calculated—and the estimate you claimed.

QUESTION: *I made a mistake on my 1990 return and, as a result, I owe an extra $210 in state taxes and a $40 penalty. How much is deductible?*

If you owe additional state taxes because you filed an *amended return* or were audited, you may also deduct these additional tax payments. Claim the write-off in the year you make the payments. Penalties and fines, however, are not deductible.

So if you file an amended 1990 state return in 1991 and pay an additional $210 in state income taxes plus a $40 fine, you deduct the $210 in 1991.

You may *not* write off the $40 penalty.

QUESTION: *I overpaid my state taxes by $400 in 1989. I received a refund for that amount in 1990. Must I report the $400 as income?*

The answer depends on whether you reduced your federal taxes by taking itemized deductions in the year you overpaid.

If you itemized deductions in 1989, you must report the $400 refund as taxable income on your 1990 return—but only if your itemized deductions in 1989, minus the amount of your state income tax refund, topped the standard deduction.

What if you claimed the standard deduction in 1989? You may pocket the $400 refund tax free.

Here's an easy way to figure out if you must report a tax refund as income on your tax return. Add up your itemized deductions for the year in which you paid the state income taxes that resulted in the refund. Then, subtract the standard deduction for that year. Next, compare this result with the amount of your state tax refund. The smaller of the two amounts is the amount of your refund that's taxable.

QUESTION: *I am self-employed, and I pay personal property taxes on the business equipment I own. Where do I write off these local taxes?*

You deduct taxes that you pay on operating your business—or on property used in the business—on Schedule C (Form 1040). Farmers use Schedule F (Form 1040).

9

Make the Most of Your Miscellaneous Deductions

Remember all of those deductions you used to take for accountants' services, financial advice, professional journals, and a host of other miscellaneous items?

As you know from sad experience with your 1989 return, these items are now only partially deductible from your adjusted gross income (AGI). To be specific, you may write off only that portion of these costs that adds up to more than 2 percent of your AGI.

Here's an example. Let's say that in 1990 your AGI totals $50,000. And you report miscellaneous itemized deductions of $1,200. That means you may deduct $200—the amount of these expenditures that tops $1,000 ($50,000 times 2 percent).

And what are these partially deductible expenses? You find out in this chapter.

BASIC RULES

First, though, let's run through a few basics.

You may write off your miscellaneous deductions only if you itemize. You claim these deductions on Schedule A of your Form 1040.

71

And Uncle Sam says you may write off as a miscellaneous deduction any expense that is related to your job, to your investments, or to your taxes.

Expenses other than these probably are not deductible.

TIP It makes sense to bunch your miscellaneous deductions in one year. By doing so, you may top the 2 percent limitation and be able to claim a write-off.

For example, you might want to accelerate these deductions into 1990. Of course, this tactic makes sense only if you are going to top the 2 percent limit in 1990.

If you fall below the limit, another strategy is to defer miscellaneous deductions until 1991, when you may be able to take a write-off.

TIP You say you're self-employed? Claim any expenses that relate to your work on Schedule C—not Schedule A. These expenses include the cost of summarizing the information and other accounting and recordkeeping for the business portion of your tax return.

EXPENSES RELATED TO YOUR JOB

The IRS wants you to play fair. So you may deduct expenses that are related to your job only if you pay them out of your own pocket. If your employer reimburses you—or would reimburse if you asked—you are not entitled to write-offs. Here's our alphabetical checklist of some of the more common costs you may deduct.

Career Counseling

The law allows you to deduct the cost of career counseling as long as you incur the expense as part of your efforts to find a new job.

Moreover, you must look for the same kind of work you are now doing. Otherwise, Uncle Sam will not help shoulder the cost. Here is an example.

Say you are a history teacher by training but are tired of the academic rat race. With the help of a career counselor, you find a position as a speechwriter for a local politician.

Pat yourself on the back. But do not even think about writing off the cost of your counseling. It is not deductible, because you landed a job in an entirely different profession.

TIP You may write off career counseling expenses even if you don't ultimately change jobs. But you may not claim a deduction if you are looking for your very first job or a job in a new profession.

TIP You may deduct career counseling expenses even if you're currently unemployed. The only catches: You must be seeking the same kind of work, and it's only been a relatively short time since your last job.

Club Dues

Uncle Sam allows you to deduct the dues you pay to a country club or any other social, athletic, or sporting club as long as you use the club more than 50 percent of the time for business. For the details on this topic, see Chapter 11.

Computers

Under the law you may deduct a personal computer only if having one is a condition of your employment. Also, you must keep the computer for the convenience of your employer. And it must enable you to perform your duties as an employee.

Say you sign on with a wire service as a reporter, and you are stationed in an outlying area. You work out of a spare bedroom in your house. As a condition of your employment the wire service requires that you purchase a personal computer and modem, so that you can transmit the stories you write.

You meet all three of these tests, so you are entitled to a deduction through depreciation or by use of a limited expensing election—on Schedule A of your Form 1040. (See Chapter 18 for more on how to write off computers.)

Dues

You may write off dues you pay to professional organizations. You may also deduct union dues and expenses, such as initiation fees.

Education

Uncle Sam allows you to deduct the cost of *employment-related education* as long as it meets one of two requirements.

Your courses must help you maintain or improve your present work skills. Or your education must be required either by your employer or by law to keep your salary, status, or job. For example, a nurse may write off the cost of continuing education courses that the state requires to maintain a nursing license.

Among the costs that you may deduct: tuition, books, supplies, lab fees, and the cost of travel to and from your courses.

☞ **CAUTION** Uncle Sam will not permit you to deduct education expenses that enable you to meet the minimum education requirements of your profession. The key word here is "minimum."

Say that you are hired as a lab technician by a large corporation. You never graduated from college, and the company requires you to complete your education.

You may not deduct the cost of attending school. Why? Your education simply allows you to meet the minimum requirements of your profession. You may, however, write off the cost of continuing education classes—but only after you secure your degree.

Also, you may not deduct professional accreditation fees, such as bar exam fees or medical and dental licensing fees, that you pay at the outset of your career.

Finally, you may not deduct education expenses that qualify you for a new trade or business. For example, even if earning a law degree would meet the requirement of improving your present work skills, you may not deduct the cost of obtaining the degree. Why? Because it will permit you to practice law, a new trade or business.

Employment Agency Fees

You may deduct employment agency and headhunter fees. But as with career counseling, you must satisfy this condition: The agency must help you find a new job in the same occupation.

You may write off these fees even if the agency fails in its mission. Again, you may not claim a deduction if you are seeking a job for the first time.

Entertainment

You may write off some or all of the cost of business entertainment. (See Chapters 10 and 11 for the rules on deducting entertainment expenses.)

Gifts

Good news. You may deduct the cost of business gifts. But do not be too generous: You may write off gifts of only $25 a year to any single person in any single year.

Here is an example. Helen makes her living as a literary agent. Every Christmas, she purchases a copy of a favorite hardcover book for each of the 50 authors she represents.

She may write off the cost of these books—up to $25 each—as long as she made no other gifts to these clients during the year. If she made other prior gifts, which, say, added up to $15 each, she may deduct only up to $10 per book per client for her Christmas gift.

Job Search Expenses

Keep track of all of the expenses you pile up that are associated with changing jobs—everything from telephone calls to the cost of postage.

These expenses are deductible as long as you are looking for a position—you guessed it—in your same profession or not seeking employment for the first time.

Here is an example. You are set to graduate from a Boston-area college with a degree in computer science. And you travel to

San Francisco for an interview with a computer manufacturer. Alas, you may not write off your travel expenses because you are looking for your first job.

A few years pass. You landed the job with the computer manufacturer and are still employed there. In fact, you are doing so well that a Boston computer company contacts you about an exciting new position. So you travel to your old stomping grounds for an interview.

This time you may deduct your travel expenses because you are seeking a new position in your current profession.

Jury Duty

A little-known provision of the law allows you to claim an above-the-line deduction—not subject to the 2 percent floor—for pay you received and paid to your employer while you're on jury duty. You deduct this amount by including it in your "total adjustments to income" on page 1 of your Form 1040. Label this amount "jury pay" on the dotted line next to the total.

You're entitled to this write-off only if your employer requires you to surrender that amount to him or her in exchange for your continuing to receive your regular salary while on jury duty. Remember, you must also include your pay for jury duty in your income.

TIP Congress changed the rules governing jury duty pay received after 1986. So if you failed to claim an above-the-line deduction for jury duty pay remitted to your employer after 1986, you may be entitled to a refund. Consult your tax adviser about whether it pays for you to file an amended return.

Medical Examinations

The cost of a physical examination required—but not paid for—by your employer is deductible as a miscellaneous itemized deduction.

CAUTION Health club expenses are not deductible, even if your job—as in the case of a police officer—requires that you stay in top physical condition.

Military Uniforms

If you're on active duty in the armed services, the law will not allow you to write off the cost of your uniforms. But it does permit people in the reserves to claim this deduction.

If you are in the reserves, you may write off the unreimbursed cost of your uniform as long as military regulations prohibit you from wearing it off duty.

☞ CAUTION The law will not allow you to deduct the cost of uniforms that replace regular clothing—uniforms worn by students at military academies, for example. But you may write off the cost of insignia, shoulder boards, and related items.

Office Expenses

Turn to Chapter 16 for information on how to write off an office in your home.

Résumé Preparation

Keep tabs on how much you spend typing, printing, and mailing copies of your resume to prospective employers. These costs are deductible—as long as you are looking for a new job in your present occupation.

Rewards

Most people do not know it, but you may also deduct a reward you pay for the return of lost business property. Say, for example, that you leave your briefcase on the train. You advertise in your local paper that you will pay $100 for its return.

Your luck is good, and a fellow commuter returns your briefcase to you. You may write off both the reward and the cost of your advertisement.

Subscriptions

The law allows you to deduct subscriptions to professional and trade journals as long as these publications relate to your work.

☞ CAUTION Do not make the mistake some taxpayers do and write off the cost of a three-year subscription all in one year. The IRS may disallow a portion of your deduction. The rule says that you may write off magazine subscriptions only one year at a time. Here is how it works.

Say you pay $300 in December 1990 for a three-year subscription to a technical business journal. The subscription begins in January 1991.

You may deduct only $100 of the subscription price in 1990—subject, of course, to the 2 percent AGI limitation. You may deduct $100 in 1991 and $100 in 1992.

The news is not all bad, though. Since you paid in December, you get to deduct the portion representing your 1990 subscription a whole year in advance.

Telephone

You may deduct the cost of the unreimbursed business portion of your telephone expenses and long distance telephone calls. These costs may even include answering services and beeper expenses, as long as they are required for your job.

You may also write off the cost of your cellular phone—but only that portion of the expenses that are attributable to business.

☞ CAUTION Sorry, but you're no longer able to deduct any portion of your standard monthly base charge for the first telephone line into your home. But you may write off the cost of additional work-related lines and work-related long distance calls.

Also, you may not deduct cellular phone expenses unless your employer requires you to maintain the phone as a condition of employment, and the phone is for his or her convenience only. Furthermore, if your cellular phone is used less than 50 percent of the time for business, you may only write off its cost using the less favorable straight-line depreciation. In other words, the same restrictions that apply to computers apply to cellular phones. (See Chapter 18 for details.)

Tools and Supplies

Say you purchase a $10 mechanical pencil for use in your work. Uncle Sam allows you to deduct this expense in the year you pay it.

He also permits you to write off the cost of larger items—a desk and couch for your office, say—but you must depreciate these items, meaning you write off their cost over several years. (See Chapter 18 for more on depreciation.)

Transportation and Travel

You may write off the cost of business transportation and travel if your employer does not reimburse you for the full cost. (See Chapters 10 and 12 for more on deducting transportation and travel expenses.)

☞ **CAUTION** Generally, the cost of commuting is not deductible, although the IRS now allows you to write off the cost of traveling between your home and a *temporary* place of work. (See Chapter 13 for information on writing off the cost of your automobile.)

Work Clothes and Uniforms

The rules allow you to deduct the cost and upkeep of work clothes and uniforms as long as you meet two conditions. Your employer must require you to wear special clothes on the job, and the clothing must not be suitable for ordinary or everyday wear.

Say you work as a manager of a store that sells fashionable designer clothing. Your employer requires you to wear only clothes sold in the shop. You may not, however, write off the cost of your fancy duds, because they are also suitable for ordinary wear.

So write off the cost of your uniforms if you are one of the following:

- Civilian faculty member of a military school.

- Firefighter.

- Jockey.

- Letter carrier.

- Nurse.

- Police officer.

- Professional ballplayer.

- Transportation worker, such as an airline pilot or bus driver.

TIP   You may also deduct the cost of protective clothing required in your work, for instance, safety shoes and glasses, hard hats, or work gloves.

EXPENSES RELATED TO YOUR INVESTMENTS

The government allows you to deduct costs associated with those investments that produce taxable income. Before we get to our alphabetical checklist of what you may write off, here a few general rules.

You may not write off sales commissions and other expenses you pay when you purchase investments. These expenses are "capital costs." That is, they are considered part of the cost of your investment and contribute to its basis—the cost of your property for tax purposes.

When it comes time to sell, you add these capital costs to the amount you paid for the investment, if your broker reported *gross* proceeds to you on a *Form 1099-B*.

However, if your broker has already subtracted them from the sales proceeds, and has reported *net* proceeds to you, then no adjustment to your basis is required. The important thing is that the proceeds you report on your tax return equals the amount reported to you and the IRS on the Form 1099-B.

Here is an example. Say you purchase 100 shares of stock at $20 a share for a total of $2,000. You pay your broker a sales commission of $150.

A year later, you sell the stock for $25 a share, or a total of $2,500. To calculate your gain, you add the amount you paid for the stock (in this case, $2,000) and your costs of acquiring your investment (your broker's commission of $150).

Next, you subtract this total, $2,150, from the amount you received when you sold the stock, $2,500. The result, $350, is your taxable gain.

Now, on to the checklist.

Accounting Fees

If you pay an accountant to keep track of your taxable investments or help you with planning, you may write off these fees.

Computers

If you use a computer to keep track of your investments, you are entitled to a deduction for the machine either through depreciation or by use of a limited expensing election. (See Chapter 18 for more information on writing off computers.)

Custodial Fees for Dividend Reinvestment Plans

No doubt you have heard of dividend reinvestment plans. These programs allow you to use your dividends to purchase additional shares. Some companies offering these plans charge participants a custodial or service fee. And you are entitled to deduct these charges on your return.

Entertainment

The law says you may claim a deduction equal to 80 percent of those meal and entertainment expenses that are associated with your taxable investments. So if you take your stockbroker to lunch to discuss her recommendations, feel free to write off 80 percent of the cost of the meal. (See Chapters 10 and 11 for more information on entertainment deductions.)

Investment Adviser Fees

If you pay someone to manage your investments, you may deduct any amounts you pay that person. The only requirement: Your investments must produce taxable income.

Here's an example. Say you decide to put all of your money in tax-free municipal bonds. And you pay someone to manage these bond investments. Under the rules, you may not deduct the fee you pay your money manager. The reason: Your investments don't produce taxable income.

☞ **CAUTION**   You may not know it, but mutual funds often charge you for investment fees. They do this by reducing the amount of dividend income you receive.

How do you handle this fee on your tax return?

Include in your taxable income the gross amount of the dividend shown on your statement. Then claim the investment fees as miscellaneous itemized deductions.

 TIP   Good news! These fees are exempt from the 2 percent floor.

IRA Administration Fees

The law allows you to write off trustees' administration fees that you pay to maintain your Individual Retirement Accounts (IRAs).

Our advice: Pay this fee separately if your miscellaneous deductions for the year top the 2 percent floor. But if you fall below the floor, save yourself the trouble of writing a separate check. Let your IRA fork over the administration fee. But be aware, if you go this route, you will have that much less in your IRA.

Legal Fees

The same rule that applies to fees for investment advisers applies to fees for legal services. You may deduct the amounts you pay as long as the lawyer's advice was related to the determination of your tax liability, tax planning or keeping track of investments.

☞ **CAUTION**   You may write off only those legal fees that are not part of the cost of acquiring an investment or defending title to it.

Here is an example. Say you purchase an apartment building, and you hire an attorney to handle the closing. The lawyer's fee is a capital cost, meaning it is related to acquiring the property. So it is not deductible.

But all isn't lost. The fee is added to your cost in the land and the building, and the portion allocable to the building increases the amount of depreciation you claim.

Office Expenses

The law won't allow you to deduct office expenses—such as rent—that are related to managing your investments and collecting taxable income from them. (See Chapter 16 for the details on how to write off home offices.)

☞ **CAUTION** The IRS says you may not write off the cost of hiring someone to guard your personal residence against burglary attempts—even if your home is loaded with evidence of your favorite hobby, collecting valuable art, for example. Nor may you write off a security system to protect coin or other collections.

Postage and Supplies

Again, as long as your investments produce taxable income, you may write off the cost of postage and supplies associated with these investments.

Safe Deposit Box Rental

Uncle Sam says you may deduct the cost of renting a safe deposit box if you use the box to store investments—or papers related to investments—that generate taxable income. But you may not write off the cost if you use the box only for personal items or tax-exempt securities.

Service Fees

You may write off fees you pay to a broker, a bank, a trustee, or other agent to collect your taxable interest or dividends on shares of stock.

But as we have seen, you may not deduct a fee you pay to a broker to buy investment property, such as stocks or bonds. You must add this fee to the cost of your property.

☞ **CAUTION** The IRS won't allow you to write off bank check-writing fees on an interest-bearing personal checking account.

Subscriptions

You're allowed to claim a deduction for subscriptions to investment-related publications. But remember, you may not write off in one year the cost of a multiple-year subscription. You may deduct subscriptions one year at a time.

Telephone

You may deduct the cost of investment-related telephone expenses, including the cost of cellular phones and long distance calls. However, as we discussed earlier, the law imposes new limits on the deductibility of cellular phones.

Also you may not deduct any portion of your standard monthly basic charge for the first telephone line into your house. But you may still write off the cost of any other investment-related phone expenses.

Transportation and Travel

The rules let you write off the cost of transportation and travel associated with investments that produce taxable income. For example, you may claim a deduction for your mileage and parking fees when you visit your stockbroker, so long as you do not invest solely in tax-exempt instruments.

☞ **CAUTION** Sorry, but Uncle Sam will not allow you to write off the cost of travel to an investment seminar or convention. Nor may you deduct the cost of the seminar or convention itself.

You are also out of luck when it comes to writing off transportation and other expenses you pay to attend stockholders' meetings of companies in which you own stock but have no other interest. You may not deduct these expenses even if you are attending the meeting to get information that would be useful in making future investments. (See Chapter 12 for more on transportation and travel expenses.)

EXPENSES RELATED TO YOUR TAXES

Here is our checklist of deductions related to tax planning and preparation.

Appraisal Fees

You may deduct these fees if you pay them to determine the fair market value of property you donate to charity. The reason: The fees go to determine the amount of your deduction.

Legal Fees

If you pay for tax advice, it is deductible. You may even deduct legal expenses for tax advice related to a divorce, as long as your attorney's bill specifies how much is for tax advice.

Tax Planning and Preparation Fees

Usually you may write off, in the year you pay them, tax counsel and assistance fees, such as fees you pay to have your tax return prepared.

So you may deduct on your 1990 return those fees you pay in 1990 for preparing your 1989 return, as well as fees for an early start on your 1990 return.

You also may write off expenses you pay for determining, collecting, or refunding any tax—including income tax, estate tax, gift tax, sales tax, or property tax. So the cost of any IRS user fee for ruling requests from the service is deductible.

And you may deduct fees you pay to a consultant to advise you on the tax consequences of a transaction.

More good news: If you contest a tax assessment, any fees you pay are deductible, even if your defense is unsuccessful. And you may deduct professional fees you pay to obtain federal tax rulings. Finally, you may also write off the cost of defending yourself if you are audited.

TIP Uncle Sam allows you to claim a deduction for tax preparation and planning books—including *The Price Waterhouse Personal Tax Adviser.*

CASUALTY LOSSES

If you itemize, Uncle Sam may let you deduct your casualty losses, but the amount of the deduction will be less than the loss you suffer. Casualty losses are not subject to the 2 percent limit discussed earlier, but are subject to other limitations, discussed below.

If you incur a loss that is sudden, unexpected, or unusual—such as an earthquake, hurricane, flood, or fire—you may have the start of a casualty loss deduction. If the loss occurs over time, say, a period of several years, such as termite damage, you're out of luck.

If you have a loss that fits the bill, you must make a few calculations before you find out how much you may write off. First you must determine the decrease in the property's fair market value and your *basis* in the property. The lesser of these amounts is the loss incurred.

Fair market value is the price you could sell the property for, not what it costs to replace it. You can support the fair market value decrease by using pictures, appraisals or published listings, such as automobile "bluebooks." The cost of making repairs to bring the property to its condition before the casualty may indicate its decrease in fair market value.

TIP The cost of pictures, appraisals and the like are deductible as miscellaneous itemized deductions, since you need this information for your tax return.

Once you figure out the amount of the loss incurred, reduce it for any insurance reimbursements you receive or expect to get. Then knock off $100.

CAUTION You must file an insurance claim if you have insurance that may cover the loss. If you don't, Uncle Sam won't allow you to deduct any part of the loss as a casualty loss. However, any portion of the loss not covered by insurance is not subject to this rule.

Do this calculation separately for each of the casualty losses you incur during the year. Add up the amounts calculated for all your losses. Whatever remains after subtracting 10% of your AGI is your write-off.

CAUTION The $100 reduction applies to each loss during the year. However, if several losses are incurred as a result of the same event, only one $100 reduction applies, no matter how many pieces of property are involved.

A single event may be two closely related causes—like wind and flood damage from the same storm. Also, a hailstorm could damage both your house in the suburbs and your car downtown—again, a single event, and only one $100 reduction applies.

TIP Casualty losses are generally only deductible in the year in which the casualty occurs. But before you claim your casualty loss deduction, consider the special rule for designated disaster losses—that is, losses incurred in areas declared by the President of the U.S. as disaster areas—such as last year's Hurricane Hugo or the California earthquake. The IRS allows you to elect to deduct these losses in the year the disaster occurred, or the immediately preceding year. The limits discussed above apply to the year you take the deduction.

TIP If the property is used for business, such as a rental condo, the casualty loss wil not be subject to the passive loss rules which may otherwise limit the deductible loss (see Chapter 19 for more information on passive losses).

QUESTIONS AND ANSWERS

QUESTION: *In addition to my regular work, I operate a small kennel. This year my little business was awash in red ink. How much may I deduct?*

It depends. Uncle Sam doesn't mind if you dabble in a small business just for the fun of it. But he doesn't want to help foot the bill—hence, the so-called *hobby loss* limitation rule.

Under these rules, you must first determine whether your operation is a hobby or a for-profit business. If it is a hobby, you may deduct hobby expenses that aren't otherwise deductible only up to the amount of your hobby income. What does "not otherwise deductible" mean? Well, let's say that you breed and sell show dogs. Dog food isn't ordinarily a deductible cost—unlike, say, real estate taxes—so it falls into the category of expenses that are "not otherwise deductible."

You aren't allowed to create a tax loss from your hobby to slash your overall tax bill. One other point: You claim your hobby expenses as miscellaneous itemized deductions, not on Schedule C.

How does the IRS determine if your enterprise is a hobby or a for-profit business?

First, the IRS provides an objective test. If you meet this test, the government presumes—at least for this year—that you are engaged in a for-profit business.

Under the objective test you must realize a profit from an activity in three out of the most recent five consecutive years. If horse breeding and racing are your passions, you need to make a profit from these activities in two out of seven consecutive years.

And second, there is a subjective *facts-and-circumstances test.* Under it the IRS considers whether you operate your business in a businesslike way. It also examines your expertise in your chosen activity, the time and effort you devote to it, and the amount of personal pleasure you derive from it.

☞ **CAUTION** The rules on itemized deductions may also restrict your hobby write-offs to an amount less than your hobby income. Here is how.

You know that hobby deductions—other than taxes you may deduct as a personal expense, such as property taxes—are classified as miscellaneous itemized deductions. And as we have seen, you may deduct them only to the extent that they exceed 2 percent of your AGI.

So although you must include the full amount of your hobby earnings in taxable income, your hobby write-offs will offset this income only to the extent your combined miscellaneous itemized deductions top the 2 percent floor. If your combined miscellaneous itemized deductions are less than 2 percent of AGI, you get no tax deduction for your hobby expenses.

QUESTIONS AND ANSWERS

QUESTION: *I now know what I may write off as a miscellaneous deduction. But what may I not deduct?*

Here's an alphabetical checklist of some items you may *not* deduct:

- Burial or funeral expenses.

- Campaign expenses.

- Commuting expenses.

- Fees and licenses, such as car licenses, marriage licenses, and dog tags.

- Fines and penalties, such as parking tickets.

- Home repairs, insurance, and rent.

- Life insurance premiums.

- Losses from the sale of your home, furniture, personal car, and so forth.

- Lost or misplaced cash or property.

- Lunches and meals you eat while working late.

- Personal legal expenses.

- Personal living or family expenses.

- Political contributions.

- Self-improvement expenses, such as the cost of attending a self-enrichment workshop.

- Voluntary unemployment benefit fund contributions.

One last word on final expenses: Whereas funeral and burial expenses are not deductible on a personal income tax return, the executor or administrator deducts such expenses on a federal estate tax return.

QUESTION: *I started a new job this year that required me to move to another city. May I write off my moving expenses?*

The law allows you to deduct moving expenses that are due to a change in your employment. So if you accept a job in a new city, you may deduct the expenses of moving to that city—as long as you meet IRS guidelines. What, you ask, are the IRS guidelines?

The rules say that you must stay in your new job at least 39 weeks. Also, you must relocate within one year of the date you assume your new post, and your new job must be at least 35 miles farther away from your existing home than your old job.

You deduct moving expenses as miscellaneous itemized deductions. But moving expenses are not subject to the 2 percent floor that applies to most miscellaneous deductions.

QUESTION: *What may I deduct as moving expenses?*

Uncle Sam says that you may write off the cost of moving your household belongings, including your car and your pets, to a new location. And he imposes no ceiling on this write-off as long as the amount you claim is reasonable in light of the circumstances of your move.

You may also deduct travel expenses, including lodging for you and your family and 80 percent of the cost of meals, that you rack up on your way to your new home.

And if you are not able to move into your new home right away, you may write off temporary living expenses—for up to 30 days.

What's more, you may deduct the cost of house-hunting trips. And if you are a homeowner, you may deduct the cost of selling your old home and buying a new one, including real-estate commissions, attorney fees, and so on. If you rent, you may write off the cost of canceling your old lease and securing a new one.

☞ **CAUTION**   The rules cap deductions for purchase and lease costs, housing-hunting expenses, and temporary living expenses to a total of $3,000. Of this amount, house-hunting and temporary living expenses may not exceed $1,500.

QUESTION: *I often buy state lottery tickets. May I deduct my losses?*

The rules allow you to deduct the cost of your losing tickets and any other gambling losses—but only up to the amount of your winnings.

Say you spend $60 on losing lottery tickets. And your winnings for the year add up to $100. You include the $100 in your income on page 1 of your Form 1040, then you subtract $60 as a miscellaneous itemized deduction, which isn't subject to the 2 percent floor.

What if you won nothing during the year? You may not write off any of your gambling losses because you have no gambling winnings.

If you are audited, the IRS may ask you to substantiate your claims. So you should maintain records of your winnings and losses.

What kinds of records?

Hold on to copies of keno tickets that are validated by the gambling establishment, copies of your casino credit records, and copies of your casino check-cashing records. In the case of slot machines, keep a log of your winnings by date and time that the slot machine was played.

As far as blackjack, craps, poker, roulette, baccarat, and other table games are concerned, write down the table number at which you were playing, and if you used credit, keep the casino card or marker.

With bingo, maintain a record of the number of games played, the cost of tickets you purchased, and the amount of your winnings.

In the case of horse or dog racing, keep a log of the races, your wagers, the amounts you collected on winning tickets, and the amounts lost on losing tickets. Likewise, with lotteries, maintain a record of tickets purchased, dates, winnings, and losses.

10

Safeguarding Your Travel and Entertainment Expenses

Expenses that you rack up for business-related travel, entertainment, and meals *may be* legitimate deductions from your taxable income. We stress "may be" for two reasons.

First, to qualify as deductions, these expenses must conform to a stringent set of rules. You can understand the reasons for the stringency: There's no reason why other taxpayers should subsidize someone's good times, unless there's a legitimate business reason for the expense.

Second, you have to be able to prove that you actually incurred the expense. That means you must maintain adequate records.

In this first of three chapters covering business-related travel and entertainment expenses, we explain the record-keeping requirements. The next two chapters cover the specific rules that apply to deductions, first, for meals and entertainment, then for business-related travel.

WHAT YOU NEED FOR THE RECORD

Suppose the IRS decides to audit you. And it asks you to prove your outlays for business travel, meal, and entertainment expenses.

What kinds of evidence should you provide? Actually, Uncle Sam considers two types. The first is *documentary evidence*, which the IRS defines as any kind of receipt that's corroborated by a third party. Cancelled checks meet this requirement, and so do credit card slips.

The second is a *log* or diary. The government, however, doesn't require you to keep a log as long as you note all the required information on your documentary evidence—on the back of credit card slips, say. Here's the information you're required to record.

Business Purpose

For each expense, note the business reason or nature of the business benefit you have realized—or expect to realize—from the trip or entertainment.

Say you purchase drinks for a customer and yourself. The drinks follow a lengthy sales presentation during which you describe your company's new computer.

The business purpose of the drinks is to try to clinch the sale. You must document the topic of business conversation that took place before, during, or after the entertainment. Example: "Discussed possible purchase by XYZ Corporation of 10 computers."

Business Relationship

You should identify each person you entertain by name and your business relationship—for example, Joe Jones, President, XYZ Corporation. Also, write down the names and business relationships of any people you visit on a business trip.

Cost

Jot down the amount you spend for each item—dinner, say, and theater tickets, followed by a round of drinks at your favorite nightspot. And don't overlook tips and incidental items, such as taxi fares and telephone calls.

Time

If you conduct a business discussion during a meal or while you entertain, there's no need to record the length of your business conversation, but you must note the date.

If you don't discuss business during the meal or entertainment, the rules require you to jot down both the date and the length of the business discussion that took place before or after the meal or entertainment.

In the case of travel expenses, write down the dates you leave and return from your trip and the number of days you spend away from home.

Place

The rules require you to record where you run up the expense—the name of a restaurant, say. If you don't discuss business during the meal or entertainment, note where the business conversation took place before or after the meal or entertainment.

When it comes to travel, jot down your destination—the name of a city will do.

TIP Special recordkeeping rules apply if you write off dues to social, luncheon, athletic, or sporting clubs. Each time you use the club, you must document whether your use was business or personal.

That's because the deductibility of dues to a club is based upon your business usage. This is one area where documentation is absolutely critical. Keeping accurate records will ensure that you collect the maximum allowable deduction.

NOTE IT NOW

You should document your expenses as close as possible to the time you take a business trip or entertain business colleagues. The reason: The IRS places greater value on records that you keep currently.

Say you dine out on business three times a week. The morning after each business meal, you jot down on the back of your charge slip all the data Uncle Sam requires—the time, date, and place of your meal, the nature of your business discussion, and so on. The IRS is unlikely to challenge the validity of your deduction.

Now let's say your office mate also wines and dines customers several nights a week. But she doesn't write down anything until the end of the month.

Uncle Sam is far more likely to challenge her evidence. The reason: The information isn't timely, and it's based on memory.

Of course, a log where you record all your business engagements and a file of your receipts are the best evidence, as far as Uncle Sam is concerned.

TIP Stationery stores offer a variety of easy-to-maintain log books that are no bigger than a checkbook. You may find one of these logs useful.

A word to the wise: Never underestimate the importance of writing down the required information. Without this documentation, the IRS may disallow your perfectly legitimate deductions.

RECORDS YOU DON'T HAVE TO KEEP

Here's one category of expenses you don't need to keep receipts for. That category includes anything, except lodging, costing less than $25.

The IRS requires you to keep documentary evidence only for outlays of that amount or more. If you spend less than $25, you don't need receipts. Simply write down the proper information in your log or on a slip of paper.

ACCOUNTING TO YOUR EMPLOYER

One more thing you ought to know. When you account to your employer for your business expenses, you generally don't have to account for the same expenses in your return. But watch out—you may be surprised.

Uncle Sam says that your employer's arrangement for advances, allowances or expense reimbursements must meet three requirements.

First, the monies you receive must be for business expenses you incur as an employee.

Second, you must provide your employer with substantiation. How, you say? That depends on the type of expense. You've read about overall record keeping in this chapter—more specifics come in the next two.

Finally, if you received more from your employer than you actually spent, you must return the excess.

Is there a benefit to you if your employer has these requirements, and you comply? You bet there is. In your return you don't need to report either the expenses or the monies you receive from your employer.

What if your employer's arrangement lacks one or all of these requirements? Or, you just fail to comply? Uncle Sam says all of the advances, allowances or expense reimbursements you receive are to be reported as income on your W-2.

Seem painful? It gets worse—the income is subject to both income tax withholding and FICA. Furthermore, you will only be able to deduct your business expenses as itemized deductions subject to the two percent floor (see Chapter 9).

Let's see how it works.

Say you receive an advance of $300 for a business trip and your actual business expenses are $300. Your employer's expense reimbursement arrangement has all three requirements. You comply.

What do you report on your return? Nothing. You show neither the business expenses nor the advance.

But say that the actual business expenses you incur are $400. You just haven't received enough in reimbursement. The amount received still isn't income, but you may be able to deduct the "excess" expenses as miscellaneous itemized deductions subject to the two percent floor.

One more twist. Say you receive an advance from your employer for business expenses you expect to incur. Your employer stipulates that amounts spent must be for its business and that you must provide substantiation. You account to your employer for how you spent the money. But say that your employer is a generous person and does not require you to return any amounts over your expenses—at least not right away.

He knows that you will use the excess to cover expenses down the road. In this case, the entire advance is considered taxable income to you because the excess is not required to be returned. And you may deduct all of the business expenses only as miscellaneous itemized deductions subject to the two percent floor.

☞ **CAUTION** This situation, or situations where you fail to account to your employer whose arrangement contains the proper requirements, can cost you real dollars. You may think that your business expenses will offset the income paid to you by your employer. But don't forget that the income may be subject to FICA. Further, the expenses may be limited by the two percent floor on miscellaneous itemized deductions.

Uncle Sam makes one exception to these rules. Say your employer imposes all three requirements. You receive an allowance of $300 but actually only spend $250 on legitimate business expenses. You provide substantiation, but contrary to the arrangement fail to return the excess. You expect to use it for business expenses sometime in the future.

You don't have to report the expenses on your return, but now you'll have an additional $50 of income to report. That $50 shows up on your W-2 and is subject to payroll tax withholding.

QUESTIONS AND ANSWERS

QUESTION: *My employer reimburses me for my travel, meal, and entertainment expenses. I don't have to keep records for the IRS, too, do I?*

If you make an adequate accounting of your expenses to your employer, chances are, you don't have to substantiate them again for your personal tax return.

But if you claim any deductions on your personal return—say, for expenses beyond those reimbursed by your employer—you must keep records to back up these claims.

The IRS also requires you to document your expenses if you're related to your employer or if your employer doesn't require you to account for your expenses.

QUESTION: *When it comes to the $25 rule, do I add up what I spent the entire evening or only at each spot?*

The IRS looks at each expenditure separately.

For example, if you take a client to dinner and a play, the cost of dinner is treated as one expenditure, the play as another. If you spend less than $25 for dinner and less than $25 for theater tickets, receipts aren't required for either expense.

☞ **CAUTION** Say you purchase several rounds of drinks at your favorite watering hole. The amount you spend is treated as one item for purposes of the $25 rule.

11

How to Write Off Business Meals and Entertainment

You and a business client attend a professional football game. And your question is, is the cost of the tickets deductible as a business-related expense?

Well, it might be deductible, or part of it might be deductible. But the answer depends on what the two of you did before or after the game, why you went to the game with that particular client, and—not least of all—where you sat.

The rules governing business-related entertainment and meals are at least as complex as those governing football, and, like the football rules, the tax law sometimes involves difficult judgment calls upon which two reasonable people might disagree.

Nonetheless, if you do any business-related entertaining or dining, the deductions available are certainly worth taking.

In this chapter we tell you what you need to know to claim the deductions without provoking a penalty flag from the IRS.

LAVISH OR EXTRAVAGANT

We start with the basics. Uncle Sam allows you to write off business meals and entertainment expenses as long as they aren't *lavish or extravagant*.

99

What, you ask, is lavish or extravagant?

The government doesn't say. But we have never seen IRS auditors disallow a deduction simply because it exceeded a certain dollar amount.

Our advice: Dine and entertain in any style you think is reasonable. It's highly unlikely the IRS will label a deduction as lavish or extravagant unless it's totally outrageous.

And *outrageous* is usually easy to spot.

Say you're a plumbing contractor, and you do business in Texas. You take your favorite customer to lunch in Paris—not Paris, Texas, but Paris, France.

You may write off the cost of the meal, but, chances are, the IRS will consider the cost of your two round-trip airline tickets as lavish and extravagant. The reason is simple: The trip to France is neither ordinary nor necessary to your business.

WHICH MEALS AND ENTERTAINMENT QUALIFY?

The law allows an 80 percent deduction for meals and entertainment expenses that are *directly* related to the active conduct of your business. An 80 percent deduction is also allowed for meals and entertainment costs that are *associated* with the conduct of your business.

What's the difference?

Uncle Sam defines *directly related meals and entertainment* as any meal or entertainment during which you *actively* discuss or conduct your business. Also, your primary purpose must be to transact business. That is, you must expect to gain some benefit from your meals and entertainment—other than goodwill.

Consider this Tax Court case as an example.

A company invited a number of people to attend the Super Bowl as its guests. Customers, employees, and friends came with their families.

When the company invited its guests, it made no mention of a sales seminar. Nor did it reserve space in the hotel for any sales meetings. A dinner meeting that the company claimed was for business was held in a hotel dining room with other patrons present.

The trip was for pleasure, not business.

The court noted that no pre-weekend correspondence referred to business meetings. No bona fide business purpose was served by the presence of wives and children. And only random conversations with some guests involved business.

Also, there was no evidence that the weekend promoted business or that other companies used similar programs to do so. The court concluded that the weekend was little more than a group social excursion to the Super Bowl and disallowed the deduction.

TIP No amount of Monday morning quarterbacking can convert a Super Bowl weekend into a business-related sales seminar once the game is over. With careful planning, though, you can deduct these expenses as long as the business purpose of the gathering is clear.

For example, you can refer to the get-together as a sales seminar from the start. You can also distribute an agenda prior to the meeting and schedule and hold business discussions in surroundings that are conducive to business, such as a private meeting room in a hotel.

Here's another example: Say you're an accountant, and you're at a client's office going over her business plan. Your meeting starts at 10 a.m. and continues through 4 p.m.

But the two of you don't break for lunch. Instead, you order out and munch your sandwiches while sitting at her conference room table. Under the rules, the meal is directly related because you continue your business discussion through lunch.

But the IRS assumes the meal or entertainment isn't directly related if it takes place in a setting that makes doing business difficult—if not impossible. For example, the IRS presumes you can't conduct business in a noisy nightclub or a theater.

Associated meals and entertainment is far more common among businesspeople than directly related meals and entertainment—and far harder to pin down.

Here's the IRS rule for this type of meal and entertainment: It must precede or follow a bona fide business discussion. Also, you must prove that your expense was for a specific business purpose—to obtain a new client, say, or keep an old one.

Simply taking your attorney to a baseball game to cultivate good feelings doesn't qualify as associated entertainment, for example. But if you met before the game to discuss your plans to acquire another company, you could write off 80 percent of the cost.

It isn't enough, in other words, that the person you take to the baseball game has a business relationship with you, as an important potential sales account, for instance. You must actually conduct business before or after the game.

TIP   When Uncle Sam says you must conduct business, he doesn't mean that you must close on a sale. Say, for example, that you are a distributor of a new product, and you are scrambling to secure retail shelf space for that product.

You take a retailer to lunch, but he does not, despite your best efforts, agree to give you the shelf space you desire.

Still, the meal is 80 percent deductible.

BUSINESS MEALS

When is a meal a *business meal*? It's a business meal—and therefore 80 percent deductible—if it's directly related to or associated with the active conduct of your trade or business. If it's not, it's not deductible at all. Here's an example.

Say you sell paper products, and one of your best customers is the XYZ Corporation. You take the president of XYZ out for a fancy dinner.

You don't discuss business before, during, or after the meal. You didn't expect to talk shop because all sales to XYZ are negotiated by the company purchasing agent.

The cost of the meal isn't deductible because it doesn't meet the requirements of either directly related or associated entertainment—that is, you and your guest didn't actually discuss business before, after, or during the meal.

Something else you should know: When we refer to the cost of the meal, we mean the cost of the food and drink you consume, plus the cost of tips and taxes.

Also included in the cost are cover charges, room rental fees, and other entertainment expenses. Here are some other rules governing business meal deductions.

Someone from the company must be present at the meal, or your write-off isn't going to fly. You may not, in other words, treat visiting clients to a deductible dinner and night on the town unless someone from the company is willing to share the repast.

But you may deduct 80 percent of the cost if your attorney, accountant, or other professional adviser attends the business meal as your representative.

The cost of including spouses—yours and your business associate's—at a meal may be 80 percent deductible. The meal must qualify as business-related. Your own expenses and those of your associate must meet all of the qualifications for deduction.

The 80 percent limit on deductibility applies to all business meals—whether you're dining with someone in your own city or dining solo at some out-of-town motel during a business trip. But the costs of getting to and from a restaurant—by taxi, say—are still fully deductible.

The 80 percent rule also applies to so-called *single sum expenditures*. What's a single sum expenditure? Here's an example to illustrate.

Say a hotel includes one or more meals in its room charge. In this case, Uncle Sam says, you must allocate part of the room charge for food and part for lodging.

The part for lodging is fully deductible, but you may write off only 80 percent of the food costs. The single-sum rule also applies to *per diem arrangements*.

What about the cost of food and beverages served at conventions, seminars, or meetings? It, too, is subject to the 80 percent limitation. And the old rule that allowed you to deduct the full cost of meals you consumed while attending certain seminars is no longer in place.

But the 80 percent rule doesn't affect employer reimbursement policies at all. Your employer may still reimburse 100 percent for the cost of your business meals, as long as you account to him or her for the money you spend. Note, however, that your employer is now limited to deducting 80 percent of the expense.

Nor does the 80 percent rule apply to most food-related employee fringe benefits. The holiday ham, the employee cafeteria that qualifies as a *de minimis fringe benefit* (one too small to really matter), and the food and refreshments served at the company picnic are still fully deductible expenses to your employer and nontaxable to you.

☞ **CAUTION** Also not subject to the 80 percent rule are taxable employee benefits, such as the vacation packages awarded to salespeople for meeting quotas. (The value of these benefits, however, must be reported on employees' W-2 forms and is subject to withholding.)

TIP Under the rules you may deduct 80 percent of the cost of business meals you prepare and serve in your own home—as long as you can prove the meals were for business, not pleasure.

BUSINESS ENTERTAINMENT

The rules for deducting business entertainment expenses parallel those for business meals—they must be directly related or associated with the active conduct of your trade or business. Also 80 percent of the cost of legitimate entertainment expenses are deductible. Of course, even after you meet this rule, you are faced with the particulars and the exceptions.

Parking costs at a sporting event, unlike the cab fare to a restaurant, aren't considered transportation expenses. Rather, your parking tab is part of the entertainment expense—and only 80 percent deductible.

Furthermore, with one exception, only 80 percent of the price printed on the entertainment ticket is deductible. If you pay a premium to an agent or a scalper, that part of the cost is strictly on you.

The only exception to this rule is the *charitable sporting event*—one in which all of the proceeds go to charity and practically all of the labor is voluntary. You may deduct as a business entertainment expense the full cost of these tickets, plus the agent's fee, if any.

Moreover, any food and beverage costs that are part of the ticket package are also 100 percent deductible. Note, sadly: High school and college games don't qualify as charity events.

CAUTION Skyboxes are out as deductible business entertainment expenses.

TIP You should know, too, that you may write off your spouse's share of entertainment costs if he or she accompanied you during entertainment that the IRS considers "directly related."

Uncle Sam also recognizes that it can be difficult—if not downright rude—to entertain an out-of-town client or customer without his or her spouse.

So, he allows you to write off the cost of the spouse's entertainment, as long as the expense of entertaining the customer or client was deductible.

And more good news: Say your spouse joined the party because your client's spouse came along. In this case, feel free to deduct your spouse's expenses.

QUESTIONS AND ANSWERS

QUESTION: *I belong to a luncheon club. May I write off the dues I pay?*

The IRS allows you to deduct the business portion of the dues you pay to a luncheon club—or dues to any other social, athletic, or country club, for that matter—as long as you can prove that you use the club more than 50 percent of the time for business.

But you may write off only that portion of your dues that you can attribute to directly related meals and entertainment, meaning meals and entertainment during which you actively discuss business.

One other catch: The amount of dues you may write off—that is, that amount attributable to business—is subject to the 80 percent rule.

Say, for example, that you use the club 60 percent of the time for directly related meals and entertainment. Your dues times 60 percent times 80 percent is the amount that is deductible.

TIP If you're near—but not over—the 50 percent mark, make a conscious effort to increase to more than 50 percent the business dining and entertaining you do at your club. If it's 50 percent or less, you get no deductions for the dues

QUESTION: *I belong to a professional society. Once a month, we hold a breakfast meeting. The cost of these breakfasts is not broken out but is included with my dues. How do I write off the breakfasts?*

You deduct these meals as meals.

It's up to you to calculate how much of the amount you pay is for dues—and 100 percent deductible if you use the club exclusively for business—and how much is for breakfasts—80 percent deductible.

QUESTION: *What's the "quiet business meal" rule?*

In the old days you could deduct the cost of a "quiet business meal." As long as the environment was conducive to a business discussion, you weren't required to discuss business before, during, or after the meal to make the cost deductible.

In 1986, Congress—in a belt-tightening mood—zapped this rule. You may no longer claim a deduction for quiet business meals.

You may deduct only the cost of business meals that meet the definition of directly related or associated entertainment.

QUESTION: *Are meals I eat while I'm out of town on a business trip subject to the 80 percent rule?*

The law says that you may write off only 80 percent of the cost of business meals. And it makes no difference if you ingest them during out-of-town business trips. (See Chapter 12 for more information on travel expenses.)

QUESTION: *I own my own company. And I pay a per diem amount to my employees when they travel. Do I write off the whole amount?*

Companies that pay their employees a per diem when they travel will have to find out how much of that goes toward meals and how much toward other expenses.

They may ask employees to document how they spend the money given to them. Then they may deduct only 80 percent of the amount that goes for meals.

In addition, if your company pays you a per diem equal to the standard federal allowance, the company may deduct only 80 percent of the amount paid for the meals portion.

Another idea: Companies may determine how much employees spend on average for meals when they travel and deduct 80 percent of that amount.

QUESTION: *My employer reimbursed me for my moving expenses, including the cost of meals we ate traveling from our old home to our new home. What are the tax consequences?*

Your employer reimburses you for your full moving expenses, including the cost of the meals you ate while you were on the road.

You report the amount you received from your employer as income. Then you write off 80 percent of the cost of the meals on your return as an itemized deduction. You report this information to the IRS using Form 3903, "Moving Expenses."

If your employer did not reimburse you for these expenses, you could claim 80 percent of the cost of your meals as an itemized expense in your moving expense deduction.

Moving expenses—including meals—are not subject to the 2 percent floor on miscellaneous itemized deductions.

QUESTION: *My employer pays me a flat $100 a month for entertainment, and I do not have to account for how I spend this money. How do I treat this amount on my tax return?*

Since you didn't account for how you spent this money, the IRS doesn't consider these amounts to be reimbursement. Rather, it considers them taxable income.

So your employer reports your monthly entertainment allowance as income on your Form W-2, and the amount is subject to all payroll tax withholdings.

If you want to claim deductions for business meals or entertainment expenses actually incurred, those are subject to the 80 percent rule and to the 2 percent floor on miscellaneous itemized deductions (see Chapter 9).

QUESTION: *I'm self-employed and run up about $2,000 a year in business meal and entertainment expenses. May I still write off at least 80 percent of this amount from my self-employment income?*

Self-employed people may deduct the expense of business meals and entertainment before they determine their self-employment income—so long as they abide by the 80 percent limit.

12

How to Write Off Travel Expenses

You may not know it, but there is still ample opportunity to collect generous write-offs for business travel. And combining business with pleasure may still pay off as well. Just be sure that you know—and follow—the IRS regulations.

In this chapter we run through the rules governing write-offs for business travel. And we tell what is deductible—and what is not.

HOME AWAY FROM HOME

When you travel strictly on business, your write-offs are clear-cut. The amount you spend for lodging and transportation—hotel bills, taxi fares, and so on—is deductible. So is the cost of tips, baggage handling, business calls, telegrams, laundry, and dry cleaning.

And Uncle Sam allows a write-off for the cost of the meals you consume while you are away from home—although these expenses are deductible only up to 80 percent of the final tab. (See Chapter 11 for more on deducting business meals.)

But your travel deductions become less clear-cut when you combine business with pleasure—sightseeing, or visiting old friends, for example.

Let's say you take a vacation or other trip primarily for personal reasons. You may not deduct any of your transportation costs. You may, however, write off any business expenses you run up once you arrive at your destination.

Here is an example. Suppose you take your family to New York for a holiday. While you are there, you take time out from your vacation to see a customer.

You may deduct the cost of the cab fare between your customer's office and your hotel. And you may also write off 80 percent of the meal you buy her.

What if your primary reason for the trip was business?

You are entitled to a deduction for transportation as well. And it makes no difference if you add a few days to a business trip to see the sights.

Say, for example, that your company requires you to attend its annual sales conference, so you fly from New York to Palm Springs where the conference is being held. You spend a week at the conference, then five days vacationing.

You could deduct your hotel bill and other expenses for attending the one-week meeting. You could also write off your air fare to Palm Springs because—in the eyes of the IRS—you took the trip for bona fide business reasons.

☞ **CAUTION** The IRS scrutinizes *borderline "business" trips*, meaning trips that are part personal and part business. But as long as you can document that the main reason for your trip was business, you may deduct the entire travel cost—even if your trip includes some personal R&R.

FOREIGN TRAVEL

When you travel overseas, the law requires you to allocate all costs between the business and personal portions of your trip.

And it makes absolutely no difference that the reason you took the trip was for business. It only matters how you spend your time on the trip.

Say, for example, that your trip consisted of 70 percent business and 30 percent vacation. You could deduct only 70 percent of your transportation and lodging costs. But there are exceptions to this rule. The IRS will allow all your transportation costs if the following apply:

- You spend less than a quarter of your travel days on personal affairs.

- You are overseas for less than seven days.

- You are not in "substantial control over arranging the trip"—that is, as far as the IRS is concerned, you are not self-employed, a managing executive, or you are not related to your employer.

- Your major reason for taking the trip was not a holiday or vacation.

Another special rule: Uncle Sam may disallow a deduction for a trip to a convention outside North America if he concludes that holding the convention in, say, Beijing or Hong Kong was less reasonable than holding it here.

Also, the rules require you to show that the convention you attend is related to the active conduct of your trade or business.

Obviously, if you belong to the International Association of Criminal Attorneys, you may write off the cost of your participation in a meeting held in London.

But if you belong to the Green County Pipefitter's Association, forget about deducting the cost of attending your annual confab in Amsterdam.

☞ **CAUTION**   Uncle Sam will not allow you to write off the cost of travel expenses that are "lavish or extravagant." What meets the definition?

Let's say you own and operate a chain of dry cleaning stores. And you charter the Concorde to take you and a customer to a business meeting in London. You can be pretty certain that Uncle Sam will disallow your deduction for the trip.

However, you do not have to suffer to avoid raising IRS eyebrows. Feel free to travel in a comfortable fashion as long as it is not "lavish or extravagant." First class is okay, and you do not have to shop around for super-saver fares unless you want to.

COMBINING BUSINESS AND PLEASURE

You say you are planning a trip to a resort in the United States, and the trip is part business and part pleasure? You also say you would like to deduct the amount you spend on travel? Here are some rules that you need to know.

Your travel expenses and 80 percent of the costs of meals and entertainment are deductible only if your trip is primarily for business.

If your trip is primarily for pleasure, then none of your transportation expenses are deductible—even if you do some business once you arrive at your destination.

But you may write off expenses that are related to your business activities, regardless of whether you deduct your transportation costs.

To determine if your trip is primarily for business or pleasure, consider the amount of time you spend on both activities.

If you decide your trip is primarily for business, document your claim with records of your business activities at the resort.

TIP Uncle Sam does not require you to hold meetings close to home in order to claim a deduction for your travel expenses.

Say that your company is in the midst of reorganizing. And you and other key executives need to discuss this new structure in a place with few interruptions.

You should feel free to hold these meetings anyplace you choose—a meeting room in a hotel a few blocks away or in a hotel at an oceanside resort.

LIMITS ON CRUISES

The law limits the amount you may write off for luxury cruise expenses, even if the ship takes you from one place to another on business.

The limit? It comes to twice the highest federal government allowance for U.S. travel by executive branch employees. Currently, that amount is $147 per day. So you may deduct no more than $294 per day for luxury cruise travel expenses.

Unless the cruise company breaks out food and beverage expenses separately, these costs are fully deductible—up to the $294 per day limit, of course. If the company does itemize your meal and beverage expenses, they are only 80 percent deductible.

What happens if you attend a convention or seminar aboard a cruise ship? You are not subject to the rules we just described for general travel.

For starters, the IRS says that you get no deduction unless you can show the convention is directly related to the active conduct of your trade or business.

Also, the cruise ship must be registered in the United States—and there are few that are—and you must sail to ports of call in the United States or its possessions.

Finally, to claim your deduction, the IRS requires you to attach a statement to your tax return specifying, among other items, the length of your trip, the schedule of business activities, and the number of hours you attended these sessions. And the statement must be signed by an officer of the sponsoring organization.

One final point: The rules cap deductions for conventions or seminars aboard cruise ships to $2,000 per year per person.

QUESTIONS AND ANSWERS

QUESTION: *May I deduct the cost of taking my spouse along with me on a business trip?*

Uncle Sam will not allow you to write off the expenses of bringing along your spouse—or any other relative, for that matter—on a business trip.

But the government provides an exception to this rule in cases where a spouse's presence serves a bona fide business purpose.

Taking notes at meetings does not fit the definition of a bona fide business purpose. But entertaining clients may. The courts have upheld deductions for a spouse's traveling expenses in cases where entertaining constituted a reason for his or her presence.

If your employer sends you on a business trip and allows your spouse to accompany you, employer reimbursements for his or her expenses will be reported as taxable income to you. These expenses include transportation for your spouse and the difference between the cost of a single room versus a double room.

QUESTION: *I took my spouse with me on a business trip not paid for by my employer. I do not intend to claim a deduction for his expenses. But how do I write off my own expenses?*

If you traveled by automobile, the law allows you to deduct the full expense—even though your companion was riding in the car with you.

But if you traveled by any other mode of transportation—an airline or train, say—you may write off only the price of your ticket.

In the case of lodging, claim a deduction for the single room rate—$100 a night, say—rather than the double room rate you paid—$120 a night, for example.

13

The Right Way to Write Off Business Automobiles

The company car has been around longer than the Internal Revenue Code. So you would think that by now the rules governing write-offs for business cars would be clear-cut and easy to understand. Well, think again.

In this chapter, we try to make sense of the complicated rules for writing off business automobiles. First, though, a few words about record keeping.

KEEPING THE RECORDS

Uncle Sam says that you must substantiate the business use of your car, and that means you must maintain adequate records. You are not off the hook if you use a car owned by your employer, either. These record-keeping rules apply regardless of whether you own the car or it is provided to you by your company.

The best way: Keep a log handy to record your business miles, your destination, and the business purpose of your trip. (See the appendix for a copy of a sample log.)

These records are not just for show. When you or your employer files annual tax returns, the IRS wants proof of your automobile expenses and usage.

It wants to see the number of miles you logged for business. It wants to know the total number of miles you drove. And if you are driving a company car, the IRS wants to know if your employer allows you to use the automobile to commute.

Finally—and most important—the IRS wants to know if you have support for your deduction. If the answer is yes, you are better off if your evidence is written.

BUSINESS DRIVING DEFINED

When it comes time to write off automobile expenses, here is the first question you must ask yourself: "What percentage of my car's use may I attribute to business?"

The IRS defines *business use* as the miles you drive your car between two business locations—your office, say, and the office of a customer.

Commuting is never business use. It makes no difference what type of work you do, how far you travel to your office, or what crisis you are about to face.

A trip to work is personal and not deductible. And making a business phone call or holding a business meeting in your car while you drive will not change that fact.

For an employee, the IRS has taken the position for years that commuting is the first trip in the morning and the last trip home. So in the past if you drove from your home to a customer's office, you were—in the eyes of the IRS—commuting. And you weren't entitled to classify the trip as business.

You were able to skirt this rule if you were temporarily assigned to work at a client's place of business, which was located some distance from your metropolitan area. In this instance, you could claim as business miles the distance from you home to you client's office.

Say you're a salesperson for ABC Furniture Co., which is located five miles from your home. You're due at a client's office at 9 a.m. on a Monday morning. And you decide to drive directly from your house to your client's place of business.

Your client is based in a city 80 miles from your home and 75 miles from your office. The IRS lets you classify 80 miles as business use, because your client is located outside your geographic work area and much farther from your home than your normal place of business.

In 1990 the IRS announced a major change in policy regarding the deduction of commuting expenses. The IRS now says that for a taxpayer who has one or more regular places of business, daily transportation expenses paid or incurred in going between the taxpayer's residence and temporary work locations are deductible business expenses whether or not such temporary locations are outside the taxpayer's metropolitan area. However, such amounts may be claimed by employees only as miscellaneous itemized deductions, which are subject to a 2 percent floor.

Thus, for example, daily transportation expenses incurred by, say an accountant (who is an employee with a regular work location) between his residence and a temporary work location is now a deductible business expense.

TIP The law also carves out an exception to the commuting rule for people who are self-employed and do business from a bona fide home office. These taxpayers may claim—as business mileage—trips to and from home.

Let's say you are a physician in private practice in Chicago, and you maintain an office on the first floor of your townhouse. You see patients in your office, but once a day you drive 12 miles to a local hospital to make your rounds.

Under the rules you may claim as business mileage the 12 miles to the hospital—and the 12 miles back—even though you are driving to and from your home. The reason is, your home is also your office. Here is another example.

Say you are employed full-time by a computer manufacturer and spend your days working at its headquarters. But at night you freelance as a computer programmer. And you maintain an office in your home for this purpose.

As a freelance software writer, your largest client is a small software manufacturing company. One evening a week, you drive from your home to that company's office, where you advise it on the development of new software.

Uncle Sam allows you to claim as business mileage the miles you drive from your home to your client's office — again, because your home is your office.

But here is where the scenario gets complicated. Say you drive from the office of your employer to the office of the software manufacturer and then drive home. You may classify the miles you drive from the office of your employer to the software manufacturer as business miles.

But—and here's the kicker—the IRS would very likely consider the drive from the software manufacturer to your home to be commuting. The reason: The IRS would say that your last trip of the day is commuting—even if the trip is not between your regular office and home.

DRIVING THE COMPANY CAR

If your employer provides you with a company car, you need to concern yourself with the following issues. The law requires your employer to report the value of your personal use of the car on your W-2 form.

And your employer must also withhold income and Social Security taxes (FICA) on the value of this benefit. However, with the exception of FICA, your employer may choose not to withhold taxes as long as he or she lets you know by January 31 of each year.

☞ **CAUTION**   If your employer does not withhold income taxes, you may need to pay estimated taxes to cover what you will owe on this fringe benefit.

When it comes time for your company to report the value of your personal use of the company car on your W-2, it has two options. It can report only the value of your personal use or it can report the total value of your use of the car as personal use.

Let's take a look at each option.

If your company reports only personal use, you must submit evidence to your employer that documents how you used the car.

Say you log 23,176 miles—based on odometer readings at the beginning and end of the year—in your company car in 1990. You drive 15,677 miles on business, 3,466 miles commuting to and from work, and 4,033 on personal trips.

At the end of the year, your employer asks you to submit a form detailing how you used your car. So you report 15,677 business miles and 7,499 personal miles — that is, the mileage you post for commuting and personal trips.

Based on these numbers, your employer determines that your business use added up to 68 percent of your total miles and your personal use 32 percent.

Now, your employer—following IRS regulations— reports the value of your personal use on your W-2 form. That amount equals your personal use multiplied by the total value of the use of the car.

And your employer may determine the value of your use of the company car in a number of ways. The most popular way: the annual lease value tables, based on fair market value, issued by the IRS. (You will find a copy of the IRS lease table in the appendix. You should know that the IRS tables include the cost of maintenance and insurance. You cannot subtract these amounts from the tables even if your employer makes you pay for insurance or maintenance.)

Another method to measure the fair market value of personal use is to use standard car lease rates in your area.

There's yet another option available to your company when it comes time to report the value of the personal use of your company car. This option applies to cars that are valued at less than a threshold amount—$13,100 for cars placed in service prior to January 1, 1990, that log at least 10,000 miles a year, and that are used regularly for business.

How does Uncle Sam define regular business use? If at least 50 percent of the car's total mileage is for business, or if the car is generally used each workday to transport at least 3 employees in an employer-sponsored car pool, then you meet the test.

The rules say that your employer may report your personal usage of the company car at a flat rate of 26 cents a mile in 1990. You may subtract 5.5 cents per mile if you pay for your own gasoline.

☞ **CAUTION** The IRS will announce a new, inflation-adjusted threshold amount for cars placed in service in 1990. In addition, the mileage rates are subject to change, so check with your tax adviser for the new amounts.

Your company may also report the total value of your use of the car on your W-2 form. In this case, you may deduct the value of the business use of your car on your personal return subject, of course, to the 2 percent floor on miscellaneous itemized deductions.

Here's an example. Say the year is 1990, and the value of your total use of the company car, based on the annual lease value method, is $5,100. Your employer adds that amount to your W-2 form.

When it comes time to file your 1990 tax return, you provide your tax preparer with a copy of your W-2 and a statement summarizing how you used your company car. Let's say you used it 12,433 miles for business and 5,321 miles for personal purposes.

You or your tax preparer multiplies the percentage of business use—in our example, 70 percent—times your car's value, as recorded on your W-2 ($5,100). The result—$3,570—is the amount you may deduct on your return as a business expense.

However, your ability to claim this deduction as a direct offset against the imputed income has been severely restricted by new legislation in 1988. Where employers simply impute 100 percent of the lease value on the employees' W-2, the business use deduction will be subject to the 2 percent floor on miscellaneous itemized deductions.

You may also write off as miscellaneous itemized deductions certain other expenses—such as parking fees and tolls—that you paid that represent business use. Again, these are subject to the 2 percent floor.

☞ **CAUTION** If your company reports the total value of your car use on your W-2, you and your employer are paying Social Security taxes on that amount. And that may mean money out of your pocket.

Here's an example. Assume your employer reports the total value of the use of your company car to you—$4,300, say. You and your employer pay Social Security taxes on the entire amount—unless you have already paid all the Social Security tax you owe (in 1990, that means 7.65 percent on income up to $51,300).

Now let's say your employer changes its method. Your company reports the value of only your personal usage of your company car, or $2,800. Clearly, you are better off paying Social Security taxes on $2,800 than on $4,300.

OTHER POINTS TO KEEP IN MIND

The rules won't allow you to depreciate your car using the accelerated method unless you use the vehicle more than 50 percent of the time for business. In other words, you're limited to the straight-line method—that is, 10 percent in year one, 20 percent in years two through five, and 10 percent in year six. (For more on depreciation, see Chapter 18.)

Also, if you aren't an officer whose compensation equals or exceeds $50,000, a director, an employee with compensation of

$100,000 or more or a 1 percent shareholder of your company, and the only personal use of your company car allowed by your employer is commuting, your employer may use a different method to calculate the value of your personal use "fringe benefit."

The compensation amounts will be indexed for inflation. The 1990 amounts are $56,990 for an officer and $113,980 for an employee.

If you drive to and from work, the value of your personal use of the car that your employer includes in your W-2 is computed at $3 a day. A one-way commute is valued at $1.50.

BUSINESS USE OF PERSONAL CAR

If you use your personal automobile for work, there are three requirements you must meet before you may deduct business-related automobile expenses on your personal tax return.

First, you must use your automobile "for the convenience of your employer"—that is, your employer must require that you have a car to properly perform your duties as an employee. Second, your employer must require the automobile as a condition of employment. In other words, no car would mean no job.

An example of an employee who would meet these two tests: A messenger service's representative who must deliver packages to customers.

Last, but most important, you need to substantiate business use and maintain adequate records.

When you deduct car expenses, you have two choices: You may claim a flat amount for each business mile you drive—known as the *standard rate*—or you may write off the *actual costs* of operating your automobile. Here is how the two methods work.

Using the Standard Rate

The standard mileage rate currently stands at a flat 26 cents a mile.

☞ **CAUTION** These standard mileage rates have historically been reviewed by the IRS each year. When the rates are modified, generally the new rates are effective retroactively to January 1—so check with your tax adviser for the rates in effect for 1991.

☞ CAUTION   Sometimes you are not allowed to use the standard mileage rate and must write off actual expenses. The two instances: when you lease your car and when you have claimed accelerated depreciation on your car in a previous year.

Actual Expenses

In most cases, your actual expenses will exceed the standard mileage deduction. So you should opt to write off actual costs.

A portion of all of the following expenses is deductible (the percentage you write off equals the percentage of your car's mileage that you attribute to business).

- Automobile club memberships.

- Batteries.

- Driver's license.

- Gasoline and oil.

- Insurance.

- Lubrication and repairs.

- Registration and other licensing fees.

- Supplies, such as antifreeze.

- Temporary rentals.

- Washing and waxing.

You also may write off tires with a life of less than one year. (You should depreciate tires that last longer and are purchased separately from the car.)

But you may not deduct on your personal return the cost of parking your car at or near your office. However, if your company provides you with parking, the value of this fringe benefit usually isn't taxable to you. So your employer does not report it as income on your Form W-2.

Nor may you fully deduct interest on a car loan if you are an employee—even if you buy the car strictly for business. This interest is considered personal interest, which, thanks to tax reform, is only 10 percent deductible in 1990. After 1990, personal interest is not deductible at all. (See Chapter 5 for the rules on deducting personal interest.) If you're self-employed, a portion of the interest may be deductible, limited to your business use of the car.

You also may depreciate your car in the same way you depreciate other personal property you use for business. If you are buying a car that will be used for business, you calculate your depreciation deduction based on the total purchase price of your car.

If you are converting your family car into a business automobile, then you base depreciation deductions on the lower of the fair market value at the date you convert or its purchase price. In either case, you must multiply the depreciation amount times the percentage of your actual business use.

But note that a special cap applies to cars.

The law limits depreciation deductions for business cars purchased after December 31, 1986, and before January 1, 1989, to $2,560 in the first year, $4,100 in the second year, $2,450 in the third year, and $1,475 in all remaining years. For cars bought in calendar year 1989 or 1990, the rules caps depreciation deduction at $2,660 in year one, $4,200 in year two, $2,550 in year three, and $1,475 in each subsequent year. When you compare this to depreciation available under regular depreciation rules, any car with a purchase price of over $13,300 will be subject to these caps.

Here's an example. On January 15, 1989, you purchased an automobile for $19,000. You start driving it—or, in IRS lingo, "place it in service"—that same day.

In 1989 and 1990 you use the car for business 70 percent of the time. So your depreciation deductions for 1989 and 1990 are $1,862 (the $2,660 limitation times your 70 percent business use) and $2,940 (the $4,200 limitation times 70 percent).

Another wrinkle: If business use of your car falls below 50 percent, you must go back to the first year you depreciated the car and recompute your depreciation using the straight-line method. The difference is picked up in your current return as income.

You are not permitted to use the more favorable accelerated depreciation. And the above limits on these depreciation deductions apply regardless of which depreciation method you use.

Also, the sales tax you pay isn't currently deductible. You may, however, add this cost to the purchase price of your car when it comes time to calculate your depreciation deduction.

☞ **CAUTION** If you take the standard mileage deduction in year one, then write off actual costs in year two, you must depreciate the car using the straightline method—that is, you write off the same amount each year.

But if you deduct your actual costs from the start, you may depreciate your car using the accelerated method—that is, you write off more in the early years of ownership.

TIP If you use the actual cost method, reimbursements that exceed your expenses always count as taxable income. But if your reimbursement is based on your use of the standard mileage rate, the excess over your actual costs is tax-free income.

TIP Whether you write off your actual automobile expenses or claim the standard mileage rate, you may still, in addition, deduct as miscellaneous itemized deductions (subject to the 2 percent floor) parking fees and tolls you pay when you travel for business. But you may not write off fines for violating traffic and parking laws.

SPECIAL RULES FOR LEASING

When Congress voted to cap depreciation deductions for business automobiles, it also imposed tough new restrictions on cars that you lease. And these rules apply whether you are an employer or employee.

The law still allows you to deduct that portion of your lease payment that is attributable to business. For example, if you use your leased car 90 percent for business, you may write off 90 percent of your payment.

But here's the rub. The law wants to put people who lease business automobiles on an equal footing, tax-wise, with those who purchase their business autos outright.

So if you lease, the law requires a certian amount to be added to your taxable income and/or applied as a reduction to your deduction. You determine this amount each year by using tables and formulas provided by the IRS. The lower a car's business use, the smaller the adjustment.

You do the second calculation only if your car was leased before

December 31, 1986. Even then, you do the calculation only once in your car's lifetime—when your business use falls below 50 percent.

QUESTIONS AND ANSWERS

QUESTION: *My employer reimburses me at 26 cents a mile for every business mile I travel. Is that amount reported as income on my W-2 form?*

The answer is no, it's not.

Uncle Sam says that if you're reimbursed at the standard mileage rate by your employer, the amount isn't reported as income to you on your W-2 form as long as your employer requires you to substantiate the miles traveled.

QUESTION: *My employer reimburses me at 26 cents a mile for every business mile I travel. But my actual costs are greater than the amount I receive. May I write off the difference?*

When you file your tax return, you also file Form 2106, "Employee Business Expenses." On that form you report your actual expenses. You also record any reimbursements you receive from your employer. If your actual expenses exceed the amount you are reimbursed, you deduct the difference as a miscellaneous expense—subject to the 2 percent floor.

QUESTION: *My company reimburses me at a flat $100 a month for automobile expenses. I do not have to account to my employer for how I spend this money or how I use my automobile. How do I treat this $100 a month for tax purposes?*

Your employer has no way of knowing whether you spent the $100 on "ordinary and necessary" business expenses. So, under the law, it must report this amount as income on your W-2 form. And your employer must withhold taxes—including FICA taxes—on your automobile stipend.

But all is not lost. You may claim a deduction for your expenses as a miscellaneous itemized deduction, subject to the 2 percent floor.

QUESTION: *Business use of my car added up to 70 percent last year. But this year my business use will fall to about 45 percent. Are there any tax consequences?*

Unfortunately, if your business use falls below 50 percent, you may have to "recapture" some of the depreciation deductions you claimed in the previous year.

Say you purchase a car in 1990 for $13,000, and you depreciate the car using the accelerated method, which allows you to claim larger write-offs in the early years of ownership. (See Chapter 18 for more information on depreciation.)

In 1991, however, your business use falls to 45 percent. The law says you must recalculate the depreciation on the car using the straight-line method. With the straight-line method, you claim the same amount of depreciation each year you own the car.

This change in depreciation methods results in a lowering of your depreciation deduction for last year. So you must add to your taxable income in the current year the difference between your deductions under the straight-line and accelerated methods.

QUESTION: *If I use the actual-cost method, what is the best way to keep the data in one place?*

Many people jot down mileage in a small pocket notebook, then attach expense receipts to the pages with paper clips.

You may also purchase a mileage log. Most mileage logs include a place to list these expenses so that you can find them easily when you summarize your tax data.

QUESTION: *I keep a log to document my automobile expenses, and I find it a real headache. Is there any way to reduce my record keeping?*

You could try a method known as sampling. But you may use it only if your percentage of business use remains consistent from month to month.

Here is an example to illustrate how sampling works. Say you have your own interior decorating business and operate out of an office in your home.

You use your automobile for local business travel: to visit the homes or offices of clients, to meet with suppliers and other subcontractors, and to pick up and deliver materials to your customers. You log no other business miles on your car.

You maintain a diary for the first three months of 1990, and it indicates that 75 percent of your use of your automobile was for your interior decorating business. Based on invoices from subcontractors and other paid bills, you can prove that your business continued at approximately the same pace for the rest of 1990.

If there are no other significant changes in your business operation in the last nine months of 1990, you may use the log that you maintain for the first three months to document your business use of 75 percent.

Another option: You could maintain a log for the first week of every month during 1990. If your invoices indicate that you did about the same volume of business during the other weeks of each month, your records—in the eyes of the IRS—would support your claim of using your car 75 percent for business each month.

QUESTION: *My company will not allow me to use my company car during off hours. Do I still need to maintain records, since I do not use the car personally?*

If you have a company car but company rules do not allow you to use the car for personal reasons—or if you use it only to commute—then you are off the hook when it comes to record keeping. You do not have to keep a log.

14

Making the Most of Your Capital Gain

Just because the law no longer gives a tax-rate break to *long-term capital gains*—profits from assets you hold for more than one year—that does not mean that you no longer have to distinguish between them and ordinary income. You do—and that means keeping records.

In this chapter, we show you the best way to handle this record-keeping chore. We also tell you how to report your profit or loss from the sale of assets.

First, though, we want to point out that the absence of a break for long-term capital gains does not mean that you should be indifferent to when you sell assets. Depending on your income and the timing of a sale, your capital gain may be taxed at 15 percent, 28 percent, or 33 percent.

You would probably prefer the former to the latter. So it is worth understanding the law as it applies to capital gains.

☞ **CAUTION**   As we noted earlier in this book, there is talk on Capitol Hill of reinstating a preferential rate for long-term capital gains.

126

LOCKING IN LOWER RATES

Back in 1986, when the tax rate for long-term capital gains rates was capped at 20 percent, many taxpayers decided they were better off selling their investments and reporting their profits that year. That way, they were guaranteed to pay a tax of no more than 20 percent on their gains.

Now that you no longer have that option, is there anything you can do to reduce your capital gains tax rate? The answer depends on your personal tax situation. As you know, in 1990, the 5 percent surcharge kicks in at $47,050 for single filers and at $78,400 for joint filers.

If you are not subject to the surcharge in 1990 but you will be in 1991 and possibly future years, consider this strategy: Sell a stock or other security now to lock in the lower 28 percent rate on your gain to date. Then, if you believe it will continue to appreciate in the future, immediately repurchase the security.

☞ **CAUTION** The best tax strategy is not always the best financial strategy. The additional brokerage charges you will incur in the repurchase may reduce or wipe out the tax savings. Also, it may make sense, when you consider the time value of money, to pay taxes later rather than sooner.

WRITING OFF YOUR CAPITAL LOSSES

Uncle Sam allows you to deduct up to $3,000 in capital losses from your ordinary income in any one year, and it makes no difference whether these are long-term or short-term losses.

In addition, Uncle Sam says, you may carry forward any losses that you are unable to write off in the current year to future tax years.

Let's say, for instance, that you have accumulated net long-term capital losses of $10,000. This year you had $5,000 in short-term gains.

You may use $5,000 of your $10,000 in long-term losses to offset your gain this year. And you still have $5,000 in long-term losses remaining. You may deduct $3,000 of these losses in the current year and carry the remaining $2,000 forward to future years.

💵 **TIP** You say you had zero or negative taxable income before you deducted your capital losses? You may be able to carry forward all or a portion of your losses to next year.

Here is an example.

Say you're single, and your taxable income—before you subtract your capital losses but after you claim your personal exemption—adds up to a $200 loss.

Now, how do you calculate how much of your capital losses you may carry forward to next year? Add back to your taxable income (in your case, a $200 loss) your personal exemption of $2,050. The result is taxable income of $1,850.

Your capital losses for the year add up to $4,000. You subtract $1,850 from $4,000 and the result—$2,150—is the amount you may carry forward to next year.

QUESTIONS AND ANSWERS

QUESTION: *Do states tax long-term capital gains at the same rate as ordinary income?*

A few states still tax long-term capital gains at a lower rate than short-term capital gains. Your tax adviser will know the rules in your state.

QUESTION: *I have heard about wash sales. What is a wash sale and what is its significance for me?*

You could be in for a large and unexpected tax bite if you plan to offset your capital gains with losses the IRS classifies in the *wash-sale* category.

Wash-sale rules are intended to prevent you from selling a stock at a loss, writing off the loss on your tax return, then immediately buying the stock back.

These regulations say that you may not take a loss if, within a period beginning 30 days before you sell your security and ending 30 days after that date (a period covering 61 days), you have acquired or entered into a contract or option to acquire "substantially identical stock or securities."

Moreover, the Supreme Court has ruled that you may not take a loss if your spouse purchases identical securities.

The rules do not apply, incidentally, if you received your stock or security through a gift, bequest, inheritance, or tax-free exchange.

Let's say on September 15, 1990, you bought 100 shares of XYZ Company stock for $1,000, and on March 22, 1990, you bought an additional 100 shares for $975. On April 6, 1990, you sold the 100 shares you purchased on September 15 for $900. Since you bought 100 shares of the same stock within the period beginning 30 days before the date of the sale and ending 30 days after that date, you may not claim a loss on your return.

QUESTION: *I hear there is a way to postpone paying taxes on my stock market investments until next year. How do I do it?*

It's possible to nail down a 1990 paper profit on your stocks and have it taxed in 1991. In effect, you freeze a profit (or loss) and postpone the tax result by using a technique known as a *short sale against the box*.

For example, you go to your broker and tell him or her you want to arrange a short sale.

It works something like this. You own 100 shares of XYZ Corp. The stockbroker allows you to borrow another 100 shares, using your existing shares as collateral. You then sell the borrowed shares in December 1990, thus fixing your profit.

You do not owe the stockbroker money. You owe the broker shares. You deliver your original shares to the broker in repayment in January 1991.

The result: The profit on the 1990 short sale becomes 1991's taxable income.

QUESTION: *I have bought several tax-exempt bonds over the years at their par, or face value. Because interest rates have fallen, these bonds are currently selling at a premium. If I sell my tax-exempts now, is my gain taxable?*

It is. The interest paid on the bond is tax exempt, but any capital gain you realize is taxed just like the gain on the sale of a taxable security.

☞ **CAUTION** If you sell a bond, tax-exempt or not, for which you paid either more or less than face value, the price you paid may not be your basis in the bond for figuring gains or losses.

Rather, the price you paid for the bond may have to be adjusted mathematically so that by the time the bond matures, your basis in the bond is equal to the bond's face value. The rules here are complicated, so you should see your tax adviser. He or she will help you make these computations and determine which rules apply.

QUESTION: *I have purchased stock in the same company on three different occasions at three different prices. Now I want to sell just some of the stock. When I am calculating my gain (or loss) for tax purposes, which of the three stock prices do I use in computing my basis?*

Use the price of the shares actually delivered. If you can't identify the specific shares you're selling by, say, certificate number or by virtue of having held them in different accounts, you must abide by the "ordering rule." It says that you're considered to be selling the stock in the order in which you bought it.

QUESTION: *I own stock in a company, and the stock recently split. How long do I have to hold the new stock before it qualifies as a long-term capital gain?*

For capital gain purposes, you calculate your holding period from the day after you originally bought the stock, not from the time the stock split.

And this same rule holds true for companies that pay dividends in the form of additional shares. The holding period for the new shares is the same as for the old shares.

What about dividend reinvestment plans that allow you to use your cash dividends to purchase additional shares of stock, sometimes at a discount? Another rule applies. The holding period for stock purchased through these plans begins on the day after you purchase the new shares.

QUESTION: *I lent money to a friend of mine to start a business. She has filed for bankruptcy, and I am not going to get my money back. May I write off this bad debt?*

Uncle Sam says that you may deduct this amount as a *short-term capital loss* on your tax return—as long as it is truly uncollectible.

QUESTION: *I lent money to my brother, and he failed to pay me back. May I write off this amount as a bad debt?*

You may claim a short-term capital loss deduction—but again, only if the money is truly uncollectible. Also, if the IRS audits you, be prepared to prove that the money you gave your brother was a loan and not a gift. The IRS likes to see a signed note, plus evidence that you charged the going interest rate.

QUESTION: *I invested in a small company that went belly up. The company's stock was classified as* **small business stock**. *How is my loss treated for tax purposes?*

Congress wants you to invest in small companies, and it is willing to share the risk with you. It says that you may deduct from your ordinary income losses of up to $50,000 ($100,000 if you are married and file a joint return). This amount has no bearing on your other capital losses.

QUESTION: *A few years ago, the law allowed taxpayers to exclude from their income dividends they received from public utility stocks, as long as they reinvested these dividends in additional shares. I did just that. Now I want to sell the stock I acquired through this reinvestment plan. What are the tax consequences?*

The entire amount you receive from the sale of stock bought with dollars that were exempt from tax is now taxable. The reason is, your basis in the shares acquired is zero.

QUESTION: *I sold stock listed on a public exchange on December 28, 1990, at a gain, but the settlement date on the slip my brokerage firm mailed to me was January 7, 1991. In what year do I report the sale?*

The law requires you to report your sale in the year you initiated the sale (your trade date), whether gain or loss—in your case, 1990.

15

Tax Rules You Need to Know When You Sell Your Home

Selling your home—and selling it at the best possible price—is never an easy job. And even when the sale is over, the transaction is not yet complete.

That is because Uncle Sam is waiting to hear from you.

If you sell your home at a profit—and we hope that you do—he wants to know how much you made on the sale and if any taxes are due.

The good news is that he allows you to defer paying taxes on that profit as long as you reinvest the proceeds from the sale of your home to purchase another home of equal or greater value.

If you recently sold your home or are contemplating a sale, read on. We tell you what you need to know about that most complicated of transactions—the sale of your home.

To begin, though, a few key definitions. We use these terms in this chapter and elsewhere, and we think you will find them useful.

A residence is a place that contains basic living accommodations. So houses, apartments, condominiums, mobile homes, and even houseboats count as residences.

A *principal residence,* on the other hand, is your primary home, meaning the one that you live in most of the time. The fact that you own a house does not make that house your principal residence. You must actually live in the house for it to qualify as your primary residence.

Uncle Sam imposes no set limits on the amount of time you must spend in your home for it to qualify as your primary residence. But we suggest you use common sense.

WHEN ARE YOU TAXED?

Say you sell your house or condominium at a profit.

And now, what you want to know is, are any taxes due? Uncle Sam allows you to defer paying taxes on your gain as long as you meet these two conditions:

One, you must buy or build and occupy a new principal residence within 24 months before or after the date you complete the sale of your old home.

And two, you must buy or build and occupy that new house or condominium for an amount that equals at least the *adjusted selling price* of your old home.

What is the adjusted selling price? Uncle Sam defines it as the amount you pocket from the sale—that is, the sales price minus any *selling costs*—less any *fixing-up expenses.* (Fixing-up expenses are the expenses you incur in fixing up your home and getting it ready to sell.)

Ordinarily, you gain no tax benefit when you fix up your personal residence. Painting and wallpapering, for example, are not currently deductible.

And they do not directly reduce your gain when you sell, either. But when you sell your home, these expenses do enter the picture.

How? They reduce your adjusted selling price, meaning the amount you must reinvest in a new home to defer tax on your gain from the sale of your old home.

The rules say that the work must be for repair and maintenance, not for improvements—a distinction we will explain shortly.

Finally, you must do the fixing up during the 90 days before you sign the contract to sell your house, and you must pay for your repairs within 30 days after the sale.

But what about direct selling expenses, such as real estate commissions? Unlike fixing-up costs, these expenses actually reduce the gain on your home, whether you get to defer the gain or not (more on selling costs and how you should compute your gain later.)

And keep this point in mind: Postponement of the gain applies only to the sale of your principal residence. A vacation cottage—or any second home—does not qualify. But a condominium, a co-op, or even a houseboat fits the bill as long as it was your principal residence.

So far, rolling over the gain from your old home to a new one sounds simple. It can be, but often there are complicating factors.

Here is an example. Say you are an up-and-coming executive transferred to another division of your corporation in another city. You put your home up for sale.

And you sign a contract to purchase a house for a slightly higher price in a suburb of the new city. You figure that you will sell your old house at about the same time that you are scheduled to move into your new home.

But it does not quite work out that way. The housing market in your old neighborhood is depressed, and although several buyers are interested in your property, you have no firm offers.

You decide to rent your house until you find a buyer. The rental agreement includes an option to buy, but your tenant never exercises the option. It takes you a year to locate a buyer.

Here is how the situation gets sticky. The rules say that you may defer the gain on the sale of a house only if it is your principal residence *at the time of the sale*. So does that mean your old home is no longer considered your principal residence, since it is occupied by a tenant at the time you sell it?

Well, not really.

TIP The courts have ruled that temporarily renting out your old house because of a depressed real estate market will not prevent you from deferring your gain. So in this case you do not have to actually occupy the house at the time of the sale.

And you get another break as well. Not only may you consider your house as a principal residence for the purpose of deferring your gain, but you may also treat the property as rental real estate and claim operating expenses and even depreciation deductions for the period you rent it.

So in this situation you are way ahead. But what if the new house you buy costs less than the adjusted selling price of your old one?

Consider this example. You are 52 years old and your spouse is 50. You commute every day from your home in Connecticut to your job in New York. Weary of your 90-minute trek into Manhattan, you suggest selling your ten-room house and purchasing a small condominium near your midtown office.

Your spouse agrees, and you put your home on the market. A buyer offers $610,000. You are delighted, since you purchased the house 20 years earlier for $150,000.

You sign a contract and pay the real estate agent a 6 percent commission, or $36,600. Since you have no remaining mortgage and no other selling expenses, you collect $573,400 from the sale.

All told, your gain amounts to $423,400—$573,400 less the $150,000 cost of your home. You begin looking for a condominium but find nothing you like.

So you decide to temporarily rent an apartment in midtown Manhattan. A year later you locate the perfect condo. Its price: $550,000, or $23,400 less than the $573,400 you pocketed from the sale of your home in Connecticut. You move into the condo immediately.

What are the tax consequences?

Since you did not reinvest all of the proceeds from the sale of your previous house, you must report on your federal tax return the difference between what you sold your old house for and what you paid for your new one—in this case, $23,400. But you still get to defer $400,000 of the gain from the sale of your old house ($423,400 less the $23,400 you do have to report).

If you had paid for your condo an amount equal to or greater than the adjusted selling price of your previous home, you would defer paying tax on all of your $423,400 profit.

TIP If you plan on making improvements to your new home, do so within 24 months before or after the sale of the old one. Then you may add the cost of the improvements to the cost of the home. Acting fast is particularly important if, as in this case, the cost of your new home is less than the selling price of your old one.

Still another complication in the law involves taxpayers who are building new homes. Say you hire an architect or a contractor to build a house or you contract the work yourself. Ready or not, you must move into your new home within 24 months after the sale of your old home. Otherwise, you pay taxes on your gain.

What is more, the house must be substantially complete when you move in. You cannot pitch a tent on the foundation and claim you occupy your new home. The IRS is strict on this point—despite the house-building delays people suffer—and the courts have backed the IRS up.

TIP Include a clause in your construction contract that calls for your contractor to pay any taxes you owe if construction is delayed beyond the 24-month limit.

HOW DO YOU CALCULATE YOUR GAIN?

Say your new home does cost less than the amount you collect when you sell your old house. Or suppose you do not buy a new residence at all but choose to rent.

In these cases, some or all of any gain you pocket is taxed. So, clearly, you should do everything you can to keep your taxable gain as low as possible.

Let's look at some strategies you should consider.

To begin with, you need to know how to determine the actual profit and the taxable gain or loss on the sale of your home. The calculation is simple.

You just subtract your basis—the cost of your house plus improvements (but not fixing-up expenses)—from your selling price, less, of course, your selling expenses.

Now, to maximize your tax savings, be sure to include every item that increases your basis, and subtract all legitimate adjustments from your sales proceeds.

And note: You may use some of the costs you ran up when you bought your home—and while you owned it—to slash your taxable profit when you later sell.

Here are some expenses you may include.

Purchasing Costs

You should add to your house's original cost any of the following fees you shelled out when you bought your home: appraisal fees, attorneys' fees, cost of removing any cloud on the title, costs for title search and insurance, fees for the recording of the deed and mortgage, late closing charge, and survey expenses.

Improvements

Also add to your cost all amounts you paid for improvements. What counts as an improvement? Anything that adds to your home's value or appreciably prolongs its life. (You will find a checklist of these items at the end of this chapter.)

☞ **CAUTION** You may not increase the basis by the cost of ordinary repairs and maintenance designed to keep up the building and grounds.

What counts as a repair?

Common examples include repainting inside or out, fixing the gutters or floors, mending leaks, replastering, or replacing broken window panes.

TIP In certain circumstances, such as the restoration of an old house, some of these items may be considered improvements. It is smart to check with your tax adviser on how to treat these items.

Now let's look at an example of how you might figure your taxable gain. Let's say the original cost of your home was $50,000. And you had purchasing expenses of $2,000. Over the years, you added a new room for $9,000 and installed central air conditioning and heating for $3,000.

Finally, you sell the old homestead for $90,000. But your broker's commission and other selling expenses total $5,000.

Is your gain $40,000 (your $90,000 sale price less your $50,000 cost)? Definitely not. As we have seen, to determine your gain, you add your purchasing expenses and the cost of improvements to your basis, and you subtract your selling expenses from the sales proceeds.

So in our example, your cost basis comes to $64,000 (your $50,000 original cost plus $14,000 in improvements and purchasing expenses).

The amount you collect in cash after you subtract your selling expenses totals $85,000 (your $90,000 sales price less $5,000 in selling costs). So your gain comes to only $21,000 ($85,000 less $64,000).

☞ **CAUTION** You must be prepared to substantiate your expenses. And doing so requires accurate and careful record keeping. So keep detailed records of all of your home-related expenses.

PUT OFF TODAY WHAT YOU CAN PAY TOMORROW

Let's go back to the example we just gave.

You pay no tax on your $21,000 profit as long as you buy a new house costing $85,000 or more—or at least you do not pay any tax now.

Say you buy a new house for $86,000. Your purchasing costs add up to $4,000. Your basis in your new home is $90,000 ($86,000 plus $4,000). Right?

Wrong. Uncle Sam says you must reduce your basis in your new house by the amount of gain from your old house that you rolled over, or deferred.

Your basis in your new home then comes to $69,000— that is, $86,000 plus $4,000 minus the $21,000 gain you rolled over.

Now, let's say it is a year later, and you decide to tour the world for two years. You sell your house for $90,000, but you do not buy a new one.

The law says you must report on your tax return the difference between the selling price ($90,000) and your basis in your home ($69,000). And your gain—$21,000—is taxable now because you did not buy a new home.

But what if you had purchased another house? You are still in trouble. Under the rules you may roll over your gain from the sale of a house only once every two years—unless you take a new job in another location or are transferred as part of your old job.

Here is another example. You sell your old house on January 15, 1990, at a $10,000 profit. Then you buy a new one on February 15. The cost of your new home tops the amount you received for your old house.

Then you discover oil in the backyard of your new home. So on March 15 you sell the second house at a hefty profit. And finally, on

April 15, you move into yet another, even more expensive home. Under the rules, you may defer only the $10,000 gain from your original home.

Why? Because Uncle Sam says that only the last principal residence purchased in the 2 years following the sale of your old residence qualifies as the replacement residence for the rollover break. So the rollover break does not apply to the sale of your second home. Instead, you must report and pay taxes on the gain from the March 15 sale of the house with the gusher in the backyard. And you reduce the basis of your last home—the one you bought on April 15—by the $10,000 gain you deferred on the sale of your first one.

☞ **CAUTION** As we mentioned above, Uncle Sam provides an exception to the once-every-two-year rule for taxpayers who take a new job in another location or are transferred as part of their old job. In such cases, the rollover break applies sequentially to *each* sale and purchase within the two-year period. Although this exception was generally designed to benefit taxpayers, and it does just that in the majority of cases, it may lead to unexpected and undesirable tax consequences.

For instance, assume that in 1989 an individual sold his home for $100,000 and moved to another state where he purchased a new home for $120,000. His basis in the first home was $50,000. Accordingly, he had a gain of $50,000, which he was able to defer, since the cost of the new home exceeded the sales price of the old. The deferred gain reduced the basis of the new home to $70,000 ($120,000 minus $50,000).

A year later, in 1990, the individual was transferred to a new location where he bought a new home for $90,000. Shortly thereafter, he sold the second home for $115,000. His gain, of course, was $45,000 ($115,000 minus $70,000). But, since the purchase price of the third home was less than the sales price of the second home, he could defer only $20,000 of the $45,000 gain. And, unfortunately, he had to pay tax on $25,000 of gain.

On the other hand, if the general rule—which permits the rollover of gain on the sale of a principal residence only once every two years—had applied, the individual would have paid tax on only $10,000 of gain because the third residence would have been the one relevant for gain deferral on the first. Thus, since the purchase price of the third home ($90,000) was less than the sales price of the first home ($100,000), he would have reported $10,000 of the $50,000 gain and deferred the remaining $40,000. The purchase and sale of the middle residence would have no effect on the deferral of gain rules. Accordingly, the individual would have incurred a nondeductible loss of $5,000 on the sale of the second home ($115,000 selling price minus $120,000 cost basis.)

In a similar case, a taxpayer asked the IRS if he could apply the general rule instead of the exception for work-related moves, since the general rule resulted in less current tax liability. The IRS declined the request and held that the exception for work-related moves requires that each sale and purchase be considered in sequence. The bottom line: The exception for work-related moves, designed to help the taxpayer, may actually result in greater current tax, in certain cases.

☞ **CAUTION** The IRS has special rules for married taxpayers when the title to the house they sell differs from the title to their new house. For example, the husband might have had sole title to the old house, but the new house is jointly owned.

Here is the rule. As far as Uncle Sam is concerned, a husband and wife can be considered one taxpayer in this situation. This means it does not matter, for purposes of the tax law, which spouse owned the old house or which buys the new house.

There are only two catches: Both houses must be principal residences of both spouses, and you must sign a consent statement (on Form 2119) that says you agree to divide any gain and cost basis of the new house. (And this rule applies whether you file jointly or separately.)

Say, for example, that you hold title to a house, you and your husband's principal residence, that you sell for $100,000. The cost basis of the house was $80,000, so you realize a $20,000 gain. Within a year you and your husband each contribute $50,000 to buy a new house in your joint names.

You pay no tax on your gain as long as you and your spouse file consent statements in which you agree to allocate between yourselves the deferred gain and the basis of your new house. You file the consent on Form 2119 in the year you realize your gain. So the basis of the new house is $40,000 to you and $40,000 to your husband.

What if you fail to file the consent form? Uncle Sam requires you to pay tax on the $20,000 gain because the amount you contributed toward the purchase of your new house—$50,000—is less than the adjusted selling price of your old house.

TIMING YOUR SALE

When Congress adopted the 1986 Tax Reform Act, it zapped favorable tax treatment of long-term capital gains. (See Chapter 14 for more information on capital gains.) And that is bad news for many homeowners.

Here is why. Nowadays, if you sell your house for a profit and do not purchase another home to replace it, your gain is taxed at the same rate as ordinary income—potentially as high as 33 percent.

Our advice: If you plan to sell your home and not purchase a replacement residence, identify your tax rate for 1990. Then identify your tax rate for 1991.

If your tax rate is lower in 1990, sell in 1990. What if your tax rate is the same? Then it makes no difference—tax-wise, at least—when you sell your home. But if it is close to the end of 1990, you may want to wait until 1991, so your reporting of the gain and payment of tax will be delayed a year.

TIP Remember, too, that Congress is considering reducing the tax rates on capital gains. If a rate reduction should become law, it could affect your strategy considerably when it comes to timing the sale of your house.

WAITING UNTIL YOU ARE OLDER

Say you are a 64-year-old widow. You owe no money on your eight-room house, because you paid off the entire purchase price of $50,000 years ago.

Tired of property taxes and the expense of maintaining your large home, you decide to sell the house and move into an apartment building near your daughter. You contact a real estate agent and learn that the property, which you bought 30 years previously, is now worth $170,000. You place it on the market at that price.

What is the tax consequence for you? The answer, simply stated, is none. Under the law, you owe no tax as a result of selling your home—even though your gain is $120,000.

And it does not matter to the IRS whether you use the proceeds from the sale to buy another house, place the entire amount in the bank, or stuff your gains into a jar. You owe no taxes.

Why? Congress voted to allow older taxpayers who sell their principal residence to pocket the profit tax-free—if they meet four conditions. The conditions are as follows:

The tax-free profit on the sale of your house may not top $125,000. This ceiling applies to a single person or a married couple filing jointly. In the case of a married couple filing separately, the limit is $62,500 per spouse. Any profit on your house above $125,000 is taxed as a capital gain.

You must be 55 years of age or older on the date of sale. The rules treat a married couple filing a joint return as one person. So a couple qualifies for the tax break if only one spouse is age 55 or older on the date of the sale.

Another important point: You may exclude a profit on the sale of a house from your taxable income only if you did not previously take advantage of this break.

☞ CAUTION Many taxpayers don't know it, but the $125,000 exclusion is a once-in-a-lifetime offer. What happens if you remarry? Neither you nor your new spouse may claim the exclusion if either of you took it previously.

☞ CAUTION Don't allow your buyer to take possession of your house before you turn age 55. Sometimes, simply taking possession constitutes a sale for tax purposes, even though title has not actually changed hands.

You own and live in the same house and maintain it as your principal residence for at least three of the five years immediately before the sale. But the house does not have to be your principal residence at the time of the sale. Under the rules, up to two years may elapse between the time you move out and the sale takes place— as long as you occupied it for the previous three years.

💰 TIP A special rule applies to individuals who become physically or mentally incapable of caring for themselves at least five years before the sale.

These taxpayers must use their house as their principal residence for periods that total at least one year— rather than three—during the five-year period.

There is a condition attached, however. They must live in a state-licensed facility, such as a nursing home, the rest of the time.

You tell the IRS that you are making use of the exclusion by filing a tax form with your annual tax return. You must inform the IRS of the sale of your principal residence and your decision to make use of this part of the law. The IRS calls filing this form "making a formal election," and it is the government's way of making sure you do not capture the break more than once. The required "formal election" actually is made on a government-printed, government-provided form telling the IRS when you sold your home and how much profit you made.

If you want to complete the form yourself, just stop by or telephone your local IRS office for a copy. (Ask for Form 2119, "Sale of Your Home.") The IRS will also provide instructions on how to prepare the form and will offer assistance if you need it. You might also ask the IRS for a free copy of its Publication 523, *Tax Information on Selling Your Home*.

The important point to keep in mind: Plan carefully for your use of this tax break. It is far too valuable to waste. Here is an example of how you may lose part of your benefits.

Say you bought a house for $30,000 in early 1962. By 1990 you're over age 55. And you and your spouse decide to sell your house. You plan to invest the tax-free profit in securities, then move to the Florida vacation cottage you purchased some years earlier.

A willing buyer pays $130,000 for the old homestead. To figure your profit, you subtract the original cost of the house ($30,000) and a 6 percent real estate agent's commission ($7,800). The result: $92,200. You notify the IRS that you intend to make use of the one-time, age-55, home-sale exclusion.

You invest your $92,200 and move south.

So far so good—until you think about your situation a little more carefully. You used only $92,200 of the amount of gain you are allowed to exclude—$125,000—on the sale. And the difference between the amount you use and the amount allowed—$32,800—is gone forever. The reason: The law lets you make use of this exclusion only once.

This provision is fine if you can exclude the maximum amount you are allowed or close to it. But you cannot exclude the difference later on.

If you could have waited a year or two before you sold your house, you might have been better off. By then, the housing market might have become stronger, and you could have gotten a better price and been able to take better advantage of this once-in-a-lifetime tax break.

TIP Here is some advice for people who own more than one home. It usually does not make sense to cash in on the $125,000 exclusion if you can make better use of it later.

Say, for example, that you just sold your home and are retiring to your vacation house in the mountains of North Carolina. Your vacation home has appreciated more in value than the house you just sold.

Why not wait to claim the $125,000 exclusion until you sell your North Carolina property? That way, you can take better advantage of the exclusion.

CAUTION Don't make the mistake that some taxpayers do and decide to claim the $125,000 exclusion without taking into account estate planning. Our advice is to seek the help of your tax adviser *before* you opt for the $125,000 exclusion.

TIP You can cash in on a really impressive tax-free parlay. How? Combine the $125,000 exclusion and the sale-and-replacement break.

And doing so is a big break for the home seller who is "buying down"—for example, a retiree who is selling his or her big home and buying a smaller one.

By combining the exclusion and the rollover, you may collect more than $125,000 in profit and buy a much less expensive home without paying one dime in taxes.

Here is how. Say you paid $165,000 for your house in 1980, then, ten years later, you sold it for $380,000. You pocketed a hefty $215,000 profit. And you opted for the one-time exclusion. So $125,000 of your $215,000 gain is tax free to you—forever.

Now you want to purchase a house of equal value to your old one, so you will qualify for the sale-and-replacement break.

But wait: When it comes time to calculate how much you must spend on a new home, the law allows you to subtract the amount of your exclusion ($125,000) from the selling price of your old home

($380,000). So you need to spend only $255,000 for a new house—not $380,000.

As long as your new house costs $255,000 or more, you defer paying taxes on your remaining gain of $90,000. And you reduce the basis of your new house by only the $90,000 gain that you do not pay taxes on now.

QUESTIONS AND ANSWERS

QUESTION: *We bought a new home, but we are holding on to our old one and plan to rent it. What depreciation period do we use?*

The length of time over which you depreciate your house depends on two factors: when you purchased your home and when you placed it in service as rental property.

If you bought your house after 1980 and you began renting in 1987 or later, you depreciate it over 27.5 years. But if you bought it before 1980 and began renting it after 1980, you must follow the depreciation rules that were in place at the time of your purchase. (See Chapter 18 for the details on how to depreciate real estate.)

QUESTION: *We sold our old house, which we bought for $100,000, for $125,000. We bought a new one for $100,000, then, six months later, spent $50,000 making improvements (we remodeled the kitchen and both bathrooms). How much of the $25,000 gain do we include in our tax return?*

You might think that you have to include the entire $25,000 on your return because the amount you paid for your new house is less than the selling price of your old home. Not so.

The law gives you a break. You may add to the cost of your new house the amount you spend on improvements within 24 months before or after the sale of your old home.

So your taxable gain equals zero. Here is why. The $100,000 you paid for your new house plus the $50,000 you spent on improvements is greater than the $125,000 you collected for your old house.

QUESTION: *The real estate market in our area is really depressed. We had to sell our house at a loss. May I claim this loss on my tax return?*

You may not deduct a loss from selling a personal residence. But you do get a write-off for a loss when you have converted a home to rental property. The reason: Your home is no longer considered your personal residence; it now qualifies as business property. The deduction is limited, however, and taking advantage of it is complicated. So check with your tax adviser.

Converting a personal residence into rental property has another plus. You may also deduct operating expenses and depreciation during the rental period, as well as any loss when you eventually sell.

TIP If you have to sell a home in a depressed market and it looks as if you are going to take a loss, rent out your house until conditions improve. That way you have converted your house to a rental and will be able to deduct your loss when you eventually sell.

QUESTION: *We sold our old home. But we will not buy a new one before we file our next tax return. Do we have to notify the IRS of the sale?*

Yes. Attach Form 2119 to your return showing how you figured your gain. Form 2119 asks for the date you sold your old residence, the sale price, and your basis in the house. Also check the box that you intend to acquire a new residence within the replacement period. Once you replace your home, let the IRS know in writing on another Form 2119.

But what if you decide later not to buy another house, or the 24-month period has passed? In these cases you report your taxable gain for the year of your sale on Form 1040X (an amended 1040) to which you attach a Schedule D (to report capital gains and losses) and a new Form 2119.

QUESTION: *Before we got married, my spouse and I each owned homes, which we have since sold. Now we have bought a new house together. Can we both defer the gains on our old home?*

The answer is yes.

Under a special rule, the IRS will let you both defer your gains under two conditions: The new home must cost more than the combined adjusted sales prices of your old homes, and you must have taken joint title to your new home and each contributed half of the purchase price. Moreover, you do not have to file the special consent statement we discussed in this chapter.

QUESTION: *How does the IRS know that I sold my house?*

The 1986 Tax Reform Act makes it easier for the IRS to uncover unreported profits by sellers of residential real estate. The reason:

The law requires that real estate sales be reported to the IRS on Form 1099-S.

For sales that close before 1991, this reporting requirement applies only to residential real estate of four or fewer units. So the rule applies to any sale of a single house, townhouse, condominium unit, duplex, triplex, or fourplex, as well as stock in a cooperative housing corporation or co-op.

For sales after 1990, the reporting requirements are expanded to include additional types of real estate—among them, land (improved or unimproved, including airspace), and commercial real estate.

Who does the reporting? Usually the person listed as the settlement agent on a settlement statement or the person who prepares the settlement or closing statement.

If there is no statement, responsibility passes in descending order to the buyer's attorney, the seller's attorney, the title company, the mortgage lender, the seller's broker, the buyer's broker, and, finally, the buyer. Or both the buyer and seller may designate someone to file Form 1099-S with the IRS.

Whoever the person is, he or she must report the total amount—with no reduction for selling expenses—received by the seller. And he or she must list the seller's name, address, and Social Security number, as well as the closing date of the sale and the address of the property sold.

The information must be submitted to the IRS by February 28 following the year of the closing. And a copy must also be sent to the seller by January 31 following the year of closing.

QUESTION: *Who pays for the cost of preparing this 1099-S? Will I, as the home buyer, have to pay?*

The answer, you will be happy to hear, is no.

Congress adopted legislation that prohibits reporting costs being charged to buyers. Rather, the person responsible for filing the 1099-S will have to pay.

QUESTION: *I do not own a house. I own a condo. Do the same rules apply?*

First a critical distinction: A condominium owner owns his or her residence outright, whereas a cooperative apartment is owned by a corporation in which the resident owns stock. Stock ownership entitles the co-op "owner" to the exclusive right to lease his or her apartment. But whether you own a condo or a co-op, you get the same tax treatment as owners of single-family homes.

You may deduct mortgage interest and taxes. Of course, if you are a condo owner, you, like the owner of a house, pay your interest and taxes directly. If you are a co-op shareholder, you pay a portion of the corporation's interest and taxes, based on the number of shares you own.

And you may deduct the portion of your co-op payment that is allocated to the corporation's interest and taxes. (Of course, your co-op or condo interest must meet the tests for deductibility. See Chapter 5 for more on interest deductions.)

When it comes time to sell, your cost is increased by the amount you spend for improvements—again, just as if you owned a house. Remember, though, to include your share of maintenance charges or special assessments that your association spends on improvements for the benefit of all of the condos or co-ops in your building.

QUESTION: *I bought a washer five years ago and added its cost ($200) to my basis in the house. Now the washer is kaput. I have bought a new one for $350. Do I also add its cost to my basis?*

Sorry, but Uncle Sam will not allow you to increase your basis by the purchase price of both machines. He says you must subtract the amount you paid for the first washer ($200) from your basis. Then you may add the price of the new machine ($350).

So your basis in your home increases by $150—the difference between the price of the first and second machines—at the time you purchase the second machine.

CHECKLIST OF IMPROVEMENTS

Uncle Sam defines an improvement as anything that adds to the value of your home or appreciably prolongs its life. Here is a checklist of what counts as an improvement.

Additional acreage	Attic improvement (converting it into living space)
Additional rooms	
Air cleaner	Awnings
Air conditioning	Barbecue grill
Alarm system	Baseboard heating
Aluminum siding	Basement improvement (converting it into living space)
Attic fan	

Basketball goalpost
Bathroom addition
Bathtub
Bathtub enclosure
Bathtub sliding doors
Beams (decorative)
Birdbath
Boiler
Bookcases
Breezeway
Built-in furniture
Burglar alarm system
Cabana
Cabinets
Carpeting
Caulking
Ceilings (acoustical)
Chimes (door)
Chimney
Circuit breakers
Circulating system
Closets and closet organizers
Clothes dryers
Cold water pipes
Concrete walks
Cooling equipment
Copper tubing
Cornice
Countertops
Cupboards
Curtains
Deck
Dehumidifier
Dishwasher (built-in)
Doors
Doorbells
Dormers
Drainboards
Drain pipes
Drainage system
Drapes

Driveway (paving or blacktopping)
Dryer
Dry wells
Ducts
Electric heat
Electrical outlets
Electrical wiring
Electronic air filter
Exhaust fans
Fences
Fire alarm system
Fireplace
Fireplace mantel
Fixtures (lighting and plumbing)
Flagstone walks
Flooring (wood, tile, etc.)
Food freezer
Furnace (replacement)
Furnace filter system
Fuse boxes
Garage
Garage door
Garage door opener
Garbage disposal systems
Garden and grounds
Gates
Glass enclosure
Grading
Grease traps
Greenhouse
Grills, air ducts
Gutters
Hamper
Hardware (fixtures and locks)
Heat ducts
Heat pumps
Heating system
Hedges
Hot tub

Hot water heater
Hot water pipe
House numbers
Humidifier (furnace)
Humidistat
Inside walls (altering)
Insulation
Intercommunication system
Kitchen
Lamppost
Landscaping
Laundry equipment
Lawn sprinkling system
Lighting fixtures
Lightning rods
Linen chute
Linoleum
Locks (door)
Mailbox
Medicine cabinet
Mirrors
Outdoor lighting
Ovens
Paneling
Partitions
Pathways
Patio
Play yard
Plumbing
Porch
Pumps
Racks (garage)
Radiator covers
Radiators and valves
Railings
Range (gas or electric)
Range hood
Refrigerator
Retaining walls
Roofing
Room dividers

Screen doors
Screens
Security system
Septic system
Sewer assessment
Sewers
Shades
Shed
Shelves (built-in)
Shower controls
Shower doors
Showers
Shutters
Shrubs
Sidewalks
Siding
Sinks
Skylights
Smoke detector
Softwater system
Solar heating unit
Solar room
Space heater
Stairs
Steam room
Steps
Storm doors
Sump pump
Supply cabinets
Survey (property)
Swimming pool
Switch plates
Telephone outlets
Television antenna
Termite-proofing
Terraces
Thermostat
Tiles
Toilets
Topsoil
Towel racks

Trees
Trellis
Vacuuming system
Vanity
Venetian blinds

Vent pipe
Walks
Wall coverings
Washer
Weather stripping

16

Answers to Questions About Home Office Deductions

You may not know it, but some 24 million Americans, or 23 percent of the labor force, now work at home at least part-time. And one reason is technology. Inexpensive computers and communications devices, such as modems, now make it easy for people to go to work without ever leaving home.

Working at home, at least as far as taxes are concerned, is both a blessing and a curse. The blessing? Uncle Sam allows you to deduct part of the cost of owning or renting and of maintaining your home.

The curse? The IRS believes that many people who maintain *home offices* and claim *home office expenses* on their tax returns are abusing the law. So the agency tends to look carefully at tax returns containing home office deductions.

Our advice? Take the deductions to which you are genuinely entitled. Just be sure that you are prepared to defend them on audit.

In this chapter, we show you which home office deductions you may legitimately claim and how to be sure you can back them up if the IRS should inquire.

WHO QUALIFIES FOR A HOME OFFICE DEDUCTION?

If you work at home—and your office qualifies—you may deduct the costs of operating and maintaining that portion of your home you use for business.

If you own your home, you may write off a portion of your operating expenses, such as utilities, and you may depreciate that part of your home that you use as an office.

If you rent your house, you may deduct part of your rent, in addition to your operating expenses for the office portion of your home.

But the qualifying rules are stringent. You must use whatever space you designate as your home office regularly and exclusively as your principal place of business. Or you must use it regularly and exclusively as a place where you meet with customers, patients, or clients, if meeting with clients is a normal part of your business.

TIP Since 1980, the Tax Court has applied the so-called focal point test to determine whether a home office qualifies as a principal place of business. The test looks to the place where goods and services are provided to customers and where the revenues are generated. So, under this test, a doctor who works on the staff of several hospitals and isn't provided an office at any of them would be denied a home-office deduction, even though he uses his home office regularly and exclusively to manage his practice.

Recently, however, the Tax Court announced that it will no longer follow the focal point test in cases where a home office is essential to the business, the taxpayer spends substantial amounts of time there, and there is no other available office location to perform the functions of the business. Accordingly even though the doctor provides his services and earns his income at the hospitals, his home office may be considered his principal place of business.

CAUTION The IRS has announced its disagreement with the Tax Court's recent decision. In other words, it will continue to apply the focal point test to determine the deductibility of home office expenses. However, unless the Tax Court's decision is overturned, taxpayers should be able to rely upon it in claiming home office deductions which might otherwise fail the focal point test. Your best bet is to consult your tax adviser if you think you might be affected by these rules.

TIP A home office you use for a *second* business may qualify for a deduction. Say, for instance, that you teach in the public schools but also sell vitamins door-to-door in the evenings. You use your den regularly and exclusively to run your business, that is, manage the books, order the vitamins, make phone calls, and so on. So you may take the write-off.

A home office that you use exclusively to manage your own investment portfolio, however, does not qualify for a write-off. Managing your personal investments may be how you make your money, but it is usually not your trade or profession.

You do not need to maintain an office in a separate room to qualify for a write-off. You need only use some separately identifiable space exclusively and regularly for business.

What happens if you maintain your office in a separate structure, say a carriage house? Then the rules are less strict.

In this case, you may claim a deduction if you use the structure regularly and exclusively in your trade or business. In other words—and this is the important point—the building does not have to be your principal place of business.

Another important rule: If you are employed by someone else, you must maintain your home office for the convenience of your employer—or you do not get a write-off.

What do these rules mean to you? Say you are an attorney with a downtown firm. You sometimes use your den to catch up on your reading and to occasionally meet with clients. Does your den qualify as a home office?

No, and here is why. You do not use it regularly and exclusively to conduct your law business. And it is not your principal place of business. Your principal place of business is your downtown office. Also, you use it only occasionally to meet clients—not regularly.

Now, let's say that you are a typist employed by a large company to perform word processing. The company requires you to work at home full-time. You set up shop in what used to be your child's nursery.

You have already cleared one hurdle—the office is for the convenience of your employer. Now, you have only one more hurdle to get over.

If you use your office exclusively as your principal place of business, that is, you do not use it as a den, say, during the evening, you are entitled to deduct the appropriate costs. (See Chapter 9 for more information on rules governing deductions for employee business expenses.)

☞ **CAUTION** If you're audited, the IRS may ask you to prove that you maintain your home office for the convenience of your employer. Protect yourself. Ask your employer to write you a letter specifying that your home office is maintained at his or her request.

☞ **CAUTION** Some taxpayers may use a home office to conduct more than one business. The Tax Court recently ruled that in order for any of the home office expenses to be deductible, each business must qualify for home office deductions. In other words, if one of the businesses fails to qualify, none of the home office expenses are deductible, even though the other businesses qualify.

In this case, the taxpayer used his home office for two purposes—in connection with his employment and for work done as an independent contractor. Because employment-related use wasn't for the convenience of the employer, the court ruled that expenses attributable to that use weren't deductible. The court treated this use as personal use. So, the use of the office for work done as an independent contractor couldn't be regarded as exclusive business use since the office was also used for personal purposes. Accordingly, none of the expenses attributable to the office were deductible.

In the past, some taxpayers used another part of the tax law to bypass the requirement that a home office serve as their principal place of business.

They would lease a part of their home to their employer. Then they would deduct the costs associated with the leased space but they would not use the home office rules to justify their write-offs.

Rather, they used the section of the tax law that allowed them to deduct expenses for rented space. Now, however, the tax law specifically forbids this practice.

Here's why. Congress worried that employees would get around the restrictions on home office deductions by arranging to have a portion of their salary paid in rent. And the legislators did not like these sham transactions one bit.

TIP   Renting a portion of your home to your employer may still provide tax benefits, even though you may not deduct your expenses.

Say, for example, that you rack up passive losses from an investment in a limited partnership. The rules say that you may deduct passive losses only from your passive income. Rental activities are almost always considered passive, so you may be able to generate passive income by renting your home office. (See Chapter 19 for more on passive losses.)

Just remember that you must charge a fair and reasonable rent, you should have a written lease, and you should use the rented space exclusively for business.

FIGURING THE DEDUCTION

The law imposes a strict limit on the total amount of home office expenses you may deduct. It says that you may not use the cost of maintaining a home office to create or increase a loss from your business and therefore reduce your other, unrelated income.

Specifically, the law says that you must first reduce your gross business income by the sum of the portion of mortgage interest and taxes attributable to your home office space and the *direct expenses* attributable to your business. (These are expenses you would incur even if you did not have a home office.) Then, it says, your deduction for home office expenses may not exceed this amount.

Here is an example. As an accountant, just out of school, you decide to work from a basement office in your St. Louis home. In your first year you earn $20,000 in client fees.

The mortgage interest and taxes on that part of your home you use for your office add up to $4,000. So you subtract $4,000 from your $20,000 of gross income to get $16,000.

The expenses for your part-time secretary, phone answering service, stationery, and so on—everything but the home office expenses we noted at the beginning of this chapter—come to $12,000. Deduct this amount from the $16,000, and you get net income, before you deduct home office expenses, of $4,000.

From this amount, you subtract your home office expenses in the following order: operating expenses, then depreciation. Operating expenses, such as utilities, come to $2,000. So you subtract $2,000 from the remaining $4,000 to get $2,000.

Your depreciation expense totals $3,000. Now, you subtract $3,000 from your remaining income of $2,000 to get a loss of $1,000.

But you may not use these expenses to reduce your taxable income below zero. So $1,000 of depreciation is disallowed for that year.

Here is a break, though. You may carry this unused office expense deduction forward to offset your business income in future years.

Assume that in the second year of your accounting practice you earn $30,000 in fees, have mortgage interest and taxes of $4,000 on that part of your house you use for your home office, rack up $10,000 in direct expenses for telephone, secretarial help, and so forth, and have home office expenses of $7,000.

First you calculate your net income by reducing your gross income by your mortgage interest and taxes: $30,000 minus $4,000, or $26,000. Then you deduct your direct expenses: $26,000 minus $10,000, or $16,000. From this $16,000 you may deduct your home office expenses of $8,000 ($7,000 in current expenses plus $1,000 in expenses you have carried forward from previous years); again, as long as they do not lower your business income to less than zero. In this case you may deduct the entire $8,000, giving you taxable income in your second year of only $8,000.

TIP Do not worry about deducting the portion of your mortgage interest and property taxes attributable to your home office or your direct business expenses. These are always deductible and, in the computations above, serve only to limit your home office deductions.

Remember, as a homeowner, you are entitled to deduct your mortgage interest and property taxes. And, if you are operating a business, you may deduct most expenses even if they create a loss. But you may not use home office expenses to increase a loss.

Say your gross business income before you deduct your home office expenses adds up to $8,000. Say, too, that interest and taxes attributable to your home office come to $10,000. Under the rules, you may not use home office expense deductions to reduce your net income below zero.

So you would write off $8,000 to reduce your gross income to zero. Then you would write off the remaining $2,000 of interest and taxes as itemized deductions.

And you may deduct your direct business expenses—secretarial wages, office supplies, and so forth—that are not exclusively related to your home office.

You may not write off any other home office costs—utilities, maintenance, and so on—since you may not use these costs to increase the loss from your business.

👉 **CAUTION** If you're audited, expect Uncle Sam to ask you to prove that you actually spent the amount you claimed for your home office. Maintain documentation of all your expenditures—utility bills, cancelled checks, and so on.

💵 **TIP** If you would like more information about home office deductions, ask the IRS to send you a copy of *Business Use of Your Home* (Publication 587). This booklet is free for the asking.

QUESTIONS AND ANSWERS

QUESTION: *I'm a physician, and I maintain an office downtown. I don't use my home office to meet with patients. But I do telephone patients from my home office in the evening. And I do use the office exclusively for business. Am I entitled to a write-off?*

Sorry, but Uncle Sam will not allow you to take a deduction. The reason is, your home office is not your principal place of business. Also, you do not meet there with patients face-to-face (phone calls do not count).

QUESTION: *I'm a musician, and am employed by an orchestra. I practice in our spare bedroom, because there is no place to practice at Symphony Hall. May I claim a deduction?*

In most cases, your employer's principal place of business is your principal place of business. But you are an exception to this rule.

Because your employer did not provide you with practice space, and practicing is essential to maintaining your skills, you are entitled to a write-off. The only catch: You must use your spare bedroom regularly and *exclusively* as a practice room.

QUESTION: *I maintain an office in my eight-room home. Do I write off one-eighth of the expense of maintaining my home?*

You may, if all eight rooms are approximately the same size. Otherwise, you may calculate the percentage of floor space your home office occupies.

QUESTION: *I operate a day-care center and use the basement of my home exclusively for this purpose. May I claim a home office deduction?*

The answer is yes. You are also entitled to a write-off if you use your home regularly to provide day care for children or people who are elderly or handicapped. But you must operate a licensed facility. And, when it comes time to calculate your deduction, you must take into account the amount of space your day-care operation occupies.

Say you use 30 percent of the floor space of your home for day care. You are entitled to write off 30 percent of the expense of operating your home. You may deduct 30 percent of your heating bills, 30 percent of your cooling bills, 30 percent of your home insurance bills, and so on.

Congress carved out an exception to the exclusively-for-business rules for day-care center operators. If, for instance, you use your living room and kitchen as a day-care center only during the day, you may still claim a home office deduction.

You are subject to the same rules as the day-care center operator above—plus one other rule. You must take into account how much time you use your home for day care and how much as a residence. And you deduct only those costs attributable to the day-care.

Here is how it works. Say that you use 30 percent of your floor space for day-care. And your business uses this space ten hours a day Monday through Friday and six hours on Saturday for a total of 56 hours each week.

During the remaining 112 hours, your family uses the space. Under the rules, you may write off 10 percent of the cost of operating and maintaining your home; that is, 30 percent of your floor space times the 33 percent of time you use the house for your day-care business.

QUESTION: *Where on my tax return do I claim a deduction for my home office?*

If you are self-employed, write off your home office on Schedule C of your Form 1040. If you are employed by someone else, claim your home office deductions on Schedule A, with Form 2106 attached, as a miscellaneous itemized deduction subject to the 2 percent floor. That is, you write off only those expenses that, when added with other miscellaneous expenses, top 2 percent of your adjusted gross income. (See Chapter 9 for the details on how to write off miscellaneous deductions.)

QUESTION: *I claimed a home office deduction for the past ten years. I am planning on selling my house. Are there any tax implications?*

If you claim a home office deduction and plan to sell your home, there may be tax implications at the time of the sale. It depends on whether you are entitled to claim a home office deduction in the year you sell your home. And the key word here is "entitled."

If you are not entitled to claim a write-off that year you may roll over the entire gain from your house into another home and defer paying taxes on your profit.

But what happens if you satisfy all the rules and you are entitled to claim a home office deduction in the year you sell your house? You are taxed on that portion of your gain attributable to that part of your home you used as a home office.

Say, for example, that the cost of your house plus improvements is $125,000, and you sell it for $150,000. From the time you purchased your home until you sold it, you used 10 percent of the floor space in your house as a home office.

So you allocated $12,500 of the cost of your home to your home office. Over the years, you claimed depreciation deductions of $5,000.

The net gain on the sale of your house is $30,000 ($150,000 less your cost of $125,000 reduced by depreciation of $5,000).

Uncle Sam says you may roll over a portion of this gain, tax-free, into a new house. But, since you were entitled to a home office deduction in the year you sold your house, the portion of your gain allocable to your home office is taxable.

Here's how to calculate this taxable gain.

You allocate the sale proceeds between the office and nonoffice portions of your home. Remember, you allocated 10 percent of the cost of your house to your home office.

So you use this same 10 percent to allocate the proceeds from the sale of your home. That is, you allocate $15,000 of your sale price to your home office (10 percent times $150,000).

Your taxable gain on the sale comes to $7,500 ($15,000 less $12,500 cost reduced by $5,000 depreciation). And you may roll over the remaining $22,500 of your gain into a new house. (See

Chapter 15 for more information on the tax implications of selling your home .)

TIP   If you are planning to sell your home, put pencil to paper to decide what is worth more to you in the tax department:

- Claiming a home office deduction in the year you sell your house, or

- Rolling over that portion of your gain on the sale attributable to your home office.

If postponing the gain gets you more, violate the home office rules. For example, do not use your home office exclusively for business.

That way, you are not entitled to claim a home office deduction in the year of the sale. You lose the write-off, but you get to postpone the gain on that portion of your house.

QUESTION: *I have a home office but also rent out part of my house during the tax year. How do I handle my home office deduction?*

For purposes of calculating your home office deduction limitation only, you must include in your gross business income the amount of money you collect from the rental.

You must also include as part of your direct business expenses all similar expenses, if any, that relate to your rental activity.

Once again, these amounts do not include expenses, such as depreciation, utilities, maintenance, and so forth, that relate specifically to the rental space.

After you figure your home office deduction, you separately compute your net rental income or loss.

17

Getting the Most from Your Vacation Home

So what do you want from your vacation home?

A place you and the family can use whenever you like? A place that you know you can always escape to? Or is your primary consideration keeping the costs down?

If getting away from the madding crowd is uppermost on your mind, then tax expense is a secondary consideration and should not interfere with your choice.

But, in either case, you ought to know the rules so that when you make the choice it is an informed one. An unexpected tax bill can put an ugly end to an otherwise pleasant vacation.

The tax treatment of a second home varies, depending on how you use your retreat. Is it strictly for personal use? Do you rent it? To whom? And for how long?

The information in this chapter will help you decide—at least from a tax perspective—how best to use your vacation home.

WHAT IS A VACATION HOME?

As far as the IRS is concerned, your second home is either a vacation home that you and your family use exclusively, rental property, or some combination of the two. How Uncle Sam treats the house depends on which of these classifications it falls into.

We cover the details in the sections just ahead, but here is an overview of the tax differences among these three categories.

A vacation home that you use personally 100 percent of the time gets the same tax treatment as your first home, even if you rent the property to others for as much as 14 days a year.

You may write off your mortgage interest and property taxes, but you may not deduct other expenses, such as repairs and utilities. And the same restrictions that apply to the deductibility of mortgage interest on your first home apply to the second. (Chapter 5 explains these rules.)

TIP The other good news about a vacation home is this: If you rent out your home for fewer than 15 days, the rental income you collect is tax-free. That's right, you pocket the money, and Uncle Sam doesn't require you to pay taxes on it.

The bad news is that when you sell your vacation home, it doesn't qualify for the same tax breaks as your principal residence. That is, any gain is immediately taxable to you.

Rental property is very different. You get income from renting the property, and you may deduct most of the expenses that you run up, utilities and repairs, for instance, from that income. You may also depreciate the property—write off a portion of its cost each year.

Combination property gets different treatment depending on how much rental use and how much personal use your vacation hideaway gets.

☞ CAUTION Just one day one way or the other, as you will see when we get to the details, can make a big difference in your tax bill.

DEFINING THE DIFFERENCE

Since, for tax purposes, the differences between a personal vacation home and rental property are so great, the tax code is very precise about which is which. If you intend to rent your second home and take advantage of the tax deductions that renting brings you, these distinctions are important to you.

The tax law says that you may classify your second home as rental property as long as you do not occupy it yourself for more than 14 days in the year or for more than 10 percent of the total number of days that it is rented at fair market value, whichever is greater.

If, in other words, you rent your second home at the going rate for 300 days, you could use it yourself for as many as 30 days, and it would still qualify as rental property.

☞ CAUTION What happens if you occupy it for 31 days? You may still claim a write-off for mortgage interest and taxes, but you are limited on the deductions you may take for operating expenses and depreciation.

Uncle Sam is quite strict about what he considers personal use. You have used your home for personal purposes—in his view—if, on any part of any day, your vacation home is occupied by you or any of the following people:

- A person who has an equity stake in the property.

- A spouse or blood relative (meaning your parents, children, siblings, and grandparents).

- A person with whom you have a barter arrangement that allows you to use another dwelling.

- A person to whom the vacation home is not rented at "fair market value" which, according to the law, is the going rate for other, similar homes in the area.

And take care: Even if you charge a relative, or someone with an equity interest in the property, a fair rent, the IRS still considers this personal use.

Say, for instance, you own a vacation home in upstate New York. You rent it to your sister, a relative, for the going rate, $1,500 for ten days.

Next, as part of a barter agreement, you allow your friend Bob to occupy your vacation home for 11 days. In exchange, you use his home in California for eight days.

Finally, you rent your vacation home to your father's boss for ten days and charge the man only half the fair market rental.

How many of these days are personal days? By IRS rules, all 31 count as personal use. What, by the way, constitutes a day? When you are counting, do it the way hotels do: each 24-hour period.

Say you occupy your vacation home from Saturday afternoon through the following Saturday morning. For IRS purposes you have used your house for seven days—even though you were on the premises for part of eight calendar days.

The law does contain one exception to the general rule on renting to relatives. Let's say you rent your property at fair market value to a relative who uses the house as a principal residence—a condo for your parents, for instance. The IRS does not consider this use personal use.

TIP You may not know it, but there's a way to reduce the rent you charge relatives. Consider this lesson from one Tax Court case.

In that case, the court allowed a taxpayer to reduce by 20 percent the fair market rent he charged his parents. The court ruled that the reduced rent was fair because it reflected the amount the man saved in maintenance and management fees by renting to such trustworthy tenants.

CAUTION If you donate time in your vacation home to a charity, you may have to claim that time as personal use time. In one ruling, the IRS held that a week's use of a vacation home that the owner donated to a charity auction counted as personal use of the home. The reason? The owner did not charge the bidder at the auction—the renter—a fair rent. Instead, the bidder paid the rental to the charity. To make matters worse, the owner could not claim a write-off for a charitable contribution, because a gift of the right to use property is not deductible.

TIP You say you want to donate use of your vacation home to a charity auction. Try this tactic: Rent your home for a week at its fair market value, then donate the rent to charity. That way, you get a deduction for your contribution and avoid piling up personal use days.

Maintenance and Repair Visits

Anyone who owns vacation homes knows that they require repairs and maintenance. If you stay at the house while doing the repairs, does the IRS count these as personal use days? Not if your "principal purpose" in staying there is to make repairs or perform maintenance chores.

Say, for example, that you own a mountain cabin that you rent during the winter. You and your spouse arrive at the cabin late Thursday evening. The point of the trip: to prepare the cabin for the rental season. But the two of you are tired.

So you enjoy dinner by the fire, then turn in early to get plenty of rest for the days ahead. You work on the cabin all day Friday and Saturday. Your spouse helps for a few hours each day, but spends most of the time catching up on paperwork.

By Saturday evening the work is done. You spend the rest of the evening relaxing, then head home shortly before noon on Sunday.

Since the principal purpose of your trip was for maintenance, none of these days are counted as personal days. They are all maintenance days.

☞ **CAUTION** In an audit, the IRS may probe to make sure your "principal purpose" was indeed repair and maintenance.

An auditor will look at the frequency with which you did your chores, the amount of time you spent on these activities, and the presence and activities of friends. If the auditor sees that you claim to spend most of your time at your home doing maintenance, but you always bring along companions, he or she may argue that your activities are not on the up and up. And the IRS might count those days as personal use, which may result in a loss of deductions.

💰 **TIP** Keep a log of your repair and maintenance days. Write down when you arrive, how much time you spend on various tasks, and what kinds of work you perform. That way, you can prove how you spent your time should Uncle Sam ever question you.

Rental Property

What is rental property worth to you in the tax department? Probably a lot of deductions. Let's take a look.

Advertising and commissions. Say you own a mountain cabin in West Virginia. And you enlist the help of a local real estate agent to keep the property occupied. Each time he signs someone up to rent your cabin, you pay him a commission.

Under the rules, you may deduct these commissions directly from your rental income. You may also write off advertising expenses.

Mortgage interest and property taxes. You may deduct state and local property taxes that are assessed on your rental property. And you may write off mortgage interest. (Of course, these same costs may be deductible even if your vacation home does not qualify as rental property; that is, you use it as a personal residence.)

(See Chapter 5 for more on writing off interest expenses. See Chapter 8 for more on deducting state and local taxes.)

Operating expenses. Deductible operating costs include utilities, maintenance, insurance, and any other expenses, such as professional fees and repairs. You may also write off any supplies, a receipt book, say, that are normally deductible for profit-oriented activities.

Depreciation. You probably can reduce your taxes by depreciating your vacation home. If you started renting your house before 1987, you may write it off using the depreciation rules that were in effect before the 1986 tax reform bill took effect.

If you began renting it after 1986, however, you must abide by the new, less generous rules. These rules require you to depreciate your house over a 27½-year period.

You may also claim depreciation deductions on furniture and appliances in your vacation home. The post-1986 rules allow you to depreciate these items over seven years, the pre-1987 rules over five years. (See Chapter 18 for the details on depreciation.)

Of course, you do not get a deduction without incurring an expense, and, as people who own them know, maintaining property that you rent out *is* expensive.

Passive investors in rental property may deduct rental losses, but only against income generated by other passive investments, limited partnerships, for instance. If you have no income from other passive investments, you have to postpone claiming your deductions from the vacation home that you operate as rental property until you do have passive income or dispose of the property. (For more information on this rule, see Chapter 19.)

MIXED USE: ALLOCATING EXPENSES

Remember there are two categories of mixed use. In the first, you may make personal use of your vacation home within the 14-day or 10 percent limits and still claim most of the deductions you would get for rental property.

If your use falls into this category, your property—in the eyes of the IRS—is not a personal residence. It's a rental property, and the rules won't allow you to write off as mortgage interest any interest allocated to your personal use. The IRS treats the interest as personal interest expense, the same as credit card interest, for instance. Take heart. If your personal use is less than 14 days or 10 percent of total use, chances are most of your interest expense will be deductible as rental expense. (Personal interest expense is partially deductible through 1990. See Chapter 5 for more information on interest deductions.)

Property taxes, of course, are fully deductible.

In the second mixed-use category, your personal use of the house exceeds 14 days or the 10 percent limit, and the tax treatment your house receives is substantially different.

The portion of your interest, taxes, and expenses allocated to rental use is only deductible against rental income. In other words, if your second home falls into this category and you post a loss from renting the house, too bad. You may not write off that loss currently against your other taxable income. Assuming this type of property qualifies as a second residence, you may write off any mortgage interest allocable to personal use as an itemized deduction. And, of course, you may deduct the personal portion of the taxes.

One other wrinkle: You must deduct your "rental" expenses in a certain order. First, you write off advertising and commission charges; then property taxes and mortgage interest; next, your operating expenses; and, finally, depreciation. Why is the order important?

Uncle Sam is forcing you to write off first against rental income the expenses (with the exception of advertising and commissions) that you are allowed to deduct in any case. And you may write off your other expenses only if you still have rental income left over after these deductions are made.

TIP You may carry forward to future tax years any expenses you may not deduct currently—subject to all the limits we have described, of course.

☞ **CAUTION** If you own a third home and use it as both a residence and rental property, different rules apply. The portion of your mortgage interest allocated to personal use is not deductible as mortgage interest, because the IRS lets you treat only two homes as personal residences.

Rather, the interest allocated to personal use is treated as personal interest and is only partially deductible in 1990 (see Chapter 5 for the details).

Interest allocated to the rental use is deductible to the extent of rental income less advertising, commission charges, and taxes, as discussed above.

No matter which mixed-use category your second home falls into, you must allocate expenses. Be careful. This rule holds true even if you use your home yourself just one day of the year, New Year's Day, say, or the Fourth of July. You now must allocate one day's worth of your vacation home's total expenses to personal use. And Uncle Sam makes no exceptions to this rule.

The allocation formula, however, is simple. Here is how it works. Calculate the number of days you actually rented your property at a fair market value. Call this number X.

Then figure the number of days you used the property for any other purpose. Do not count days it was standing vacant, and do not count any repair or maintenance days. Call the resulting number Y.

You allocate expenses by multiplying your total expenses (including property taxes and mortgage interest) for the year by the fraction: X divided by the sum of X plus Y. The product of that multiplication is the amount that you may allocate to rental use.

WHAT A DIFFERENCE A DAY MAKES

Now let's use a couple of examples to see how to figure the allocation of expenses. The examples also show the big difference just one additional day of personal use can make in the tax cost of owning your second home.

Assume the following facts: Your principal residence is in Connecticut, and you also own a vacation home in New Mexico, which you actively participate in renting.

You take out a mortgage to buy the home in New Mexico, and the interest expense totals $4,000, taxes are $2,000, operating expenses (utilities and maintenance) equal $2,000, and depreciation comes to $5,000. You realize rental income in 1990 of $7,500, after you subtract commissions, for the year, and your adjusted gross income is $80,000.

Example A:

You rent the house at a fair rental value for 126 days. You use it for family vacations for 14 days, and you spend four days there to take care of repairs and maintenance.

The IRS figures you used the house for 140 days (126 rental and 14 personal). The four days you spent on repair and maintenance are not included in your total use days.

You may allocate 90 percent—that is, 126 divided by 140—of the costs associated with the house to its rental use.

Since you used the house yourself for only 14 days, and since your AGI is $80,000, the rules allow you to claim a loss up to $25,000. (Any remaining loss is subject to the general passive loss rules.) You compute rental income and expenses as follows:

- Total rental income: $7,500.

- 90 percent of taxes: $1,800.

- 90 percent of mortgage interest: $3,600.

- 90 percent of operating expenses: $1,800.

- 90 percent of depreciation: $4,500.

- Result: a rental loss of $4,200.

You may also write off the other 10 percent of your property taxes, or $200 as an itemized deduction on Schedule A of your Form 1040. The remaining interest, however—the part allocated to personal use—is classified as personal interest. And in 1990 only 10 percent is deductible, or $40. So, in total, you have deductions against your normal taxable income of $4,440: $4,200 plus $200 plus $40.

Example B:

Let's say, though, that you increase your use of the house by just one day, bringing your personal use to 15 days for the year.

Since 15 days exceeds the maximum 14-day limit and is more than 10 percent of the total rental days (126 days), your vacation home is now classified as a residence.

So your deductions for costs allocated to rental use—that is, 126 divided by 141, or 89 percent—may not exceed the rental income you received. And you must write off expenses allocated to rental use in the following order:

- Commissions and advertising.

- Property taxes and mortgage interest.

- Operating expenses.

- Depreciation.

On the plus side, the IRS counts the portion of mortgage interest you allocate to your personal use of your home as deductible, just like the interest expense on your principal residence. You may write this amount off on your personal return.

So, in this instance, rental income and expenses are as follows:

- Total rental income: $7,500.

- 89 percent of taxes and interest: $5,340.

- 89 percent of operating expenses: $1,780 (not limited since the $7,500 rental income exceeds the interest and taxes by $2,160).

- 89 percent of depreciation: $4,450 in reality, but limited to just $380, since that is the amount by which rental income ($7,500) tops interest, taxes, and operating expenses ($7,120).

The result: You had a loss of $4,070, but you are not able to claim it currently. The reason: Your expenses cannot exceed your rental income. You may, however, still deduct the remaining 11 percent of property taxes and interest, or $660.

As you can see, using your house more than the maximum days allowed can cause your taxes to rise sharply. That extra day's use in our example cost you $3,780 in deductions (the difference between the $4,440 in deductions in Example A and the $660 in Example B). But remember you may carry forward the excess not currently deductible—in this case, $4,070—to future tax years.

There is an alternative method for allocating taxes and mortgage interest (approved by the courts, but not the IRS) that you may use. Sometimes it works to your benefit.

How? It reduces the amount of interest and taxes allocated to the rental portion, giving you room to use more of your other expenses as deductions against rental income. And it increases the amount of interest and taxes allocable to personal use, giving you a bigger itemized deduction.

Under the alternative method, you divide the number of rental days by the total number of days in the year. You use the resulting percentage to determine the portion of mortgage interest and property taxes that you write off against rental income.

The percentage you calculate under the alternative method is usually smaller than the percentage you figured earlier. That is because the earlier method required you to divide the number of rental days by the number of days the property was actually in use.

So the alternative method usually results in greater savings. But to be sure, you have to perform both calculations with your own numbers and compare the results.

Here is an example. We assume the same facts as in Example B, but we allocate interest and taxes using this alternative method.

- Gross rental income: $7,500.

- Taxes and interest: $2,071 (allocated based on the ratio of rental days to total days in the year, that is, 126 divided by 365 times $6,000).

- Limit on other deductions: $5,429 ($7,500 minus $2,071).

- Operating expenses: $1,780 (89 percent times $2,000).

- Depreciation: limited to the lesser of $4,450 (89 percent times $5,000) or $3,649 ($5,429 minus $1,780).

- Rental income or loss: zero.

- Remaining taxes and interest deductible as an itemized deduction: 239 divided by 365 times $6,000, or $3,929.

In this situation the alternative method works out much better for you. It gives you $3,929 in tax and interest deductions, compared to $660 using the other method.

QUESTIONS AND ANSWERS

QUESTION: *In addition to my principal residence, I own a small houseboat. Does my boat count as a vacation home?*

Uncle Sam is quite liberal when it comes to defining a vacation home. It does not much matter if you have an A-frame in the woods or a townhouse in the city.

Any dwelling unit, even a boat or house trailer, that contains basic living accommodations—kitchen, bathroom, and sleeping space—qualifies as a vacation home. So if your boat is equipped with a bunk, a head, and a galley, you are all set.

☞ **CAUTION** The $25,000 passive activity rental exception only applies to real estate; a boat is not real estate, even if you do use it as a vacation home. (See Chapter 19 for more information on these rules.)

QUESTION: *I own three homes. May I deduct mortgage interest on all of them?*

Sorry, you are out of luck as far as the tax laws are concerned. If you have three or more homes, you may claim the mortgage interest deduction on only two of them, your principal residence and one other. You decide which one—and you may change your mind from year to year.

The mortgage interest on other homes gets the same tax treatment as interest on personal loans, provided you use the mortgage money to buy or improve the house.

Otherwise, the interest is classified by how you use the money. For example, if your mortgage proceeds go to purchase common stock, the interest is investment interest. (See Chapter 5 for more information on how to write off interest.)

TIP You will want to put pencil to paper to figure out which house—in addition to your principal residence—you should designate as your second home in order to collect the maximum interest deductions.

QUESTION: *I rent my second home only ten days each year. The rest of the time my family and I use it personally. What rules apply to my situation?*

There is good news and bad news. On the plus side, if you rent your second home for 14 days or less during the year, the rental income is yours tax-free.

The trade-off is that the only deductions you get to take are for mortgage interest and property taxes—no maintenance or repair costs and no depreciation.

But this could be a really good deal if your second home is in a location that commands sky-high rents for a very short period of time, the host city for a national political convention, for example. Rent it out for fewer than 15 days and enjoy the income—tax-free.

18

What You Need to Know About Depreciation

Some parts of the tax code adhere to a consistent logic. Understand the logic and you have mastered the rules. Unfortunately, the rules governing *depreciation* are not one of those parts. And yet, depreciation is one of the most important techniques that have an impact on business, tax, and financial matters.

So, complex or not, depreciation rules are something that anyone with business property, including rental property, must understand. Ignorance here can be costly.

In this chapter, we cover depreciation procedures. And we suggest strategies you can use to make the depreciation rules work for you.

PERSONAL PROPERTY CLASSES

First, a key definition: The tax code refers to *personal property* when it is talking about depreciable business assets other than real estate. We use the same term in this book, even though there is nothing very personal about the property we are discussing. (We show you how to depreciate *real property*—real estate—later in this chapter.)

The law assigns personal property, both new and used, to one of six classes. These classes really describe *recovery periods*—that is, the length of time it takes to recover the money you paid for these assets.

That, after all, is what depreciation is all about: writing off a certain amount each year until you have written off the amount you paid for your property. In this way, the government compensates you for the wear and tear your business assets receive over the years.

Recovery periods range from three to 20 years.

The *three-year class* includes small tools.

In the *five-year class* are light trucks, automobiles, computer equipment, typewriters, calculators, and copiers. Also included: assets used in research and development, oil and gas drilling, construction, and the manufacture of certain products, such as chemicals and electronic components.

Assets in the *seven-year class* include office furniture and fixtures and most other machinery and equipment.

There are also *10-*, *15-*, and *20-year classes*, but only a small number of assets—including land improvements, such as drainage pipes—fall into these categories.

Should you have any doubt into which class a particular asset falls, contact your local IRS office or ask your tax adviser.

ACCELERATED DEPRECIATION

You may depreciate your business assets—except those in the 15- and 20-year classes—using the *200-percent-declining-balance method* (which is also known as the *double-declining-balance method*). You may also opt for the *150-percent-declining-balance method* for all classes of personal property.

Both methods are types of *accelerated depreciation*, which means you get to write off greater amounts in the first years of ownership.

In fact, in the first year of an asset's life, the 200-percent-declining-balance method yields deductions that are twice the amounts you would get using *straight-line depreciation*. (The straight-line method produces the same write-offs from year to year.)

In each subsequent year, however, the 200-percent-declining-balance method lets you deduct progressively smaller amounts until, at some point, the write-offs you calculate under that method become the same or smaller than your annual deductions figured under the straight-line method. At that point, you switch to straight-line to finish depreciating your property.

The 150-percent-declining-balance method, which is used for assets in the 15- and 20-year classes is, as you would expect, 1½ times the straight-line depreciation in the first year of an asset's life.

You have a choice when the time comes to calculate write-offs on your business assets. You may use IRS-approved formulas, and later in this chapter, under "By the Numbers," we will tell you how: Or, you may use the depreciation tables published by the IRS.

You may obtain a copy of these tables from your tax adviser or local IRS office. But even if you use the tables, you should understand the conventions, or rules, incorporated in them that apply to depreciation. Let us run through them.

IMPORTANT CONVENTIONS

The first important rule: a *half-year convention* applies when it comes to depreciating personal property. This convention provides for depreciation for just half the taxable year in which you place it in service—IRS jargon for put to use.

Moreover, the half-year convention applies regardless of the date that you actually begin using your asset. So the deduction you may take the first year is one-half the amount that you would take for a full year of depreciation.

One exception to the rule: You get no depreciation deductions at all if you buy and sell an asset in the same year.

☞ CAUTION Uncle Sam does not want taxpayers who place a large number of assets in service during the last quarter of the year to claim a full six months' depreciation, so he imposes a 40 percent rule. This rule says that you cannot use the half-year convention if, of the personal property that you first place into service during the year, 40 percent of it is placed in service in the last quarter of the year.

You must, instead, use a *mid-quarter convention* for all personal property you place in service during the year, even those assets you place in service *before* the last three months. The mid-quarter convention assumes that you placed your assets in service halfway through the quarter in which you actually put them into use.

When you have to use the mid-quarter convention, you may end up with smaller total depreciation deductions than you could claim under the half-year convention.

BY THE NUMBERS

Let us run through an example of how the 200-percent-declining-balance method of depreciation and the half-year convention actually work.

Say you buy a new car on January 1, 1991. You use the car only for business. The car, which falls into the five-year class, costs $10,000.

And you depreciate it using the 200-percent-declining-balance method. To figure the first year's write-off, you divide $10,000 by five years and get $2,000.

Your depreciation deduction equals two times the amount you would write off using the straight-line method, which, as we have seen, allows you to deduct the same amount each year. In this case, you multiply $2,000 times 2 and get $4,000.

But the half-year convention only allows you to write off one-half of this amount, or $2,000, in the first year of ownership.

In the second year, you depreciate your car by $3,200. How do we get this figure? Divide the remaining *un*depreciated value of the car, $8,000, by the depreciation period, five years. You get $1,600.

Now, since we are using the 200-percent-declining-balance method, multiply this amount by two. The result: $3,200.

Follow the same formula to calculate how much you may depreciate the third year under the 200-percent-declining-balance method: $10,000 minus $2,000 minus $3,200 equals $4,800; $4,800 divided by 5 equals $960; now you multiply by two to get $1,920 depreciation in the third year.

Let us run through the formula one more time, for the fourth year: $10,000 minus $2,000 minus $3,200 minus $1,920 equals $2,880, divided by 5 equals $576.

And $576 times 2 equals $1,152.

As we pointed out earlier, at some point during your car's depreciation life, straight-line depreciation begins to yield the same or a greater write-off than the 200-percent-declining-balance method. In our example, that point is in the fourth year.

Here is how to figure straight-line depreciation.

Simply divide the remaining *un*depreciated cost of your car

($2,880) by the total number of years remaining in its five-year useful life (2½, because of the half-year convention). The answer, $1,152, is the same as you would get using the 200-percent-declining-balance method.

And you will see that in year five your straight-line depreciation of $1,152 tops the $691 you would get using the double-declining-balance method.

So, in the fourth and fifth years, you will switch to the straight-line method of depreciation until you have written off your entire $10,000 purchase price.

To save you the trouble of calculating when it is time to switch from the double-declining method to straight-line depreciation, we have put together a simple chart. (**Note:** This chart uses the half-year convention.)

WHEN TO SWITCH

Recovery Class	Year to Switch
3 Year	3
5 Year	4
7 Year	5
10 Year	7
15 Year	7
20 Year	9

EXPENSING VS. DEPRECIATING

You may not know it, but Uncle Sam allows you to deduct up to $10,000 of the amount you spend each year to acquire depreciable personal property.

Here's an example to illustrate how this tax break works. Assume that you are in the restaurant business. And you buy tables and chairs for the new restaurant you are opening. The price tag: $15,000.

The law allows you to depreciate the furniture over seven years. But the expensing rules give you another option. You may deduct $10,000 of the purchase price this year and then depreciate the remaining $5,000.

☞ CAUTION There's one catch, though. The $10,000 annual ceiling is reduced dollar-for-dollar for every $1 in personal property you place in service in any one year over the first $200,000. So if you place $201,000 worth of assets in service, you may expense only $9,000.

LUXURY AUTOMOBILE LIMITATIONS

The law caps the depreciation you may claim for luxury cars used for business. For cars placed in service after 1986 and before 1989, you may deduct no more than $2,560 in the first year, $4,100 in the second year, $2,450 in the third year, and $1,475 in each succeeding year, including years following the applicable five-year recovery period.

For cars placed in service in 1989, the depreciation limitations were adjusted for inflation to $2,660 in the first year, $4,200 in the second year, $2,550 in the third year, and $1,475 in each succeeding year. The same dollar limitations apply to cars placed in service in 1990.

This means that your depreciation deductions are limited during the normal five-year recovery period on business automobiles costing more than $13,300.

Here's an example. Say you bought a new car in 1989, and you use it exclusively for business. The automobile's price tag was $20,000. The law caps your depreciation write-offs at $2,660 in year one, $4,200 in year two, $2,550 in year three, and $1,475 in each succeeding year.

Under this schedule, you would have to hold on to your car for 11 years before you would claim depreciation write-offs equal to the $20,000 you paid for your car.

The law is even more strict if you use your automobile less than 100 percent of the time for business. Say your business use adds up to 75 percent. Your depreciation deductions are capped at $1,995 in year one (75 percent times the $2,660 ceiling), $3,150 in year two, $1,913 in year three, and so on.

☞ **CAUTION** You think you can use the $10,000 expensing allowance to boost your first-year write-off? Think again. The $2,660 cap applies to the expensing allowance, too.

DEPRECIATING REAL PROPERTY

Unlike personal property, which may fall into one of six different property classes, real property, that is, real estate, is assigned to one of only two classes—residential rental property and commercial property.

You write off the cost of residential rental property over 27.5 years and commercial property over 31.5 years. And you write off only the cost of the building, not the land under it, since, as far as the law is concerned, land does not decay.

In addition, instead of using the accelerated methods of depreciation allowed for personal property, the law requires you to use the straight-line method when it comes to depreciating real property. In other words, you write off the same amount each year.

And the law says you must abide by its so-called mid-month convention. This rule, which goes for both residential and commercial investments, means that you figure your first year's depreciation deduction from the middle of the month in which you place your property in service. The mid-month convention applies even if you place your property in service on the first, or the last, day of the month.

Here's an example of how you would figure your depreciation deductions. Say you and a colleague buy a small office complex on August 1, 1990, in a nearby suburban development. The property costs you $500,000—$400,000 for the building and $100,000 for the land.

You spruce up your property and put it on the rental market on September 1, 1990. How much may you now write off on your 1990 tax return?

Even though the complex was placed in service on September 1, the mid-month convention says the property is placed in service on September 15. So in 1990, you may deduct 3-1/2 months in depreciation write-offs, or $3,704.

Here's how it adds up. You take the cost of your building, $400,000, and divide it by 31-1/2 years, the number of years over which you must depreciate commercial property. Then you divide the result, $12,698, by 12 months and multiply by 3-1/2 months.

While the mid-month convention may seem unfair, it can actually work to your advantage. The reason: You're entitled to a half-month's depreciation no matter when during the month you place your property in service—even if, in the above example, it is September 30.

CHOICES, CHOICES

Under some circumstances, the law requires you to use an alternative method to depreciate your property—one that is usually less generous.

You must use the alternative method when you finance your property with tax-exempt bonds or when the property is used outside the United States. And, you must use the alternative method for certain "listed property," including luxury automobiles and computers used no more than 50 percent in your trade or business.

TIP The 1989 Tax Act added cellular telephones placed in service after 1989 to the list of "listed property" that is subject to the special depreciation limitations and other restrictions. So, if you use a cellular phone or other similar telecommunications equipment no more than 50 percent of the time for business, you must determine depreciation based on the alternative depreciation system instead of the more accelerated, general system.

In addition, if an employee buys a cellular phone that he or she uses for business, no deduction for any business use is allowed unless the employee's use of the equipment is for the convenience of the employer and is required as a condition of employment. Finally, in order to claim any deductions for cellular phones or any other listed property, you must comply with the IRS's strict recordkeeping requirements.

To figure depreciation under the alternate method, you use the property's useful life as specified in the *asset depreciation range (ADR) system*, which is a system that was used before 1981. If your asset isn't listed in the ADR system, use 12 years. What if you're depreciating real property—that is, residential rental real estate or commercial property? You use 40 years.

Then you depreciate your property using the straight-line method. And you use the same half-year, mid-quarter, or mid-month conventions we explained earlier.

When it comes time to compute your alternative minimum tax (AMT), you must use a modified version of the alternative depreciation method. Instead of the straight-line method, you use the 150-percent-declining-balance method for all property other than real property.

TIP As we have just seen, in some cases, the law *requires* you to use an alternative depreciation method. You may also *choose* to use an alternative method.

You may, for instance, use the straight-line method over the regular recovery period for any or all classes of personal property. You may also elect to use the alternative depreciation method for any class of property. And, in the case of real property, you may elect to use the alternate method with respect to any single property. Remember, though, that the alternative method periods are usually longer than the regular recovery periods.

If you choose either of these methods for personal property, then you don't use the 150-percent-declining-balance method when computing your alternative minimum tax.

Alternatively, you may use the 150-percent-declining-balance method for regular tax purposes and switch to straight-line at some point.

As you recall, you must use the 150-percent-declining-balance method for AMT purposes when depreciating personal property, unless you use the straight-line method for regular tax purposes.

Why would you want to use one of these alternative depreciation methods? Many taxpayers just find the straight-line method easier to use. Other taxpayers may want to use the 150-percent-declining-balance method to compute personal property depreciation for their regular tax and for AMT. That way, they do not have to make two calculations. Similarly, when you use the 40-year method for real property, you don't have to add back to your AMT income the difference between the depreciation write-offs you took over 27.5 years or 31.5 years and those you took over 40 years. (See Chapter 20 for more information on the AMT.)

TRANSITION

In general, these depreciation rules apply to all assets you place in service after 1986. But some property may still fall within one of the transition rules.

These rules allow you to depreciate property under provisions that were in place before 1987. You may, in some cases, gain a larger deduction using these rules. (Of course, property you placed in service before 1987 continues to be depreciated under the old rules.)

You may, for example, use the old depreciation rules for property constructed, rehabilitated, or acquired under a contract that was binding on March 1, 1986, or earlier.

You may also use the old rules if you spent or committed to spend at least the lesser of $1 million or 5 percent of the cost of your property by March 1, 1986, as long as construction or rehabilitation of the property actually began by that same date.

But for any of this property to qualify under the transition rules, it must be placed in service by January 1, 1991 (that is, if the ADR life is greater than 20 years). And only property with an ADR life greater than seven years qualifies for the transition rules.

QUESTIONS AND ANSWERS

QUESTION: *My partner and I opened a flower shop on June 1, 1990. That same day, we purchased a small van to make deliveries. We paid $10,000 for the van. Our partnership's tax year ends on December 31. May we claim the half-year convention?*

Your partnership was in business only seven months in 1990. In other words, you had a short taxable year. And the IRS has special rules for calculating depreciation in a short taxable year.

First, you do not use the half-year convention in the same way we described earlier. Instead, you compute your depreciation from a "deemed placed-in-service date," which—for property subject to the half year-convention—is the midpoint of your short taxable year, or September 16, 1990.

You then allocate your annual depreciation amount over the number of months in your short taxable year, beginning with the deemed placed-in-service date.

Your depreciation deduction for the van adds up to $1,167; that is, the $10,000 purchase price divided by 5 years equals $2,000; $2,000 times 2 (for the 200-percent-double-declining-balance method) equals $4,000 (the first annual depreciation amount); $4,000 times 3.5/12 (because you allocate the annual amount over the number of months from the deemed placed-in-service date) equals $1,167.

For the 1991 taxable year, you calculate your depreciation using either the allocation approach we just described or a simplified method. Under the allocation method, you take the remaining 8.5/12 of the $4,000 first annual depreciation amount, or $2,833, plus

3.5/12 of the second annual depreciation amount of $2,400 ($10,000 minus $4,000 equals $6,000; $6,000 divided by 5 times 2 equals $2,400), or $700. The result: $3,533.

Under the simplified method, you take your adjusted basis of $8,833; that is, your cost of $10,000 minus 1990 depreciation of $1,167, and divide by 5 years, then multiply the result by 2 (for the 200-percent-declining balance method). The result is the same: $3,533.

Usually the two methods give you the same depreciation amount, with two exceptions: the year you sell the asset or in a second short year, when using the simplified method results in a smaller amount.

☞ **CAUTION** If you use your personal automobile in your trade or business, you may be subject to the limitations on luxury automobiles ("listed property") discussed earlier in this chapter.

QUESTION: *I am employed by a large corporation. I bought a personal computer so that I can do some of my work at home. Am I entitled to a depreciation deduction?*

Uncle Sam is strict when it comes to writing off computers. He allows you to claim a deduction for your computer only if it is required for your job. In other words, you must need the computer in order to perform your job properly. And it must be for the convenience of your employer, *not* for your convenience.

So, if you have access to a computer at work, you will not be able to write off the cost of your home computer, even if you use it to do some work at home.

Another rule you should know, and this one applies to self-employed people as well: You may depreciate your computer using accelerated depreciation or claim the expensing allowance only if you use your computer more than 50 percent of the time for business.

What if you fail to meet the 50 percent test? The rules allow you to claim a depreciation deduction but you must use the straight-line method, not the accelerated method. In addition, you may not opt for the expensing allowance.

QUESTION: *I want to use the $10,000 expensing allowance. How do I go about it?*

You opt for the expensing allowance simply by taking it. You take your deduction for these expenditures—up to $10,000, of course—on Form 4562, the same form that you use to calculate and claim depreciation deductions.

QUESTION: *My partner and I own a trucking company. This year, we bought several open-road trucks. The total cost was $204,000. We decided to use the expensing allowance. I also own and operate a locksmith business. And I bought a van this year for $15,000. May I claim the full $10,000 expensing allowance on the van in addition to the $10,000 our partnership claimed?*

The answer, in a word, is no. The rules say that a taxpayer may not claim an expense allowance of more than $10,000 in any single year.

So here is how your situation adds up.

Your partnership may claim an expense allowance of only $6,000—not $10,000. The reason: It purchased property that added up to more than $200,000.

Your half of the $6,000 expense allowance comes to $3,000. So you may claim an expense allowance of only $7,000 on the purchase of the van; that is, the $10,000 expense allowance ceiling less the $3,000 expense allowance from your partnership. You may depreciate the remaining cost of $8,000.

 TIP The partnership reports your share of the expense allowance on Form K-1, the same form that lists your share of income, losses, and credits from the partnership. You note the amount of the expense allowance reported on the Form K-1 on Form 4562, which you attach to your personal return.

QUESTION: *I am a 50 percent partner in three separate partnerships. Each has elected to take the full $10,000 expensing allowance. My three K-1s show that I should report $15,000— $5,000 for each partnership. May I deduct this amount on my individual return?*

No, you may deduct only $10,000. The $10,000 expensing limitation applies both to the partnerships and to you, individually. And you would permanently lose the additional $5,000 deduction.

TIP If you are a partner in several partnerships and expect your total share of expensing allowances to exceed $10,000, voice your concerns to the general partners. That way, one or more of the partnerships may decide not to elect the expensing allowance, and you will not lose any of the deductions to which you are entitled.

19

Making Sense
Out of the
Passive Loss Rules

Did you know that it is only since Congress adopted the 1986 Tax Reform Act that the terms passive activity, passive income, and passive loss have become part of our tax vocabulary. These concepts aren't always easy to grasp, nor are the regulations governing them.

Here, we detail the strict rules governing passive investments. First, though, a few words on who is affected by the passive activity rules. When our national legislators passed the law governing passive activities, their intent was to discourage tax shelters, but the rules went far beyond that simple goal.

Instead, they ended up affecting nearly every person engaged in business. If you're a shareholder in an S corporation, a shareholder in a closely-held corporation, a self-employed person, or a partner in a partnership, you're potentially affected by these rules.

You're also affected if you own rental real estate or rent out other types of property such as video tapes, hotel rooms, or tools. And, as a result, you may face burdensome restrictions and paperwork requirements.

DEFINING THE TERMS

What's a passive activity? In the eyes of the IRS, a passive activity—subject to the rules we're about to discuss—is either a trade or business activity in which you invest but aren't a material participant, or it's a rental activity.

☞ CAUTION You should know also that limited partnership investments are almost always passive. Here's why: Limited partners almost never materially participate in managing the trade or business of the partnership.

Here's something else you need to know. Passive activities are investments that can generate two kinds of income.

One is passive income, meaning income from a trade or business or rental activity. The other is portfolio income, which includes interest, dividends, royalties, and so on. The law also says that income from personal services—that is, payment you receive for services rendered—and retirement plans is nonpassive income.

If all this seems a bit confusing at first, it is nonetheless important to master. That is because, as a general rule, only likes may offset likes.

Passive activity losses, for instance, may offset only passive activity income. Or, put another way, your passive losses may not reduce taxable income from nonpassive sources—salary or portfolio income, for instance. Here's an example to show what we mean.

Say you're a doctor in private practice, and you invest in a real estate limited partnership in 1989. In 1990, the partnerships produces a $10,000 loss. Meanwhile, income from your medical practice adds up to $120,000, and your interest income from other investments is $5,000.

Because your real estate partnership is a passive investment, the losses it generates can't offset your nonpassive or portfolio income.

So under the law, your AGI comes to $125,000.

What's a Passive Rental Activity?

What's passive when it comes to rental activities?

The IRS considers all rental investments, with several exceptions listed below, to be passive regardless of whether you materially participate. And rental activities include any investment that generates income from payments for the use of tangible property, rather than for services.

Included, then, are real estate rentals, equipment leasing, and rentals of airplanes or boats—as long as no significant services (flying or fishing lessons, say) are provided in making the property available to your customers.

PASSIVE ACTIVITY EXCEPTION FOR RENTAL AC- TIVITIES

Uncle Sam carves out several narrow exceptions to the passive activity rules for businesses whose main activity is renting either personal or real property.

What are these exceptions? Let's take a look.

Exception 1—The average rental period of your property is seven days or less. You usually determine the average rental period by dividing the total number of days you have rented the property by the number of rental periods. (But the calculation becomes more complicated if you charge more rent for some units in the same complex— for example, you pocket more for the handful of chalets nearest the slopes of your ski resort. You should see your tax adviser if your property falls into this category.)

Uncle Sam defines a rental period as a period during which a customer has a continuous or recurring right to use the property.

This exception exempts most hotels, motels, and bed and breakfasts from the rental property rules, as well as such businesses as short-term auto rentals, tuxedo rentals, and video cassette rentals.

Exception 2—The property isn't rental property if the average rental period is 30 days or less and if you or someone you hire provides significant personal services to your rental customers. Examples of rentals of this type include resort accommodations.

☞ CAUTION   In the eyes of the IRS, significant personal service doesn't include routine repair, maintenance, security, and trash collection nor services required for the lawful use of the property. In addition, significant personal services must be performed by individuals, so telephone and cable services don't apply.

The IRS has stated that in determining what services are significant, all relevant facts and circumstances are taken into account. These include the frequency of services provided, the type and amount of labor required to perform the services, and the value of the services relative to the amount charged for the use of the property.

Exception 3—Extraordinary personal services are provided by the owner of the property without regard to the average period of customer use. The IRS included this exception so that operations such as hospitals wouldn't be subject to the rental activity limitations.

What are extraordinary personal services? They're services provided in connection with a customer's use of the property, but the "rental" is incidental to the receipt of the services. For example, a patient in the hospital is renting the bed, but the bed rental is merely incidental to the major service of the visit, which is hospital care.

Exception 4—The rental of the property is treated as incidental to a nonrental activity of the taxpayer. Take, for example, a developer who has constructed a condominium. During the marketing period, some of the units are temporarily rented. Under these circumstances, the rental won't be considered a rental activity.

Exception 5—Property is customarily made available during defined business hours for the nonexclusive use of various customers. A golf course, for example, might qualify under this exception. While golfers pay a fee to use the course, the course is available during defined business hours and for the nonexclusive use of various customers.

Exception 6—Property you provide free of charge to a partnership or S corporation isn't rental property if you're a material participant in that partnership or S corporation. This rule applies to any property that you may own that you provide free of charge to your business. And it can include buildings and equipment.

☞ **CAUTION** When your rental investment meets one of the exceptions, your income isn't automatically deemed passive. Instead, you determine whether you must treat your business as a passive activity by running through the material participation rules (which we describe in the next section).

PASSIVE TRADE OR BUSINESS

Now you know what's automatically passive when it comes to rental activities. But what's passive when it comes to a trade or a business or when it comes to a rental activity that meets one of the above exceptions?

Let's start with the activity rules. Under these rules, you must first determine whether your involvement with many trades or businesses constitutes a single undertaking or multiple ones. What's a single undertaking? It's a trade or business that's conducted at the same location and owned directly—that is, not through a partnership or S corporation—by the same person.

Say you're the sole owner of an auto dealership, and your company both sells and repairs cars on the same lot. Your dealership qualifies as a single undertaking, even though you're engaged in two businesses; that is, you both sell and repair automobiles.

What if you sell cars on one lot and repair them in a building two miles away? In this case, your auto dealership no longer qualifies as a single undertaking, because you failed the location test. Instead, you have two undertakings.

Here are a few more twists.

Say you're the sole owner of a company that sells and installs electric garage door openers. The location requirement doesn't apply to you. Why not? Because that's the law.

Or say you're a partner in a partnership that owns a neighborhood convenience store. And you also own, by yourself, a convenience store in a nearby town.

Each store qualifies, by itself, as a single undertaking. That is, you may not lump them together and treat them as a single undertaking. Each qualifies as a single undertaking because—when they're combined—they fail the location test and the ownership test.

Now, you ask, why should I care whether my trade or business is a single undertaking or more than one separate undertakings? Here's the reason: Uncle Sam may require you to combine your multiple undertakings into a single activity. So what, you say.

You must pass the material participation test for *each* activity, not each undertaking.

What's a single activity? The rule is, a single activity is a single undertaking. But Uncle Sam doesn't stop there. He also says that multiple undertakings that are similar and controlled by the same people fall as well into the single activity category.

One undertaking is similar to another if more than half their operations are in the same line of business; that is, they fall into the same IRS business classification, which are based on the Standard Industrial Classification (SIC) codes. (Your tax adviser will have a copy.)

Two undertakings meet the second test if they're controlled by the same people; that is, the same five or fewer people own 50 percent or more of it and the other undertaking.

Here's another test, and it applies to businesses that are vertically integrated. Under the test, an undertaking is similar to another if either undertaking supplies or obtains more than 50 percent of its products or services from the other.

TIP You say you want to treat your numerous rental real estate properties as separate activities? The IRS allows you to do so by electing to report them separately on your return.

But you should know that once you make this election, you may not break your properties into any additional activities. For example, if you combined two apartment complexes into a single activity, you may not later divide those two complexes into two separate activities.

TIP Since rental real estate is always passive (subject to the exceptions we outlined previously), it usually pays to treat them as separate activities. The reason? It may help you when it comes time to dispose of or sell the units, because you can use any suspended losses you've incurred at that time. The same is true, of course, with non-rental real estate activities. (We discuss the treatment of suspended losses later in this chapter.)

MATERIAL PARTICIPATION

Now, on to the material participation rules. If you pass the material participation test, your trade or business (or your rental activity that fell into one of the exceptions) will not be classified as passive. In Uncle Sam's eyes, you materially participate in a rental or trade or business if you're involved in its operations on a 'regular, substantial, and continuous basis.'' But what does that phrase really mean?

Not surprisingly, the IRS has devised some tests—seven in this case—to help you tell whether you're a material participant in an activity. If your involvement satisfies just one of these, you're a material participant. If you don't satisfy any, Uncle Sam considers your investment passive.

And note: You may be a material participant one year and a passive investor the next. It's not enough, that is, to satisfy one of the tests in just any one year. The IRS requires you to reevaluate your participation annually.

Test 1—More than 500 hours of material participation. If you spend more than 500 hours in an activity during the year, you're a material participant for the year. When applying this test, you may count any work that you do in connection with the activity as long as it is the type of work normally done by owners.

Moreover, say your spouse also performs the work of an owner. In this case, you may add his or her participation to your own for purposes of this rule—and the other tests outlined in this chapter.

TIP It doesn't matter that your spouse isn't a part owner of the business or whether the two of you file a joint return for the year.

If the total hours the two of you worked tops 500, you meet the requirements of the first test, and your investment isn't subject to passive activity rules.

Let's say, for instance, that Patrick and Meghan, a married couple, together put in more than 500 hours of work managing a restaurant that Meghan owns.

They meet the requirements of test one. But if Patrick's work had consisted of dish washing, a job that owners don't usually perform and the purpose of his taking on this task was to avoid the passive loss rules, his hours wouldn't count toward the 500-hour threshold.

CAUTION For purposes of this test and the ones that follow, Uncle Sam won't allow you to count the number of hours you spend in your capacity as an investor, unless you're directly involved in the day-to-day management of the business.

What's the role of investor? The IRS says it includes studying and reviewing financial statements, preparing or compiling summaries or analyses or monitoring the finances or operations of the business in a nonmanagerial capacity.

Test 2—Substantially all participation. If your participation, or the participation of you and your spouse, represents substantially all of the participation by anyone in an activity for the year, you're a material participant.

Test 3—More than 100 hours of participation and not less than anyone else. This test has two parts.

First, you must spend more than 100 hours during the year operating the business. Second, you must spend more time than anyone else, including nonowners, working in the business. Meet both conditions of this rule in nonrental activities, and the business isn't a passive activity.

Test 4—More than 500 hours worked in several activities with more than 100 hours in each. This test itself isn't tricky, but the

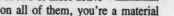

consequences can surprise you. The test says that if you spend more than 100 hours on each of two or more activities and a total of more than 500 on all of them, you're a material participant in each of those business ventures.

But that could be bad news. Maybe you wanted one of the activities to give you passive income or losses. Why? Consider this example.

Assume that Joseph, a full-time attorney, invested in several real estate limited partnerships. He expects these investments to lose money for several years.

Joseph is also a general partner in two other, very profitable activities—an auto parts store and a dry cleaning business.

He spends about 300 hours per year in the auto parts store and about 250 hours per year in the dry cleaning business. Both businesses have several full-time employees.

Joseph hopes to write off the passive losses from his real estate investments against the income from the dry cleaning and auto parts businesses.

After all, he figures, he isn't involved in either of the businesses for more than 500 hours, and others spend more time than he does working there.

But Joseph has a problem.

Since his participation in each of these businesses comes to more than 100 hours and his total participation tops 500 hours, he meets the requirements of the fourth test.

So, as far as Uncle Sam is concerned, he's a material participant in both the auto parts store and the dry cleaning business. And the income from these businesses isn't passive. The result: Joseph can't use his passive real estate losses to offset the income from his two part-time businesses.

What if you invested in two business and both are posting a profit and your hours spent on both of these activities doesn't exceed 500 hours? A special rule applies. Let's take an example where you participate 140 hours in one business and 160 hours in the other.

Under test four, you aren't a material participant, but your profits aren't passive either. The IRS treats them as nonpassive income, and you may not use these earnings to offset any of your passive losses.

Now, let's change the scenario. Say the two businesses are operating in the red. You lose again because of the special rule we outlined above. Uncle Sam now treats the losses as passive losses.

Test 5—Material participation in any five of the last 10 years. If you've been a material participant in a business for any five of the most recent ten years, the IRS considers you a material participant in the business for the current year—no matter how small your actual involvement.

What's the point of this test? Uncle Sam wants to prevent people from shifting income from the passive to nonpassive category—or vice-versa—just to reduce their tax liability. Here's an example to show how that tactic might work.

We'll assume that Joe is the sole owner of Joe's Tool and Die, a very profitable sole proprietorship. He's also an investor in several real estate limited partnerships.

These limited partnerships produce sizable losses, which Joe wants to offset against the profits from his business.

Joe worked full time in his business since he started it in 1981. But he has decided to reduce the amount of time he spends at the tool and die company beginning in 1990, so he can pursue other opportunities.

Since Joe reduced his involvement, he thought his income from the business would be passive. Unfortunately, he's been tripped up by the fifth test.

He has been a material participant in the business since 1981, or nine out of the last ten years. Consequently, even though he doesn't participate in the business currently, the IRS treats him as a material participant for purposes of the passive loss rule.

Test 6—For personal service businesses, material participation in any three previous years. Say you have materially participated in a personal service business—law, engineering, accounting, architecture, health, consulting, performing arts, actuarial science, and so on—in any three preceding years. What are the tax consequences?

In the eyes of Uncle Sam, you're considered a material participant for the current year and into the future.

This test means that once you've been a material participant in, for instance, an architectural firm for any three years, any income you receive from the firm in the future is nonpassive no matter how few hours you toil for the firm.

The IRS considers residual fees, for instance, that inactive partners might receive from a personal service firm as nonpassive income.

Test 7—Facts and circumstances. This test is easy to state, but difficult to apply. It says simply that the facts and circumstances in any specific case will be the final determinant of whether you are or aren't a material participant.

Unfortunately, the IRS hasn't issued much guidance on how it will look at facts and circumstances. Still, we do have a few guidelines.

First, you may not automatically add, as time spent in the business, the number of hours you devote to management. You may include your management hours only if no one else performs and gets paid for managing the business, and no one else spends more time than you managing the business.

Second, you must devote at least 100 hours to the business during the year to qualify under the facts and circumstances test.

If your participation comes to fewer than 100 hours, you're out of luck. Uncle Sam says you aren't a material participant in the business under this test regardless of any other facts and circumstances.

What about limited partners? Can they materially participate in a business? Generally they can't because state laws normally prohibit limited partners from being active in a business. And limited partners who do become active risk losing their limited liability.

Since limited partners do not normally participate in limited partnerships, the material participation tests we just discussed don't apply.

Exceptions exist, though. The first exception deals with the first tests, the 500 hour test. Even limited partners are material participants if they put 500 hours of more into the business.

The second exception relates to tests five and six. If a limited partner meets either the five-of-10 year test or the any-three-previous year test, he or she is a material participant regardless of the limited partner designation.

A third exception applies to people who are both general and limited partners in the same activity. The IRS considers them, on balance, to the general partners who must go back through test one through six above to determine whether they are material participants.

One final note: Although the law doesn't require it, anyone who anticipates that material participation could be an issue would be smart to keep a daily log of the hours he or she puts into a business. If the decision is a close call, the log could tip the balance.

LOSSES

Losses you rack up in 1990 from passive activities are good for offsetting your profits from other passive activities. (However, see our discussion of the phase-in rules later in this section.)

But what if you don't have profits from passive activities? All isn't lost. You may carry your passive losses forward and use them to offset passive income in future years. The passive losses that you carry forward are called suspended loses. And you must keep track of losses from each of your passive activities from year to year.

Here's an example to illustrate how suspended losses work. Say that the year is 1990, and you have invested in three limite partnerships—A, B, and C. All these partnerships are passive investments and, under the tests, are considered separate activities.

Partnerships A and B each generate $10,000 in losses this year. But partnership C rewards you with a $5,000 profit. In total, you lost $15,000 on passive investments—that is, $10,000 plus $10,000 (or $20,000) minus the $5,000 profit.

The passive loss rules won't allow you to deduct your $15,000 on your current tax return. So you carry forward the suspended loss to future years.

The losses from partnerships A and B are used *pro rata*—meaning in proportion—against C's $5,000 passive income, resulting in $7,500 of suspended loss you can carry forward for each partnership, A and B.

Here's how we do the calculation: Multiply the suspended loss of $15,000 by the ratio of each partnership's loss to your total losses.

For example, partnership A's suspended loss is $7,500—that is, $10,000 (A's loss) divided by $20,000 (A's loss plus B's loss) or 0.5 times $15,000.

Now, say the year is 1991. Partnership A earns a $20,000 profit. Partnership B once again generates a $10,000 loss, and partnership C posts another $5,000 profit. You have a net $15,000 profit for the year ($20,000 from A plus $5,000 from C minus $10,000 from B).

And here's the good news. You carry forward your total $15,000 loss for 1990 from partnerships A and B and apply it against 1991's $15,000 profit. The result: You've reduced your income from passive investments in 1991 to zero.

Remember, the law says you may carry forward these suspended passive investment losses indefinitely. But that isn't all.

When you sell a passive investment, the law allows you to use all suspended losses from the activity you sold right away. And you may use these losses to offset not only your passive income but any other income including earned income, or wages, and portfolio income as well.

☞ CAUTION What if selling your passive activity results in a loss and the passive activity was a capital asset? In this case, the loss on the sale is treated both as a passive loss and as a capital loss subject to the capital loss rules (see chapters 4 and 5 for more information on capital losses).

You add suspended losses from an activity you dispose of this year to any current losses from the same activity and any losses you recognize at the time you dispose of the activity. If these losses come to more than your net income or gain from all your passive activities during the current year, calculate the difference. You may use the result to offset any other income or gains, including wages.

To illustrate this rule, let's return to our previous example. Now, say the year is 1991, and you decide to unload Partnership A. On June 30, you sell your entire interest to your neighbor, Lisa.

For the first six months of 1991, partnership A produces income of $2,000. And, when you sell, you realize a gain of $1,500. Partnerships B and C don't produce any income or loss during 1991. Your only other source of income: your $120,000 salary.

You would obviously like to use at least some of your suspended losses to reduce your hefty income. And you may. In fact, you may use all your suspended loss from partnership A in 1991. But you must determine the suspended losses you're allowed as follows:

- Start by adding the following: the amount of your suspended loss from the previous year (in your case, $7,500); the amount of your loss from the current year (none); and the amount of loss you realize when you dispose of or sell the activity (none).

- Now, subtract from the result your net income from all your passive activities (in your case, $3,500).

- You may use the resulting amount—$4,000—to offset your salary.

What about the $7,500 suspended loss from partnership B? It's still suspended and will carry forward to 1992. You may not deduct it in 1991. The reason: You didn't dispose of your interest in B.

PHASE-IN RULES

The rules we've described so far apply to investments you make after October 22, 1986, that is, the date the 1986 Tax Reform Act was enacted. But the law provides a four-year phase-in period for investments you made on or before that date. (These investments include a binding obligation to purchase that was in effect on October 22, 1986.)

To qualify for this special treatment, you must have acquired your interest in the business, and it must have begun operations, by October 22, 1986. Even if it hadn't, though, it will still qualify for phase-in treatment if the business had a binding contract in effect on August 16, 1986 to acquire assets to use in its operations—as long as at least 50 percent of the business' assets were acquired by that date.

For these four years, you may use tax shelter losses and credits that the law will zap completely in 1991 to offset earned or portfolio income according to the following percentages:

- 1987—65 percent

- 1988—40 percent

- 1989—20 percent

- 1990—10 percent

- 1991 and future years—zero percent

So if you own both preenactment and postenactment interests in passive activities, you're going to have to do a little calculating to figure out how much of your current year passive loss qualifies for the partial deduction or phase-in.

Why? The tax rules let you apply the phase-in only to the lesser of:

- Your total net passive loss for the year, or

- Your net passive loss for the year taking into account only preenactment interests.

Let's say your passive investments produce the following results for 1990.

Activity A	Acquired Pre-enactment	$(6,800)
Activity B	Acquired Pre-enactment	2,800
Activity C	Acquired Post-enactment	1,000
Activity D	Acquired Post-enactment	(500)

How much in passive losses may you take in 1990? The answer: $3,800 of passive losses plus $350 of phase-in losses.

Let's take a look at how we arrived at these figures.

As we have seen, the first step is to add up all your losses from passive activities. Then subtract this amount from all your profits. You now have the amount of the year's passive loss that would be disallowed—if you didn't consider the phase-in provisions. In this calculation, you also determine how much of your passive losses you utilize without any phase-in limitations.

Now we get to the next step, which determines the amount of phase-in losses you may take. The rules require you to add up your net losses from passive investments you bought before October 23, 1986.

Then, it mandates that you compare your total net loss from these preenactment investments with your total net loss from all passive activities and see which figure is lower. You multiply the phase-in percentage times this lower number to get the loss you're allowed to write off against your regular income.

Here's how the numbers add up. The first step determines your passive loss disallowed without regard to the phase-in treatment.

Your total passive losses: $7,300 (the sum of activities A and D). Your total passive income: $3,800 (sum of activities B and C). Your net passive loss: $3,500. In the offsetting process, you use $3,800 of passive losses.

The second step requires you to figure your net passive losses from investments made by October 22, 1986 (the sum of activity A and B): $4,000.

The phase-in allowance applies to the lesser of $3,500 or $4,000, that is, $3,500. So multiply the phase-in percentage (10 percent) times $3,500. The result—$350—is the phase-in loss you may take for 1990 against your regular income.

Although the rules are phased in for regular tax purposes, don't expect this generosity for the alternative minimum tax (AMT). When you compute the alternative minimum tax, you must add back to your taxable income any loss that the phase-in rules allow you for regular tax purposes. (See Chapter 20 for more on the AMT.)

PASSIVE INCOME GENERATORS

If you have substantial passive losses from old tax shelter investments, consider PIGs. And no, we're not talking about farm animals.

PIGs, or passive income generators, are, in effect, reverse tax shelters. A PIG may generate a positive cash flow as well as taxable passive income.

Among the more common types of PIGs are limited partnerships that operate ongoing, profitable businesses—a ski resort, golf course, or conference center, say.

The benefit of these investments is that the income they generate is passive, and you may use your passive losses to offset this passive income.

But how do you know which PIGs might make sense for your circumstances? First, you should know that may PIGs are syndicated— that is, they're offered to the public through public offerings—and are actively marketed by brokers. However, special rules may limit the benefits from such syndicated offerings. These rules are covered in the discussion of master limited partnerships.

Once you've decided that a passive income generator may help you at tax time, you should compare a specific PIG to other investments and consider the investment merits of the PIG exclusive of any associated tax benefits.

Using the same methods, compare rates of return. Also, take a look at how the deal and the promoter stack up against others in the same industry. And make sure to include in your analysis any fees that might be involved in buying or selling both investments.

If you're interested in investing in PIGs, you should have no trouble finding them. Your investment adviser, stockbroker, or financial planner will know the names of some of these partnerships. You may also run across names of PIGs in financial publications.

Other options

Here's a useful strategy if you own a profitable corporation that isn't organized as a personal service corporation or an S corporation.

Transfer ownership of investments that generate passive losses to your corporation. The reason: The law allows a corporation to use passive losses to offset its regular business income. And it makes no difference if the corporation is closely held.

☞ **CAUTION** This strategy doesn't make sense if your passive investments generate income (not losses) currently or will do so in the not-so-distant future. That's because the income a corporation earns is taxed twice—once at the corporate level, then again when the income is passed along to you in the form of dividends.

Another drawback is that if the shelter has phantom income, such income may be triggered upon transfer. We discuss phantom income in the question and answer section later in this chapter.

TIP If you're the owner of a profitable corporation but don't materially participate in business operations elect S corporation status.

Since you don't materially participate, your income from the S corporation is passive. And you can use your passive losses to offset profits from your S corporation.

Remember, you add together income and losses from all your passive investments. So if you find yourself locked into some older investments that you expect will generate passive losses, follow the obvious strategy: Invest in vehicles that generate passive incomes. You may then use this income to offset your loses.

CAUTION Make sure your investments make economic sense apart from the tax benefits.

You may also qualify for a special exception designed to help the "moderate-income" taxpayer get around the passive loss rules.

This exception allows you to deduct rental real estate losses of up to $25,000 from your regular income under two conditions: You meet certain income guidelines, and—you guessed it—you must actively participate in the operation of your rental property.

Let's look at the income guidelines.

As long as your adjusted gross income (AGI) is $100,000 or less—figured before you subtract any rental or passive losses—you may deduct from your ordinary income up to $25,000 in rental losses from residential or commercial rental property.

But you lose the deduction for part of the loss if your income falls between $100,000 and $150,000, and you're entitled to no deduction if your AGI tops $150,000.

What if your AGI is between $100,000 and $150,000?

You must reduce the $25,000 limit by 50 percent of the amount by which your AGI exceeds $100,000. Here's an example to illustrate how to perform this calculation.

Say your AGI comes to $140,000—that is, it tops $100,000 by $40,000. So you multiply 50 percent times $40,000 and subtract the result—$20,000—from $25,000. In your case, you may deduct $5,000 in rental losses from your regular income—as long as you actively participate in managing the property. What if your losses top $5,000? You treat the excess the same as you treat other passive losses (i.e., you may subtract these losses from your passive income to the extent that you have any).

You should know, though, that this $25,000 limit applies cumulatively to all your rental property. No matter how many rental buildings you own, the loss you claim, which offsets regular income, may not exceed the $25,000 total. And Uncle Sam makes no exceptions to this rule.

GIFTS

When you give away an interest in a passive activity to a friend or relative, you lose your right to claim suspended losses. In this case, the recipient of your generosity must add these suspended losses to his or her basis in the investment.

What if, later on, the recipient sells the investment at a loss? Then, for purposes of determining the donee's loss, his or her basis is limited to the fair market value of the interest on the date you made the gift.

Moreover, sales you make to related parties—relatives, your closely-held corporation, and so on—will also not let you immediately use your suspended losses. In this instance, you carry forward the losses until the related party disposes of the investment in a taxable transaction.

For example, say you sell your limited partnership interest to your dad in 1990. You won't be able to use 1989's suspended losses from the partnership when you make the sale. Instead, you continue to carry these losses forward as suspended losses until your dad sells the investment to an unrelated party, at which time you may deduct the losses.

INTEREST EXPENSES

The law says that if an investment is a passive activity, interest expense on loans associated with that investment isn't subject to the personal or investment interest limits.

The rules say you may write off such passive activity interest only from passive activity income. If you report no passive activity income, you may not pocket a deduction.

But you may carry forward your passive activity interest indefinitely. In other words, you may use the interest you carry forward to offset passive income in future years. And in the year you dispose of a passive activity, you may deduct all passive activity interest that you hadn't been able to deduct before. In essence, this passive activity interest is treated just like it was a passive loss.

And it makes no difference whether the interest expense is "inside interest"—that is, incurred by the limited partnership itself—or "outside interest," that is, interest on money you borrow to invest in the limited partnership.

What does this rule mean? When you borrow money to purchase a passive activity investment, the interest is combined with your income or loss from the investment to determine your overall passive income or loss from the activity.

The one exception to this rule: passive investments that report portfolio income, such as a real estate partnership that earns interest income on its excess cash reserves. In these cases, you must classify a portion of your interest expense as investment interest, and it is subject to the investment interest limits.

Here's an example. You're a new limited partner in ABC Partnership in 1990. And, for 1990, you have a passive loss before interest expense of $10,000. In addition, the ABC partnership itself racks up $2,000 in interest expense. ABC reports no portfolio income.

The partnership isn't required to treat any of its interest as investment interest. The entire $2,000 is added to your passive loss for the year. You don't need to treat this amount separately as investment interest on your return.

What if ABC did have portfolio income? In this case, the partnership must allocate some of the $2,000 of interest expense to the portfolio income. ABC would then report this amount separately to you. And you would have to treat it as investment interest expense on your return.

Usually, losses you take from your passive investments won't have an impact on your investment interest limitations. But there's one exception. Losses allowed under the phase-in provisions reduce net investment income for the investment interest limitation. (See Chapter 5 for more information about interest deductions.)

CREDITS

The same rules that apply to losses apply to credits. You may use tax credits passed along to you by shelters only to offset the tax on the net income from these investments.

Consider this example. Let's say you would owe Uncle Sam $50,000 in tax if you disregarded your net passive income. But you would have to shell out $80,000 if you took into account both your net passive income and your other taxable income.

So the amount of tax that you attribute to your passive income comes to $30,000. And you're allowed to take any credits from your passive investments that don't top $30,000.

This provision applies mostly to a tax shelter that passes along such tax credits as energy credits, rehabilitation credits, and research and development credits.

Like losses, you may carry forward suspended and unused credits to a future tax year. However—unlike losses—you can't use credits to offset tax on earned income and portfolio income when you sell your shelter.

In these cases, however, you may increase your basis by the amount of the suspended credit (limited to the original basis adjustment) before you sell. This provision gives you a lower gain or higher loss when you sell your property. If you go this route, you may no longer carry forward the suspended credit to offset other passive income.

QUESTIONS AND ANSWERS

QUESTION: *Last year I invested in a building. And this year I lost my only tenant. It is virtually impossible for me to sell the building or convert it for use by someone else. Is there some way I can dispose of it, so I don't have to treat my loss for the year as passive?*

The answer is yes, you can abandon the property. The law also considers so-called abandonments as dispositions that let you escape the passive loss limitations. So you may claim your entire loss in the current year. The law can be tricky, though, when it comes to abandoning property. If you plan to go this route, consult your tax adviser beforehand.

Also, if you abandon your building after 1987, the suspended loss rules let you take all the losses you have been carrying forward in the year the abandonment occurs.

How do you abandon an investment?

Uncle Sam considers your building abandoned if you can prove that you originally had a profit motive for investing in the building, and the property became useless. You must also show that you have permanently deserted the building and discontinued trying to rent or sell it.

But note: Just not using the building—or a decline in its value—isn't conclusive evidence that you have abandoned your property. You must show that you have actually forsaken it. For example, the IRS would consider cutting off utilities, boarding up windows, and cancelling insurance as proof of abandonment.

QUESTION: *Can a limited partner materially participate in a business?*

Generally, no, because state laws normally prohibit limited partners from being active in a business.

Limited partners who do become active risk losing their limited liability. Consequently, the material participation tests discussed above don't apply.

Exceptions exist, though.

The first exception deals with the first test, the 500 hour test. Even limited partners are material participants if they put 500 hours or more into the business.

The second exception relates to tests five and six. If a limited partner meets either the five-of-10 year test or the any-three-previous year test, he or she is a material participant regardless of the limited partner designation.

A third exception applies to people who are both general and limited partners in the same activity. The IRS considers them, on balance, to be general partners who must go back through test one through six above to determine whether they are material participants.

QUESTION: *My accountant says I should look into "paired investments." What are these vehicles and are they appropriate for me?*

Only you can decide whether an investment is right for your circumstances. But paired investments do hold appeal for many investors.

What are they? As their name implies, they are limited partnerships with two distinct businesses. One business generates income and, hopefully, cash. The other business generates losses—at least for tax purposes—to offset that income.

Paired investments are just another variation on the tax shelter theme. Our advice: Invest in one of these vehicles only if it makes economic sense.

QUESTION: *I owned a limited partnership interest in a piece of rental real estate. We sold out in 1985 on an installment-sale basis, so I am still receiving income. Is this income passive?*

The answer is yes. Uncle Sam treats the income as passive, even though the passive-loss rules weren't in place when you sold your partnership. However, note that any interest income received would be treated as portfolio and not passive income.

QUESTION: *I am the sole owner of a small company that provides word processing services. My business is organized as an S corporation, and it is the only company in which I have an ownership interest. My son is in charge of the day-to-day operations, but I am actively involved in consulting, arranging financing, and monitoring the corporation's financial success. I spend about 400 hours a year in these efforts. In fact, my financial analysis is used regularly in the actual decision making process of the business. In 1989, my business reported a loss. Do I report this loss as a passive loss?*

It depends. You spend only 400 hours a year on the business; that is, you fail to meet the 500-hour material participation test.

The only material participation test that you might pass is the facts-and-circumstances test. But the IRS has yet to issue guidance on what criteria would allow the losses to be treated as nonpassive for purposes of the facts and circumstances test. However, the IRS is slated to issue further guidance on this test.

QUESTION: *I am a partner in a partnership that owns five convenience stores, each in a different location. The partnership is owned by two unrelated partners. Do we categorize the stores as a single activity or multiple activities?*

The stores probably fit into the category of a single activity. Why? They share the same owners and fall into the same SIC code. In this situation, businesses are usually treated as a single activity even though they are located in different places.

QUESTION: *I own an 8 percent interest in one partnership and a 6 percent interest in another. Both partnerships own the same type of business—a fast food restaurant. Do I classify these restaurants as a single undertaking or as multiple undertakings?*

The restaurants are single undertakings—and single activities—because your ownership isn't direct (that is, it is through a partnership) and it isn't substantial (meaning, in the eyes of the IRS, that it adds up to 10 percent or less).

QUESTION: *I own interests in four partnerships and all are engaged in similar ventures. My percentage of ownership in the four partnerships—partnership A, 30 percent; partnership B, 52 percent; partnership C, 15 percent; and partnership D, 8 percent. I am a material participant in partnership B. How many activities am I engaged in?*

Since you own a substantial interest (greater than 10 percent) in partnerships A, B, and C, you combine them and treat them as a single activity.

You don't hold a substantial interest in partnership D, so you treat it as a single activity separate from your other partnership interests.

QUESTION: *I am a partner in a partnership that owns a hotel. In the hotel lobby are five commercial stores that the partnership leases to tenants. These commercial rentals make up 15 percent of the gross income of the hotel. Are the rental operations of the commercial stores considered a separate rental activity from the operations of the hotel?*

The answer is no. The rental operations of the commercial space don't constitute a separate activity from the hotel.

Where an undertaking consists of both rental and nonrental operations and one of the operations is dominant, then that operation constitutes the single activity. In your case, the hotel operations are dominant— that is, they contribute more than 80 percent of your revenues—and accordingly, the rental operations aren't considered a separate activity.

QUESTION: *I have heard a lot about publicly traded partnerships. How do I treat for tax purposes income and losses from these partnerships?*

Interests in master limited partnerships—that is, MLPs or publicly traded partnerships—are traded on public exchanges, just like shares of stock. So they're much more marketable and much more liquid than other types of partnerships.

Originally, these publicly traded partnerships were thought to provide passive income to investors with passive activity losses. These investors could then use the losses to offset their income. The partnerships came under Congressional scrutiny, not only because they offered this opportunity to save on taxes, but also because they paid no tax and had characteristics of a publicly traded corporation. Instead, the individual partners paid tax on their share of any profit.

As a result of Congressional action, Uncle Sam now treats net income from publicly traded partnerships as portfolio income. That means you may not use this income to offset passive losses from other investments.

What's worse, losses from publicly-traded partnerships are treated as suspended loses. And you may subtract these losses only from net income from the partnerships. But you may claim any unused suspended losses when you dispose of your interest in the partnership.

Moreover, the IRS taxes publicly traded partnerships formed after December 17, 1987 as corporations. So profits and losses no longer flow through to the partners.

There is, however, an exception to the corporate treatment rules. If 90 percent of the partnership's gross income comes from interest, dividends, real-estate rents, gains from the sale of capital assets, income or gains from certain oil and gas activities, and gains from the sale of certain trade or business assets, Uncle Sam will still treat the MLP as a partnership.

QUESTION: *Given the dramatic change in the tax-shelter rules, does it still make sense to highly leverage my investments?*

Generally, no.

It used to make sense to leverage your deal to the greatest extent you could. That is, it paid to borrow as much money as possible. The reasons?

You could collect significant deductions with only a minimal cash investment. Also, you could deduct fully the interest you paid on any borrowed funds.

Now, however, you may want to minimize leverage in your passive investments, so you reduce your interest expense. When you do minimize leverage and cut your interest expense, you also may end up creating passive income or perhaps even breaking even in operations or at least reducing your passive losses.

Also, it's possible that your investment will produce positive cash flow in excess of the passive income. This can happen as a result of noncash deductions, such as depreciation and depletion, that don't require a cash expenditure.

QUESTION: *I invested in an oil and gas limited partnership and sold it at a loss. If this loss is a capital loss, how is it treated for tax purposes?*

The capital loss rules take precedence over the passive loss rules in determining what losses you may take on your return when you sell your passive investment. (See Chapter 14 for a discussion of capital gains and losses.)

Let's say that you sell your entire interest in your oil and gas limited partnership in 1990. As a result, you have a $10,000 long-term capital loss. Your investment also produces $5,000 of suspended passive losses in 1989. And in 1990, your investment brings you $3,000 in passive income. You have no other capital gains or losses.

The law allows you to claim only $3,000 in capital losses in one year. You must carry forward any remaining losses. So the long-term capital loss you deduct in 1990 is $3,000, and the loss you carry forward adds up to $7,000.

But you may also claim in 1990 your $5,000 in suspended passive losses. And this $5,000 offsets the $3,000 in income you realize in 1990 from your partnership. Moreover, you may use the remaining $2,000 in losses to offset your wages or portfolio income. The reason: You have disposed of your passive investment.

QUESTION: *What is phantom income, and what can I do about it?*

In the past, tax shelters were structured so that investors could claim tax deductions—accelerated depreciation, say—in the early years of ownership. But these deductions diminished over time. Then the shelter was often left with only paper profits or phantom income.

A shelter that generates no further losses and may produce taxable income but doesn't generate cash is known in investment circles as a "burned-out" shelter. The phantom income generated by this burned-out shelter usually occurs when you sell or dispose of the shelter. You must report on your return an amount of income on the sale or disposition that exceeds—often by a considerable amount—the sales proceeds you actually receive. In other words, the phantom income represents a "reversal" of those tax shelter deductions you took in prior years.

TIP   If you find yourself with a burned-out shelter producing taxable income, consider this strategy:

Phantom income is, in fact, passive income. So you can invest in a new tax shelter that generates passive losses to offset phantom income from your old shelter, if you have no other passive losses to offset the phantom income.

TIP Here's another idea to consider: Sell the investment, but be warned that you'll usually have to sell at a deep discount. And besides losing money on the sale, disposing of the investment may create taxable—and phantom—income for you.

Selling the shelter, however, may help you minimize the amount of phantom income that you'll have to report on your tax return.

QUESTION: *I own some rental property that I actively participate in managing. Now, I am thinking about investing as a limited partner in a rehabilitation deal. May I claim both losses up to $25,000 from my rental property and the credit equivalent of $25,000 from the rehabilitation partnership?*

Unfortunately, the answer is no. You may deduct from your ordinary income no more than $25,000 a year in combined losses from rental real estate and credit equivalents. How do you calculate how much you may write off?

Here is an example. Say you report a $25,000 loss from an apartment building you manage yourself. You post a loss of $5,000 from an oil and gas limited partnership. But you record a $15,000 gain from a research and development limited partnership.

The rules require you to first count up all your losses from rental properties in which you actively participate; in your case, the total comes to $25,000. Then you add up any profits, and subtract your losses from your profits. You post no profits. So you are left with a $25,000 loss.

Next, you add up your gains from passive investments: $15,000 in your case. Then you subtract your losses from passive activities: $5,000. The result: $10,000 is your net passive income.

Now subtract your $25,000 of rental losses from your $10,000 of passive income. The result—$15,000—is the amount you may write off on your return as a rental loss. But remember: You may deduct rental losses up to $25,000. So if you also invest in a rehabilitation partnership, say, you may write off as much as $10,000 in credit equivalents.

QUESTION: *I am in the situation you describe above. But I have exhausted the $25,000 limit and still have losses and credit equivalents left. What do I do?*

You may carry these losses and credit equivalents forward for use in future years. But, even then, you are subject to all the limits we described earlier, including the $25,000 ceiling on rental losses.

QUESTION: *I subtracted my passive losses from my passive income, and I came out $23,000 in the red. I also have a loss of $2,000 from my rental property in which I actively participate. May I deduct this entire $25,000 loss from my regular income?*

Alas, no. The rules say you may deduct passive losses only from passive income. You subtracted your passive losses from your passive income and you are still $23,000 in the red.

But the news is not all bad. You may carry forward this loss to future years. And you may deduct your $2,000 rental loss, as long as your AGI falls within the limits we have described.

QUESTION: *I own a condo—part of a 200-unit complex—in Denver. It is a full-service building, with a housekeeping staff and a switchboard. Each year I put my unit in a pool that rents the condos by the week. A team of employees hired by our management group takes care of advertising, renting, and maintaining the units. And I limit my personal use of my condo to 14 days. What rules apply to my situation?*

Unfortunately, the news is bad. Uncle Sam does not consider your condo a rental unit for the purpose of the $25,000 rental exception to the passive loss rules. Hard as it is to believe, he looks upon your condo as a hotel or motel.

Why? You rent your unit to "transients," that is, people who stay in a place for fewer than 30 days. Moreover, your association provides "significant services," among them maid service and a telephone switchboard.

But even if your condo did qualify as a rental unit, you would fail the "active participatice" test. The reason: Your management group runs the rental operation and makes the final decisions.

So you are only a "passive" investor. And any loss you post is subject to the passive loss rules—that is, you may deduct these losses only against passive income.

20

Calculating the Alternative Minimum Tax

It's possible, through the use of deductions, deferrals, and credits, to reduce the tax bite on even a healthy income to a nice small number.

But the IRS has a response for people who manage to do so. It's called the *alternative minimum tax*, or AMT for short. And the idea is that no matter how clever you are at cutting your tax bill, Uncle Sam is still going to see to it that you pay your fair share.

Think of the AMT as a completely separate tax system. First you calculate your tax under the regular system. Then you calculate it under the AMT.

You compare the two results and pay the higher one. Does Uncle Sam require everyone to pay the AMT? Not at all, but if you have claimed lots of deductions in the categories listed below, you may be a candidate for this alternative tax.

- State and local real-estate taxes, income taxes, and personal property taxes

- Passive investments, such as oil and gas limited partnerships and real estate

- Interest on a refinanced mortgage if the amount refinanced is greater than your original mortgage (interest on the excess amount over your original debt)

- Donations of appreciated property you give to charity

- Investment interest, personal interest and home equity interest

- Miscellaneous deductions

Maybe you're uncertain whether or not you're subject to the AMT. Perhaps, too, you don't want to take the time to do the AMT calculations.

If this is the case, you should see your tax adviser.

However, if you think you probably will have to ante up the AMT, read on. We'll help you pay no more tax than is absolutely necessary.

Who pays the AMT?

As we just noted, if you claimed many deductions—particularly in the categories we mentioned—you may be in trouble. Chances are high that you'll have to pay the AMT.

Other circumstances may also make you liable for the AMT. For example, you may have exercised incentive stock options (ISOs) or invested in what are known as *private-activity bonds*. (State and local governments issue these bonds, so they can raise money for private purposes. For instance, a state may issue industrial bonds, which small businesses then use to build factories.)

☞ **CAUTION** If you just can't tell whether you'll be subject to the AMT, there's only way to know for sure. You must "run the numbers."

In this chapter, we tell you what you need to know in four steps. The first step: We tell you how to figure out how much of your income is subject to the AMT. Second, we explain about an exemption that may help you offset some of this AMT taxable income. Third, we show you how to figure out what Uncle Sam calls your tentative minimum tax and minimum tax credit. The fourth step is to provide strategies to enable you to keep your AMT to an absolute minimum.

Okay, first things first. Before you can save any money, you must calculate exactly how much of your income may be subject to the AMT. This amount is called, appropriately enough, alternative minimum taxable income, or AMTI. To get started, take your regular taxable income and make the following adjustments.

Standard deduction and personal exemptions

The AMT rules don't let you claim the standard deduction—the one people take who don't itemize. Nor may you take the deduction for personal exemptions. So you must add these items back.

Itemized deductions

Alas, the regular tax system allows for many itemized deductions that the AMT prohibits. So when you figure your AMTI, you must add most of these deductions back to your regular taxable income.

Which deductions specifically? The items you must add back are: real estate and personal property taxes, state and local income taxes, personal interest, and medical expenses that total less than 10 percent of your AGI. (As you may recall, for regular tax purposes, you may deduct medical expenses that come to more than 7.5 percent of your AGI).

In addition to these items, you must add back those other miscellaneous deductions —professional dues and tax preparation fees, for instance—that you deducted under the regular tax system.

The law does allow some itemized deductions. You may continue to deduct under the AMT: investment interest that doesn't exceed your investment income (however, the phase-in rules that apply for regular tax purposes don't apply here), home mortgage interest (unless you refinanced after July 1, 1982 for more than the outstanding balance on your mortgage in which case interest on the excess is not deductible; also, interest on home equity loans is usually not deductible), charitable contributions of nonappreciated property, and casualty losses. (We'll tell you more about the rules governing appreciated property shortly.)

You should also keep these points in mind: As you recall, Uncle Sam has in place phase-in rules for investment and personal interest for regular tax purposes. But these rules don't apply when it comes to the AMT. The law says you may not deduct personal interest from your AMT income. However, although you may not deduct any investment interest in excess of investment income, you get a break when it comes to investment interest expense. You may carry forward indefinitely, until you use it up, any of this expense that you're unable to use for AMT purposes in the current tax year.

Also, the rules are different when it comes to interest you pile up when you refinance your home mortgage or take out a home-equity loan. Under the AMT, you may deduct interest only on that part of the refinanced mortgage that doesn't top your outstanding mortgage before you refinance.

And if you take out a home-equity loan in order to duck the rules on deducting personal interest, the AMT rules could foul up your plans. You usually may not collect an interest deduction on home-equity loans for AMT purposes. (See Chapter 5 for the rules on deducting interest.)

The law does, however, allow for an exception to this rule: Say you use the money you get from the home-equity loan to pay for major home improvements or renovation, a trade or business, or investments. In this case, Uncle Sam says you may still write off for AMT purposes the interest on this loan. When it comes to investments, though, you may write off only as much interest as you have investment income.

Here's another rule that you should keep in mind. Say you buy a luxury boat, and it qualifies as a second home. There's a good chance that the interest on the money you borrow to purchase the boat is deductible under the regular tax system. But you may not deduct this amount under the AMT. That's because, according to the AMT rules, a boat doesn't qualify as a dwelling unit.

Passive activities

You recall from Chapter 19 that passive activities are essentially tax shelters. And they come in many forms, including an investment in a limited partnership or rental property.

The precise definition of a *passive investment*: The IRS considers any investment passive if it constitutes a trade or business in which you do not materially participate in managing. Moreover, all rental activity, by definition, is a passive investment. It makes no difference whether you materially participate.

The 1986 Tax Reform Act's four-year phase-in period is now reaching its end. In 1990, you may still use 10 percent of your passive investment losses to offset your earned income and portfolio income for regular tax purposes. However, you get this break only if you made your investment before the enactment of the 1986 tax law. (See Chapter 19 for more information on the passive loss rules.)

When it comes to the AMT, however, it's a different story. The law prohibits you from using these losses to cut this category of income. Passive losses serve only two purposes when it comes to calculating your AMT income.

Say you sell or otherwise dispose of your entire interest in a passive investment at a loss. In this case, you may use the losses to compute your AMT income. Be careful, though. Under the law, your disposing of the tax shelter must result in a taxable transaction. That means you may not give the shelter away and still qualify for this break. If the shelter is a gift, you may not use any of the losses you have carried forward. Under the AMT rules, you may also carry your passive losses forward and deduct them against any passive income you may have in future years.

TIP A good rule of thumb if you think you may be subject to the AMT: Think about making investments that will spin off enough passive income to soak up your passive losses. If you don't, it may take years before you get any tax benefits from these losses for AMT purposes.

Another point: Before you add back any passive activity losses you were able to claim for regular tax purposes but not for AMT purposes, you must recalculate your loss for AMT purposes.

It's important to realize that the loss you may have from a passive activity for regular tax purposes is not necessarily the same as that loss for AMT purposes.

Here's the reason: You may write off some items, such as depreciation deductions, faster for regular tax purposes than for AMT purposes. (We'll have more to say on this topic shortly.)

Here's an example: You invested in a real-estate limited partnership before the enactment of the 1986 Tax Reform Act, which produces a loss of $800 in 1990.

For regular tax purposes, you may still write off 10 percent of this loss in 1990, or $80. However, you have the loss in the first place because you depreciated the property using the accelerated method, which lets you take bigger write-offs in the earlier years of ownership.

The AMT rules say that you may depreciate property only using the slower straight-line method, which gives you the same deductions each year.

Now, let's say the partnership recalculates its depreciation deductions for AMT purposes. Instead of reporting to you an $800 loss, it reports a $200 gain. This means, of course, that for AMT purposes, you realized an additional $200 of income on the same investment that produced an $80 loss for regular tax purposes.

Stock options

The big advantage of incentive stock options (ISOs)? When you exercise them, you usually pay less for the stock—sometimes much less—than the stock's fair market value. According to the tax code, this difference between the price you pay and the stock's fair-market value is the "bargain element," which isn't subject to the regular tax.

☞ **CAUTION** That's usually good news. The bad news? As you may have guessed, the difference counts as a "preference" item when it comes to the AMT.

What's a preference item? It's one that receives favorable tax treatment under the regular tax rules. So, in the year you exercise your options, you're generally required to add back the bargain element to your AMT income.

All is not lost, though. The difference becomes part of your stock's cost basis. And that means when you finally sell the stock, your gain—for AMT purposes—totals less than it does for regular tax purposes.

Say, in 1986, your company grants you 1,000 ISOs at an option price of $11. You exercise the options in 1990. The fair market value of the stock when you buy it comes to $61 a share. So you have a tax "preference" of $50,000—the difference between the option price ($11,000) and the fair market value ($61,000). By 1991, you're ready to sell the 1,000 shares, which you do for $71 a share. Your gain for regular tax purposes totals $60,000—an amount equal to $71,000 less your option price of $11,000.

But you face a different situation for AMT purposes. Here your gain totals only $10,000—$71,000 less your AMT basis for the shares, or $61,000 (the $11,000 option price plus the $50,000 bargain element you had to add to your AMT income in 1990).

When you calculate your AMT income in 1991, you subtract the $50,000 difference in the gain.

☞ **CAUTION** If you're an insider—meaning an officer or director of the corporation offering the ISOs—you're required under the rules to add back to your AMT income the bargain element of your ISOs six months after you exercise the option.

How do you calculate the bargain element in this case? It's the difference between the option price and the fair market value of the stock six months from the date of exercise. So if you exercise an ISO in July or later, you wouldn't report the preference item until the following tax year.

What if you think the bargain element will be higher on that day than on the actual date of exercise? You may elect to report the AMT preference item at the earlier exercise date. Your tax adviser can help you decide the best strategy and advise you how to make the election.

TIP You should never put tax considerations front and center when it comes to investment decisions. And that bit of advice applies as well to the AMT. If it makes economic sense to exercise your options now, then go right ahead.

Depreciation

You must add back or subtract from your regular taxable income the difference between the depreciation you claimed for regular tax purposes and depreciation you figured using alternative depreciation. What do we mean?

Consider this example.

Say in December 1989, you bought the land and building where you have an office. The price came to $125,000. You allocate $100,000 to the cost of the building and $25,000 to the cost of the land.

Now it's time to file your 1990 return, and you write off depreciation for the building. You use the straight-line method over 31.5 years to calculate this deduction. In 1990, then, you may deduct $3,175 in depreciation.

What happens when you figure out your AMT liability? Under the alternative method, you depreciate real property (the building) using the straight-line method over 40, not 31.5, years. So your depreciation deduction would have come to $2,500. That means the difference between the two methods—the amount you must add back to your income for AMT purposes—totals $675.

We'll now project your situation way into the future and imagine that 32 years have gone by. You're still the owner of the building, and you've fully depreciated it by now for regular tax purposes.

Congratulations. After all this time, you get a break. Under the AMT rules, you may still collect a $2,500 deduction each year in years 33 through 40. You no longer must add back dollars; instead, you get to take an additional deduction from your AMT income.

Uncle Sam makes one exception to this rule. The exception applies to real property and leased personal property, which is placed in service—that is, put in use—before 1987.

If this is the case, you must, in calculating your AMT, add back to your regular taxable income the excess of the depreciation you claimed using the accelerated method over the old straight-line depreciation. However, you don't later get to subtract the difference between the straight-line method and accelerated depreciation.

Other preference and adjustment items

A number of other preference and adjustment items apply to the AMT. Let's review them.

The excess of percentage depletion over the tax basis of property that generates the mineral deposit. What does this bit of tax jargon actually mean?

We can explain it best by providing an example. Say you own a 10-percent partnership interest in an oil and gas operation. In 1990, your proportionate share of the percentage depletion, which is simply a deduction that reflects the fact that the value of the operation has fallen, is allocated to you.

Your share of the percentage depletion on the gross income of the oil and gas operation totals $20,000. Your share of the adjusted basis of the land that produces the oil and gas comes to $15,000. That means the tax preference comes to the $5,000 difference—the amount you must add back to your AMT income.

Interest on tax-exempt "private-activity" bonds issued after August 7, 1986. You pay no tax on the income you collect from these bonds under the regular tax system. But—you guessed it—you do pay tax under the AMT. However, the AMT rules let you write off interest expense you incur to buy these bonds, to the extent of your tax-exempt income. The regular tax rules, by contrast, do not let you deduct this interest.

The difference between (1) the fair market value of property you contribute to a charitable organization and write off—as an item-ized deduction—for regular tax purposes, and (2) the cost of the property. Here's an example. A loyal supporter of your local symphony, you decide to donate 100 shares of stock to this venerable institution. The stock cost you $2,000 two years ago, but it now commands a fair market value of $5,000. Under the regular tax rules, you write off the $5,000 as an itemized deduction. However, the AMT rules let you write off only the price you paid for the stock. So when you calculate your AMT income, you add back to your regular taxable income the $3,000 difference.

Excess intangible drilling costs that total more than 65 percent of the net income from productive oil and gas wells. As you probably can tell by now, the adjustments you must make when you own shares in oil and gas partnerships are quite complicated. So complicated, in fact, that we strongly advise you to consult with your tax adviser if these form part of your investment portfolio.

Research and development costs. For purposes of the regular tax system, you may write off these expenses in the year you incur them. The AMT rules, however, require you to capitalize the R&D expenses—that is, write them off over several years. In this case, you must write them off over 10 years.

You deduct 10 percent of the R&D costs each year of the 10-year period. And this holds true, even though you already deducted them in full for regular tax purposes.

TIP The law does provide a loophole of sorts when it comes to R&D expenses. You may avoid treating them as a preference item by amortizing all or a portion of them for regular tax purposes and deducting them over 10 years.

This strategy, of course, is far from perfect. When you employ it, you get a much smaller deduction each year for regular tax purposes. Therefore, you should run the numbers to see which method of treating these costs saves you the most tax.

Now you've made all the adjustments to your regular taxable income and accounted for all tax preference items. What's left is your AMT income, or AMTI.

Fortunately, the law lets you cut your AMTI by these exemptions: $40,000 for married taxpayers filing a joint return, $20,000 for married taxpayers filing separate returns, and $30,000 for single taxpayers. But there's bad news, too. If by Uncle Sam's standards, your

AMTI remains high, you have to cut your exemption. You reduce it by 25 percent of the amount by which your AMT income tops:

- $150,000 for married taxpayers filing jointly

- $75,000 for married taxpayers filing separately

- $112,500 for single filers

What this rule means, in effect, is that you'll collect no exemption at all if you and your spouse file jointly and your AMT income exceeds $310,000. As a single taxpayer, your ceiling comes to $232,500.

Here's an example. Say you and your spouse file jointly and your AMTI comes to $213,725. So your exemption falls from $40,000 to $24,069.

How did we arrive at that figure? We took your AMTI of $213,725 and subtracted $150,000. The answer: $63,725. Then we multiplied this amount by 25 percent. The result comes to $15,931. Next, we subtract $15,931 from the $40,000 AMT exemption to get $24,069.

We're almost finished with all the AMT calculations. So far, you've figured out your AMT income and adjusted it by the appropriate exemption amount. We're almost ready to help you compute your alternative minimum tax. You simply take your adjusted AMT income and multiply it by 21 percent. The result you obtain—after you subtract any foreign tax credits, recomputed for AMT purposes, the law allows—is your tentative minimum tax (TMT).

Now, compare your TMT to your regular income tax. (Again, first take any allowable foreign tax credits.) If your TMT comes to more than your regular tax, you must pay the difference—the alternative minimum tax—in addition to your regular tax.

But wait. There's more. You still must calculate what's known as the *minimum tax credit* (MTC). What's that? Think of it as a credit for taxes you paid earlier under the AMT system that you wouldn't have paid under the regular tax system.

Why this benefit? Uncle Sam recognizes that some of your AMT liability may come from the fact that the AMT sometimes speeds up your income. In other words, the AMT rules sometimes require you to report income before you would have to for regular tax purposes. One example is paper profits you ''realize'' when you exercise ISOs.

Since, under the AMT system, you pay taxes on this income earlier than you otherwise would under the regular system, you've already paid a portion of your regular tax liability. In a later year, the MTC can reduce your regular tax liability by the amount of AMT taxes you paid in prior years.

So far, in computing your AMT income, you've made adjustments to your regular taxable income that fall into one of two categories. These adjustments are either "deferral items" or "exclusion items." What's the difference? We'll tell you in a minute. But first you should know that the difference affects the amount of your MTC.

Deferral items, as the name suggests, won't reduce the amount of tax you owe permanently. They only defer your tax liability until later.

Exclusion preference and adjustment items are another story. Unless you're subject to the AMT, you never have to ante up the taxes that you attribute to these items. And that's good news.

There are only four exclusion preference items: all itemized deduction adjustments, the appreciated-property charitable-contribution preference item, the percentage-depletion preference, and the tax-exempt bond preference item. Everything else counts as a deferral preference item.

That's nice you say, but how does knowing the difference between these two items help me cut my taxes in the future. Here's how: Once you've finished calculating your AMT as we described, calculate it again. This time, however, use only the exclusion preferences. Your minimum tax credit (MTC) equals the difference between this adjusted AMT and the AMT you first calculated. In other words, your MTC is the amount of AMT attributable to deferral items only.

Uncle Sam says that you may carry this credit forward indefinitely (although you may not carry it back) to offset your regular tax liabilities in the future. You may reduce your regular tax, however, only to an amount that equals the TMT in the year you carry forward this amount.

Confused? Here's an example.

Say in 1990, you pay $16,000 in AMT. The entire amount you pay results from your exercising incentive stock options, which count as a deferral tax preference item. So the $16,000 now qualifies as your MTC carryover.

In 1991, you rack up a regular tax liability of $61,000 and a TMF of $59,000. So you may use $2,000 of that $16,000 MTC carryover from 1990 to reduce your 1991 tax payment to Uncle Sam.

Say, however, that you must pay the AMT year after year. Or say your AMT liability and your regular tax bill are similar. In these situations, the minimum tax credit doesn't help you much at all.

It's important to think about both short-term and long-term strategies when you plan for the AMT. Your short-term strategies should involve accelerating or deferring income and deductions. But you must also consider the impact of the minimum tax credit. For your long-range planning, you must focus on the kinds of investments you make.

Here's an example. Say over the last five years, you've invested heavily in real estate or oil and gas limited partnerships. In fact, these are practically your only investments. You suspect you may have to pay the AMT either this year or in future years. What should you do? It may make sense for you to shift your money into corporate bonds, say, or stocks or mutual funds. The reason? These investments don't have any effect on the AMT.

Also in the realm of long-range planning: Focusing on the kind of tax treatment you elect for rental property and other depreciable assets.

 TIP One tack you might take: You may choose, for regular tax purposes, the longer alternative method of depreciation. If you do, you won't be required to add to your AMT income the difference between accelerated depreciation and alternative depreciation.

Of course, you may be out of luck when it comes to preferences from limited partnership investments. With these investments, you don't have much influence over decisions.

TIP You should always assume that you will be liable for the AMT. Then run the numbers each and every year.

You should also project your tax situation two years out. That's because the actions you take this year affect your AMT situation next year. Obviously, making these calculations can be burdensome.

Remember, you can't wait to worry about the AMT until you're ready to send in your tax return. The rules say that you must pay 90 percent of the tax you'll owe for any one year in withholding and estimated tax payments. And that means you may have to fork over more in estimated taxes if you're subject to the AMT.

QUESTIONS AND ANSWERS

QUESTION: *Let's say I sell property that I placed in service after 1986. Will I have the same gain or loss for regular tax purposes and for the AMT?*

The answer is no, and here's the reason: You are depreciating your property by a different method for the AMT. So you end up with a different AMT basis—that is, your adjusted cost or your cost less depreciation—which, in turn, affects your gain or loss.

Consider this example. Say you purchase a building on May 1, 1988, for $200,000. You sell it on June 1, 1990, for $250,000. For regular tax purposes your depreciation deductions for 1988, 1989 and 1990 amount to $13,227. For the AMT, however, your depreciation deductions total $10,417.

So your basis for the regular tax system is equal to $200,000 minus $13,227 of depreciation deductions, or $186,773. And your gain comes to $63,227. But your basis for AMT purposes totals $200,000 minus $10,417, or $189,583.

So your gain comes to $60,417. And your AMTI is reduced by $2,810—the difference between $63,227 and $60,417—in 1990.

QUESTION: *I overpaid my state income taxes in 1989 and received a refund in 1990. I know I have to report my refund as income for regular tax purposes in 1990 since I took the deduction in 1989. But how do I treat it for AMT purposes?*

As we've seen, Uncle Sam won't allow you to deduct state and local income tax payments for AMT purposes. The good news: You don't have to report any state and local tax refunds as income when you calculate your AMTI.

QUESTION: *I've run the numbers for 1990 and 1991. It looks like I'm subject to the AMT in 1990 but not in 1991. What is the best course of action for me?*

At a minimum, you want to make sure that the MTC that is generated is not less than the AMT you pay for the year. As we've seen, deferral preferences do not permanently reduce your tax liability. They only defer that liability until some later time.

On the other hand, the government never recaptures the tax revenue it loses when you reduce your liability by using exclusion preferences. And an MTC is generated only by deferral preferences.

Our advice: Run the numbers. Ask your tax adviser to help you divide your deductions into two categories: deferral preference items and exclusion preference items.

One strategy to consider is to postpone until 1991 paying expenses that you may claim as deductions. If you pay these expenses in 1990, you'll get a smaller tax benefit if your item was deductible for AMT purposes (for example, charitable contributions). Or you could waste potential deductions if the items weren't deductible for AMT purposes (for example, state and local taxes).

Alternatively, try accelerating income into 1990 since it will be taxed lower under AMT than it would in 1991 using the regular tax rates; for example, take your bonus this year rather than next. Be aware, however, that each of these strategies must take into account the impact on, and the effect of, your MTC. In fact, these strategies may not save you any tax in the long run. So remember to project your tax situation at least two years out—and always consider the MTC consequences.

21

Stock Options as Employee Incentives

It would be hard to imagine better aids to employee recruitment and retention than *stock options* and *stock appreciation rights*.

Both let employees share in the success of their employer. And from the company's perspective both boost employees' incentive to work for that success.

Some companies restrict options to top executives. Others spread this benefit down the line. Often, options are a negotiable part of a total compensation package.

You can use stock options and stock appreciation rights to your best advantage if you understand the tax rules that govern them. These rules are not difficult, and they do provide lots of flexibility, which means that you have choices to make. This chapter helps you make those choices.

HOW OPTIONS WORK

When your employer grants you a stock option, you've gained the right to buy a specific number of shares of your company's stock at a specific price within a specific period of time. You don't have to buy, but you may—at your option, so to speak.

The beauty of optioned stock—which you purchase through your company, not through your stockbroker—lies in the price you pay.

Say, for instance, that as a result of your outstanding performance last year, your boss gave you a bonus, an option on 2,000 shares of company stock.

The *option price* is $12 a share. Wait a minute, you say. What do we mean by option price? It's the amount you pay for the stock when you *exercise* your option and, in most cases, is the *fair market value* of the stock on the date your option was granted.

Now, a year later, the *market price* of the stock has soared to $20 a share, and you decide to exercise the options. When you do, you pay $24,000—that is, $12 times 2,000 shares—for stock that is currently worth $40,000. Not a bad deal.

But it's an even better deal if your options are *incentive stock options* (ISOs). As it happens, options come in two varieties: ISOs and *nonqualified stock options* (NQOs for short). The difference lies mainly in the tax benefits that ISOs provide.

There's no tax due on an incentive stock option until you eventually sell or exchange the stock, and then only if you sell or exchange it at a profit.

With NQOs, on the other hand, there's an immediate tax bite when you exercise the option, as well as the tax you pay when you sell the stock at a profit.

Let's return to our example.

If your boss had granted you NQOs instead of ISOs, you would have incurred a tax liability when you exercised them. The IRS taxes you on the difference between the option price—$12—and the market price—$20—at the time you exercise the option. So you're taxed on $16,000 when you exercise your NQO, and this income is treated as ordinary income.

If you're able to sell the stock, say, a year later for $30 a share, you're taxed again, this time as capital gains on the difference between $20 and $30. With an ISO, you're taxed just once, when you finally sell the stock for $30 a share.

But, with an ISO, the entire amount of your gain—that is, the difference between the $30 a share you receive at the sale and the $12 a share option price that you originally paid—is taxed as a capital gain. (For more information on capital gains, see Chapter 14.)

You can see the advantage of the ISO. You pay no tax until you actually realize a gain when you sell or exchange your stock, and all of that gain is treated as a capital gain.

With the NQO, on the other hand, you pay tax on your *paper profit* as ordinary income when you exercise the option. That means that you not only must have cash to buy the stock when you exercise an NQO, you also need the money to pay Uncle Sam his due.

But there's one plus with NQOs. You increase your *basis* in the stock—that is, the stock's cost to you—by the amount of your reported gain.

You should know, though, that the *bargain element*—the difference between the price at which you buy your stock and the fair market value—on the exercise of ISOs is a preference item when you compute your *alternative minimum tax (AMT)*.

So, timing is an issue. You may not want to exercise an ISO if it will throw you into an AMT situation. (See Chapter 20 for the details on the AMT).

Which is the better deal? ISOs? NQOs?

The answer is, it depends. You may be better off from a tax perspective with ISOs. But ISOs do come with a set of rules that can make them less desirable for other reasons.

These rules are what define an ISO. If a stock option doesn't conform, it is, by definition, an NQO and is automatically treated as such. Even if an option qualifies as an ISO, you may be able to treat it as an NQO if its terms give you that option, or, if you violate the rule, your ISO will be treated, taxwise, as an NQO. So, let's take a look at these rules and the restrictions they impose.

Employee status

From the day you receive the ISO until three months before you exercise it, you must be employed by the company (or a related company) granting it.

So you may, if your employer's plan allows, exercise the option within three months after you leave the company, and still obtain the favorable tax benefits.

But if you leave a company due to permanent and total disability, and if your employer's plan allows it, you have up to one year to exercise your ISOs. Sick leave or any other company-approved leave doesn't count, however.

What if you die? Your options go to your *beneficiaries*—meaning the people you specify as your heirs—and they may, in turn, exercise them.

Option period

You must exercise your ISO within 10 years of the date it's granted, unless you own more than 10 percent of your company's stock. In that case, the option period may not top five years.

Another rule you should know: The company must grant ISOs within 10 years of the date the shareholders formally approve the stock option plan or the plan is adopted, whichever is earlier.

Fair market price

The rules say that the option price must not be less than the fair market price of the stock on the date the option is granted.

But a special rule applies to individuals who own more than 10 percent of a corporation's stock. In their case only, the option price must at least be equal to 110 percent of the fair market value of the stock on the date the ISO is granted.

$100,000 ceiling

Of all the ISOs you are granted after 1986, no more than $100,000 worth (valued at the time they're granted) may become exercisable for the first time in any one year.

If you violate this rule, the first $100,000 of options still qualifies as ISOs. But the remainder falls into the category of NQOs.

You calculate the first $100,000 of options that qualifies for ISO treatment by adding together your options in the order you receive them. Here's an example.

Say your company grants you two options that are first exercisable in 1990. You receive the first—to purchase 6,000 shares at $10 a share, or $60,000—on January 15. You receive the second—to purchase 7,000 shares at $10 a share or, $70,000—on July 15.

The first option—of $60,000—qualifies as an ISO.

So does $40,000 of the second option. The remainder of the second option ($70,000 minus $40,000, or $30,000) falls into the category of an NQO.

Understand, though, that this limit isn't on the value of the options your employer may grant you. Your company may grant you any amount in options it sees fit.

Rather, the limit is on the value of the stock options that are first exercisable by you in any year. You determine the value of the option by multiplying the number of shares in the option by the fair market value of the stock at the time the option is granted.

Say, for instance, that your employer grants you $300,000 worth of options in 1990. The entire amount would qualify as ISOs as long as the option states that you could exercise no more than $100,000 in 1990, and the second and third $100,000 worth in 1991 and 1992, respectively.

You don't have to exercise them, or you could exercise all three in 1992. But you may not first exercise more than $100,000 in any one year.

What if your employer grants you $150,000 worth of options in 1990, all of which can be exercised in the same year?

In this case, you should instruct your employer at the date of exercise to issue you separate stock certificates, and to identify the certificates as an ISO exercise in the stock transfer records, for $100,000 of the stock.

Otherwise, each share of stock will be treated as two-thirds acquired by ISO and one-third acquired by the exercise of an NQO. The separate designation will provide you with greater flexibility in recognizing income in future years.

Order of exercise

You must exercise ISOs granted to you in 1986 and earlier in the order in which they were granted. But you may exercise ISOs granted *after* 1986 in any order you like.

Let's say you hold an option to purchase 2,000 shares of stock at $15 a share, another to buy 1,000 at $10 a share, and still another to purchase 5,000 at $5 each.

You received the $15-per-share option in 1985, the $10-per-share option in 1986, and the $5-per-share option in 1987. You may exercise the post-1986 option—the $5-per-share option issued in 1987—before the other two.

But you must exercise options issued before 1987 in the order in which they were granted. So you must exercise the 1985 option before you exercise the 1986 option.

Capital gains

This rule is less important now since long-term capital gains no longer enjoy preferential tax treatment—that is, they're taxed at the same rate as ordinary income. But the law says you must still keep track of long-term and short-term gains and losses.

You may claim long-term tax treatment of gains from the sale of stock bought with ISOs only if you hold the shares for the later of more than two years from the date the option was granted, or more than one year from the date the shares were actually transferred to you.

Otherwise, your gain—the difference between the option price and the amount you collected when you sold your stock—is taxed as ordinary income.

Say you receive an option on July 3, 1990. You exercise the option six months later, on January 3, 1991. Under the law, in order to have your gain considered long-term, you must hold the shares until after July 3, 1992—that is, two years after the option was granted to you.

Transferability

You may know that only you and your heirs may exercise ISOs. But did you also know that you may not contribute your options to an IRA or other retirement plan? The IRS doesn't want you deferring gains on options even longer than the options themselves permit.

No one else, not even your spouse, may exercise your ISOs during your lifetime, and you may not assign options in a divorce settlement.

It's not surprising that options are often an issue during separation or divorce negotiations. Both sides must devise a formula to compensate for the fact that much of an executive's wealth may consist of nontransferable stock options.

This rule also means that you may not sell your right to exercise an option or use the right as collateral for a loan.

With all the restrictions that apply to them, why might you still prefer ISOs to NQOs? Tax deferral is perhaps the best reason. As we pointed out earlier, you report no gain for regular tax purposes until you sell or exchange your ISO stock.

TIP This and the fact that you may use company stock you already own to pay for ISO stock allows you to use a powerful strategy.

Say that you join a young company whose shares are selling for $2. At the time you come on board, you buy 1,000 shares of stock and receive ISOs for 5,000 shares at $2 a share. In five years the stock price hits $10, and you decide to exercise your option.

You do so by paying with the 1,000 shares you bought earlier. Now, you own 5,000 shares worth $50,000 at the current market price, but your investment cost just the $2,000 you paid for that initial stock. And this transaction is tax free until you sell the option shares.

Now, let's say that you use this same strategy, but instead of paying with shares you bought, you pay with shares acquired under an ISO.

The same rules apply, but only if you have held the stock for more than two years after your ISOs were granted or more than one year after the shares were transferred to you, whichever is longer. Otherwise, the shares you exchange no longer qualify for treatment as ISOs.

You have made a so-called *disqualifying disposition*—that is, you have disposed of ISO stock before meeting the holding period requirement. So you must pay tax on your profit—that is, the appreciation—at ordinary income rates when they are exchanged.

TIP The capital gain income that ISOs yield, even though subject to ordinary tax rates, is sometimes useful for tax purposes. For instance, you may use these capital gains to offset your capital losses. (For the details on capital gains and losses, see Chapter 14.)

NQOs, however, have their place.

With NQOs, you don't have to worry about the AMT. Nor do you have to worry about any of the special rules affecting ISOs, including limits on when you can exercise your options or sell the stock you have acquired.

STOCK APPRECIATION RIGHTS

At the beginning of the chapter we mentioned stock appreciation rights, SARs for short. With SARs you never actually buy your company's stock.

But you still profit from the stock's appreciation.

Let's say your company gives you a one-year SAR on 5,000 shares of stock when the market price is $2 a share. A year later the stock price has risen to $3.

You could get a check for $5,000 (less any withholding tax, of course). Or your company could give you $2,000 (again, less any income tax withholding) plus 1,000 shares of stock valued at $3 a share. At any rate, your total compensation comes to $5,000.

The gain is taxed at ordinary rates, just like the gain on an NQO. But, unlike stock options, you never have to put up any cash of your own with a SAR.

Because you put up no cash with SARs, companies sometimes use them in tandem with ISOs to provide employees with the dollars they need to exercise their ISOs.

Say, for example, that your company grants you a one-year SAR on 5,000 shares of stock. At the end of the year, it yields $1 a share or a total of $5,000.

You receive a check for $4,000, though—that is, your $5,000 minus 20 percent of the total for federal income-tax withholding taxes.

Say, too, that along with your SAR your company grants you an ISO to purchase 2,000 shares of company stock at an exercise price of $2 a share.

You use the dollars you receive from your SAR at year end to exercise your option. You're out of pocket only the additional taxes you pay on income from your SAR.

QUESTIONS AND ANSWERS

QUESTION: *I'm a corporate insider. Any tips for me?*
If you're a corporate *insider*—an officer, a director, or a more-

than-10-percent shareholder of a public company—you must conform to special requirements regarding ISOs and NQOs. Among these requirements is the so-called six-month rule.

Here's an example to illustrate how this complicated rule works. Say you're the president of a company. You sell company stock at a gain within either six months before or after exercising your option. Under the six-month rule, you may have to forfeit to your company your entire profit on that sale.

Insider regulations are quite strict and complex. You need to choose carefully when you exercise and when you sell your stock.

TIP Since Uncle Sam restricts when you may sell your stock, he also allows you to postpone when you report your paper gain from the exercise of an NQO.

How long may you put off reporting this gain?

The answer is until the end of the six-month period. (In this case, your holding period begins when you recognize the ordinary income.)

TIP What if it's to your tax advantage to report the income at the time of exercise? Uncle Sam allows you to do so—as long as you file a statement within 30 days of the exercise telling him that you've made this election and attach a copy of this statement to your Form 1040.

TIP You may also elect to recognize ISO income when you exercise your options for alternative minimum tax purposes. (See Chapter 20 for more on the AMT.)

You should consider this election when you exercise ISOs in the second half of a taxable year in which you expect to pay regular tax.

You may not know it, but making this election is especially valuable if you expect to pay the AMT in the year following the year in which you exercise your options, or if you think the value of the stock will increase substantially during the six-month period.

TIP If you're an insider, our advice is to ask your tax adviser or attorney to help you evaluate your personal situation. And enlist his or her help as soon as you get an option. That way, you won't unknowingly violate these rules and jeopardize your gain.

22

Putting Money into a Retirement Plan

Putting money into a so-called qualified retirement plan, either your company's or your own, is one of the best ways to prepare for your financial future.

It is also a great way to reduce your current tax bill. So understanding your retirement plan options under the tax law is doubly important, but not necessarily easy.

The variety of retirement plans that qualify for special treatment under the tax law can be bewildering unless you understand that the principle underlying most of them is the same: The money you put in now will not be taxed until you take it out at retirement.

Having said that, we must also warn you that there are important differences among retirement plans. In this chapter, we show you how the tax laws affect the ways that you can put money into your retirement plan.

And we will try to make it simple for you to understand the distinctions among retirement plans—*individual retirement accounts (IRAs)*, *Keoghs*, *401(k)s*, and all the rest. This knowledge will allow you to make intelligent choices among the retirement plans available to you, whether you work for yourself or someone else.

237

TYPES OF PLANS

There are really only three types of retirement plans: those you create and contribute to yourself, those your company runs and contributes to, and those to which both you and the company may contribute. Most people may participate in more than one type of plan.

Let's look briefly at each type. Then, after we have run through the menu of retirement plans, we come back to take a longer look at two specific types: IRAs and 401(k)s.

Individual Retirement Accounts. No doubt you have heard of IRAs.

They are retirement plans that you contribute to and create. IRAs, unfortunately, lost much of their appeal as a result of changes made by the 1986 Tax Reform Act.

They are no longer as useful to individuals who are covered by employer-sponsored retirement plans. Still, they are not totally without value.

The law allows you to contribute to an IRA the lesser of $2,000 or 100 percent of your compensation each year; $2,250 if you and your nonworking spouse file jointly.

But you may deduct this contribution only if neither you nor your spouse is covered by a tax-deferred retirement plan or your adjusted gross income (AGI) falls below a certain level.

Whether your annual contribution to an IRA is deductible or not, the account earnings still accumulate tax free until you withdraw your money at retirement.

If you have an IRA, or if the information we have just outlined suggests that you should have one, you will find more detailed IRA information later in this chapter.

Keoghs. If you work for yourself, you should have a Keogh for saving and sheltering part of your self-employment income. Keoghs are bona-fide wealth-building tools.

To have a Keogh plan, you must be self-employed. That is, you must have income from your own unincorporated business, such as a sole proprietorship or partnership. And if you have employees, you must include them in your Keogh plan.

Having a Keogh does not preclude you from having an IRA. But you should know that a Keogh is a qualified plan under the tax law.

So if you set one up, you are in the same deductibility boat as someone who is an employee. That is, your income must fall within certain levels, or your IRA contributions are not deductible. (Again, more on the topic of IRAs later in this chapter.)

You pay no tax on your Keogh contributions or on any earnings that accumulate until you begin to collect benefits, usually at retirement.

Keoghs come in two varieties: a *defined-contribution* or *defined-benefit plan*. A defined-contribution plan allows you to contribute a specified amount—10 percent of your earnings, say—to the plan each year. To make matters more complicated, these plans themselves come in two varieties: *profit-sharing plans* and *money-purchase plans*.

You may contribute up to 15 percent of your self-employment income with a profit-sharing plan or up to 25 percent with a money-purchase plan. But in either case, your contribution must not total more than $30,000.

You should know, too, that you have to subtract your contribution to figure your net self-employment income. So, in practice, you are contributing only 13.043 percent of your self-employment income to your profit-sharing plan or 20 percent to a money-purchase plan.

With a defined-benefit plan, you contribute annually whatever amount is required to fund a specified retirement payout. The payout is fixed, and the contribution is based on actuarial tables for your life expectancy.

The only limit: The annual benefit after retirement may not top the lesser of $102,582 for 1990 (adjusted annually for increases in the cost of living) or 100 percent of your average earnings for your three consecutive years of highest earnings. Note, though, that your contribution cannot top your current annual income.

Many people steer clear of setting up a defined-benefit Keogh. The reason is that the paperwork and the cost of maintaining the plan are greater than with a defined-contribution plan. But for many people, the benefits outweigh the hassles involved, especially if you are over age 45.

Here is why. Let's say you are 55 years old and currently earn $100,000 in self-employment income. The most you could put away with a defined-contribution money-purchase plan is $20,000 (20 percent × $100,000).

But say you want to fund a benefit of $59,000 after you retire at age 65. Based on actuarial computations, you could sock away as much as $41,000 this year in a defined-benefit plan—$21,000 more.

☞ **CAUTION**   If you have employees you must provide them with comparable benefits. And you must weigh the cost of doing so with the benefits you will realize from the plan.

TIP   To take advantage of a Keogh, you must create your plan no later than the last day of your taxable year, which for most people is December 31. But generally you do not have to make your actual contribution until the due date of your tax return, including extensions.

☞ **CAUTION**   You may not know it, but Uncle Sam requires you to make contributions to defined benefit plans quarterly.

If you do business as a sole proprietor, you set up your Keogh plan. But if you are a partner in a partnership, the partnership must establish the Keogh plan.

TIP   Although the amount of your contribution to a profit-sharing plan may be more limited than it is for the other two types of plans, this type of arrangement does have one important advantage. You may vary the amount you set aside each year. You are thus free to base your contribution on how well your business performs. In other words, if your business does poorly one year, you aren't required to make a contribution. You are even free to skip a contribution any year you like. If you have a money-purchase or defined-benefit plan, you must make an annual contribution designated in the plan each year.

TIP   You may also "pair" or combine a money-purchase plan with a profit-sharing plan. The advantages: You may, if you want, contribute and deduct a full 20 percent of your self-employment income, just as if you chose to fully fund a money-purchase plan. But you have more flexibility in the amount you *must* contribute each year.

Here is how pairing works. You set up a money-purchase plan to shelter, say, 8 percent of your income. Now you may contribute up to an additional 12 percent (for a total of 20 percent) to a profit-sharing plan.

And the amount you put into the profit-sharing plan is entirely up to you. So you may still protect from Uncle Sam's long reach as much as $30,000, or 20 percent of your income, whichever is less.

We recommend this paired strategy for people who want to set aside more than 12 percent of their earnings in a retirement plan but do not want to tie themselves to contributing a hefty percentage of their incomes year after year.

Employer-sponsored retirement plans. These are plans created, and for the most part funded, by the company that employs you. As with Keoghs, employer-sponsored plans come in two flavors: defined-contribution plans and defined-benefit plans.

And, as with all retirement plans, any earnings that accumulate in employer-sponsored plans remain untaxed until you begin withdrawing funds at retirement.

Hybrid plans. There are several retirement plans that combine some features of employer-sponsored plans with the IRA concept. For instance, 401(k) plans are a hybrid.

Your employer will create and administer a 401(k) plan and may contribute to it. Employees use 401(k) plans much as they do IRAs—as a place to stash a tax-deferred portion of their salary or wage income until they need to withdraw it, usually at retirement. (We include more information on 401(k) plans later in the chapter.)

Another hybrid, the *simplified employee pension (SEP)* plan, is quite similar to an IRA. An employer, rather than maintaining its own pension fund, makes contributions to the IRAs of its employees.

And the employer may deduct its contributions. Moreover, you do not have to count your employer's contributions to your SEP as part of your income.

You may also, if your plan allows, make contributions to your own SEP, up to a cap of 7,979 (in 1990) or 15 percent of your compensation, whichever is less.

TIP If you missed the December 31 deadline for setting up a Keogh plan, consider a SEP instead. The deadline for establishing and funding a SEP is the due date of your tax return, including extensions.

Individuals who participate in union pension plans, called Section 501(c)(18) plans, may also make deductible contributions to these union plans, subject, however, to the same limitations that apply to 401(k)s. That is, no more than 7,979, or 25 percent of compensation, may be contributed by any one person during any one year to any single plan or combination of plans.

☞ **CAUTION** For plan years beginning after December 31, 1988, the IRS classifies as a 401(k) plan any partnership plan, no matter what type you think it is, that directly or indirectly lets individual partners vary the annual contributions made on their behalf. In this case, the $7,979 limit will apply to the discretionary contributions you make.

THE WHOLE WORD ON IRAS

IRAs were among the best retirement saving plans around. They were, that is, until Congress clipped some of their more generous features back in 1986. And now? Well, do not dismiss IRAs. They are still a useful part of many retirement portfolios. Just know their new limitations.

The greatest appeal of an IRA used to be that as long as you were not more than age 70½, the contributions you made—up to the $2,000 annual limit—were fully tax deductible.

Today, that is true for only two types of people: those who are not eligible for an employer-sponsored retirement plan or those whose incomes fall below specified levels.

If both you and your spouse are not eligible for a company retirement plan, the rules governing your ability to make tax deductible contributions to an IRA were not affected by the 1986 Tax Reform Act. Both of you are still free to write off IRA contributions equal to the lesser of your earned income or $2,000 a year ($2,250 if you have a spouse who does not work outside the home or who earns less than $250 a year).

But if your company has a retirement plan and you are an active participant in it, you may lose some or all of the deductibility of your annual IRA contribution.

How? Let's take a look.

For people with company retirement plans, the first test of IRA deductibility is income. If you are married and file jointly, you may still make a fully deductible IRA contribution as long as your joint AGI is no greater than $40,000.

In this case, AGI is your adjusted gross income before you claim a deduction for your IRA but *after* you have deducted any losses from investments. Also, your AGI includes any taxable Social Security benefits you receive.

If your joint AGI falls between $40,000 and $50,000, part of your contribution is still deductible. Couples with AGIs of $50,000 or more may not deduct IRA contributions at all.

Figuring the partial deduction is easy. Just subtract your joint AGI from the $50,000 cap. Then divide the result by $10,000. That answer is the fraction of the maximum IRA contribution that you may deduct. Confused? Here is an example.

Say your joint AGI is $42,000. Subtract that amount from $50,000 to get $8,000. Divide $8,000 by $10,000 to get 80 percent. This is the percentage of the IRA base, $2,000, that you may contribute to an IRA and deduct. So you may deduct $1,600. (See the IRA deduction worksheet in the appendix.)

Of course, you are free to *contribute* the full $2,000, but do not count on pocketing a deduction for the extra $400.

The rules and the calculations for single people are just the same, except that the income limits are different. With an AGI below $25,000, a single person may deduct the entire IRA contribution. Over $35,000, none of it is deductible.

Between the two, there is a partial deduction.

A single person with a $30,000 AGI, for instance, may deduct half of his or her maximum IRA contribution (the $35,000 cap minus $30,000 of AGI equals $5,000, which, when divided by $10,000, comes to 50 percent).

TIP You may contribute at least $200 to an IRA and write off the full amount, as long as your calculation shows that your deductible contribution is limited to no less than $10. Why? Because Uncle Sam says so.

What Happens When You File Separately?

It does not matter that only one spouse participates in another retirement plan. If you file jointly, you are treated as if both of you do.

The same is true if you file separately, and another strict set of requirements applies. The IRA deduction for each spouse is phased out beginning with the first $1 of AGI. When your AGI reaches $10,000, you cannot get any deduction.

Say, for example, that you and your spouse lived together during the year and file separate returns. And one of you is covered by a retirement plan.

Your separate AGI adds up to $5,000, so you subtract $5,000 from $10,000 to get $5,000. Then you divide $5,000 by $10,000 to get 50 percent. Finally, you multiply 50 percent times the maximum IRA contribution of $2,000 to get the amount you may deduct: $1,000.

The rules are different if you are married, file separately, but live apart from your spouse for the entire year. In this case, the spouse who is not covered by a qualified plan may contribute up to $2,000 to an IRA and deduct the contribution. If you are an active participant in a plan, the phase-out begins at $25,000.

Whatever limit the rules place on the size of your or your spouse's annual deductible IRA contribution, you will pay a penalty if you contribute too much, meaning more than $2,000 in any one year.

If you exceed your contribution limit, the IRS will demand that you pay an excise tax equal to 6 percent of the excess contribution. And, as we will see later, you also face a 10 percent penalty when you withdraw the money. You can avoid both these penalties if you withdraw your excess contribution before you file your tax return for the year.

How Active Is Active?

There is room for confusion about what the IRS means by being an active participant in a company-sponsored retirement plan. So let's clear the matter up.

As a general rule, the IRS considers you an active participant in a defined-benefit plan, if the plan's rules say that you are covered, even if you decline to participate. So just being eligible in one of these plans makes you an active participant.

In the case of defined-contribution plans, you are considered an active participant if any money is added to your account during the year. One exception to this rule is allocations to your account in the form of investment earnings. If investment earnings are the only amount added to your account, you are not considered an active participant.

How do you know if you're an active participant? One quick way is to look at your W-2 form. It provides a box for your employer to check. If this box is blank, though, you've got some work to do. And you'll need to familarize yourself with the active participation rules.

Participation in any of the following plans can make you an active participant and not eligible to deduct your IRA contributions:

- Qualified pension, profit-sharing, or stock bonus plans, including Keogh plans

- Qualified annuity plans

- Simplified employee pension plans (SEPs)

- Retirement plans for federal, state, or local government employees

- Certain union plans (so-called Section 501(c)(18) plans)

- Tax-sheltered annuities for public school teachers and other employees of charitable organizations

- 401(k) plans

Say you meet the eligibility conditions under your employer's defined-benefit pension plan. But under the plan rules, you will not be credited with any contributions your employer makes on your behalf unless you contribute to the plan. Even if you do not make a contribution, and therefore are not credited with benefits, you are considered an active participant.

Vesting also has nothing to do with determining whether you are an active participant.

Say, for example, that your company offers a profit-sharing plan. You are an active participant once your employer contributes something to your account for the year. It makes no difference that you are not vested for, say, five years.

Uncle Sam also considers you an active participant if you participate in a retirement plan for just part of the year.

Suppose you change jobs in November 1989. You move from Old Company Inc. to New Corp. Tough luck, says New Corp. You are not eligible for our pension plan in 1990, your first year on the job. So you say to yourself, "I will just make a tax-deductible IRA contribution that year."

Oh no, you will not. Old Company's pension plan does not end its tax year until January 31. You are eligible and therefore "active" in that plan for part of 1990. So the deductibility of your IRA contribution is limited for the whole year.

The point to take away from this example is simply that timing is an issue when it comes to determining the deductibility of your IRA contribution.

TIP You calculate your AGI *after* you make your Keogh contributions. Say, for example, that you are self-employed, and that you and your spouse file a joint return. Your earnings from your business add up to $40,000, and the two of you report interest and dividend income of $5,000. You contribute $8,000 to a Keogh account. Under the rules, you may make a fully deductible $2,000 IRA contribution, because your joint AGI— $37,000 before you subtract your IRA contribution—is less than the $40,000 threshold amount.

For Better or Worse

You do not have to hold a job to have an IRA. A nonworking spouse may start a so-called spousal IRA, as long as both file jointly and the nonworking spouse's earned income totals less than $250.

If you meet these two requirements, each of you may open and make contributions to an IRA. The limits? Together, collectively, you may contribute as much as $2,250 in any single year. No more than $2,000 of that amount, however, may go to either account.

How much you write off on your tax return depends on your circumstances. You are subject to the same rules on deductibility as other taxpayers.

So, how do you split up your contribution? The answer depends on your long-term objectives. If you want to keep your savings in an IRA as long as possible, make the greater contribution to the IRA of the younger spouse. If you want to get at your savings sooner, put it in the older spouse's account.

Here is another strategy if you may not deduct the $2,250. Deposit the majority of the money in the account of the person who has the largest proportion of nondeductible dollars. That way, if that person withdraws part of his or her IRA funds from that account before age 59½, the amount subject to the 10-percent early withdrawal penalty will be minimized.

Of course, if your spouse's earned income exceeds $250, you do not lose out. Your spouse just opens his or her own IRA and contributes as much as 100 percent of his or her income (up to $2,000) to it.

TIP If you own your own business, and your spouse helps out from time to time, consider paying him or her for services rendered.

Here is why. Your spouse may sock away all or part of his or her earnings in an IRA and claim a tax deduction for the contribution.

Let's say the year is 1990, and you pay your spouse $2,000 a year for bookkeeping services. She reports income from no other source.

The two of you file a joint return listing AGI of $30,000. The result: Each of you may make a tax-deductible contribution to an IRA of up to $2,000.

CAUTION Make sure you pay your spouse with a payroll check. The IRS may not consider a deposit in a joint bank account as an actual payment of wages. And be prepared to show that your spouse's employment is genuine.

You should also know that wages paid to a spouse are subject to Social Security taxes. In 1990 the combined rate is 15.30 percent; that is, 7.65 percent paid by the employee and 7.65 percent paid by the employer.

HOW MANY IRAS?

If you are eligible, it does not matter how many IRAs you have—one or a dozen. Set up as many as you like. But you should know that many institutions charge an annual maintenance fee for each IRA. The fees can run as high as $50, which can get expensive if you open lots of accounts.

The effect of these fees is to reduce the net return on your investments. The fees are deductible, but only if you pay them from non-IRA funds and only to the extent that they and all your other miscellaneous itemized deductions top 2 percent of your AGI.

The rules also allow you to borrow money to make an IRA contribution. The only question: May you deduct the interest on the loan?

The answer depends on whether the interest is classified as personal interest or investment interest. And the rules are not clear on this point.

You may deduct only 10 percent of your personal interest expenses in 1990. After 1990, you cannot deduct anything. You may deduct investment interest only from your investment income. (For more on the rules governing interest deductions, see Chapter 5.)

Choosing the Right Account and Manager

Who should manage your IRA, and what sort of investments should be in it? You may choose as the manager of your IRA the institution where you have an account: a bank, for instance, or a savings and loan or brokerage house. Or you may manage it yourself.

As to what investments belong in an IRA, almost any investment vehicle makes sense, with just a few exceptions.

What you obviously do not want in an IRA are tax-free investments—municipal bonds, for instance. The yield on tax-free bonds is almost always lower than on taxable investments. And the beauty of an IRA is that it allows you to defer taxes on an investment's earnings. If the earnings are already tax free, you lose. Here is how.

The income from tax-exempt bonds, say, is tax-free; that is, it is not subject to federal taxation. The income from an IRA is tax deferred; that is, you pay tax on it when you withdraw it. If you use IRA dollars to invest in tax-exempt bonds, income from those bonds is paid to your IRA. And when the income is withdrawn, it is taxed. In effect, you have turned tax-free income into taxable income.

Among the IRA investments you should consider:

- Bank certificates of deposit (CDs) that pay market rates of interest. Deposits are insured up to $100,000 at most institutions.

- Money market mutual funds offered by brokerage houses and other financial institutions.

- Mutual funds of all types (except municipal bond funds).

- Stocks, including individual issues. You may, for example, open a self-directed IRA at a brokerage firm. You select the stocks you like and reinvest any dividends, thereby preserving the year-to-year tax-free feature of your IRA.

- Flexible-premium annuities offered by insurance companies (these are known as Individual Retirement Annuities).

About the only investments the law says you may not make with IRA dollars are those in art objects, antiques, stamps, and other collectibles. You also may not invest IRA dollars in gold or silver coins (except gold and silver eagle coins minted by the U.S. Treasury and coins issued by a state).

Also, you may not use your IRA dollars for "self-dealing," that is, you may not use IRA funds to purchase assets from yourself or from a company you own. For example, you could not use IRA dollars to purchase stock in a corporation you own.

What is more, you may not borrow from your IRA. Nor may you use your IRA as collateral for a loan. If you do use IRA dollars in any of these forbidden ways, the IRS treats the amount you invested as if you had withdrawn it from your account.

What happens then? You pay tax at your normal rate on that amount of income, and, if you are younger than 59½, you pay a 10 percent early withdrawal penalty, too.

Whichever investments you choose for your IRA, you are no more stuck with them than you are with non-IRA investment choices. As far as the IRS is concerned, you may buy and sell stocks and mutual funds, switch to CDs, or move into the money market as often as you see fit.

The institutions with which you place your IRA, however, may put the brakes on some of this activity. For instance, a bank may penalize you by an amount equal to three months of interest if you withdraw funds early from a certificate of deposit.

You may withdraw and roll over your IRA from one institution to another without penalty just once each 365 days. So if you withdraw and roll over only part of the balance in your IRA, you are not allowed to withdraw and roll over the remainder until after 365 days later. But this limitation need not inhibit you if you have your IRA at an institution that offers a variety of investment vehicles. You may switch among these vehicles as often as you choose.

Say you maintain your IRA at a brokerage firm. You may, for instance, switch from stocks to mutual funds to bonds and back again without penalty. You do, of course, pile up commission fees and other transaction costs.

TIP Here is a way around the once-every-365-days limit on withdrawals and rollovers. Switch your funds by a "trustee-to-trustee" transfer.

You authorize the trustee of the institution that now holds your IRA dollars to transfer these funds directly to the trustee of another institution. Since you never touch the money—it goes from one institution to another—it is not technically a rollover. And it is not subject to the once-every-365-days limit.

TIP Uncle Sam says that your IRA may not lend you money. But here is a way to borrow from your IRA using the rollover rules.

As we have seen, the law says that you may withdraw your IRA funds as long as it has been at least one year since your last withdrawal was rolled over. You pay no taxes and no penalties as long as the money is transferred back into another IRA within 60 days. The result: You may withdraw your IRA dollars, use the money for up to 60 days, then roll it over into another IRA—all without any tax consequences.

Here's something else you should know about borrowing from your IRA. Up until now, tax practioners have assumed that a rollover of an IRA must be from one IRA to another. But that's not what the IRS told a taxpayer we'll call Pat in a recent private-letter ruling.

Pat withdrew $1,500 from his IRA in 1986, then redeposited that amount in the same IRA 60 days later. He did that again in 1987.

The IRS says Pat is not subject to tax on the rollover. In private ruling 9010007, the IRS writes that "an individual" usually may take out IRA funds for his or her personal use, and do so tax-free as long as he or she redeposits the funds in the same or another IRA in time.

You should know, that private rulings apply only to the taxpayers involved, although these rulings do hint at the IRS's position on a given subject.

Note: In the eyes of Uncle Sam, IRAs you maintain at several institutions are considered separate accounts. What does it matter?

Say you maintain two IRA accounts, one at a bank, the other at a brokerage firm. On October 1, 1990, you withdraw and roll over the money from the bank to a mutual fund company.

Delighted with the mutual fund's performance, you decide—four months later—to withdraw and roll over the money from the brokerage firm to the mutual fund company.

Rest easy. You can do it without penalty. The reason: The 365-day rule applies separately to each account.

Alternatively, as we discussed earlier, you could have the bank or brokerage firm transfer your IRA dollars from either one or both of the IRA accounts directly to the mutual fund and you would have accomplished the same result.

Should You Make a Nondeductible Contribution?

If you are not eligible, for whatever reason, to make deductible contributions to an IRA, should you make any at all? It is not an easy question to answer, even though the pros and cons of this decision are relatively straightforward.

The pros?

The most obvious is that even though you may not deduct your annual IRA contribution, the earnings from your IRA investments accumulate and compound tax deferred. That means they build up faster than if you were paying tax on them every year.

And the cons?

Once you put money into an IRA, it is locked in until you reach age 59½ unless you are willing to pay a 10 percent penalty for early withdrawal.

The penalty applies to the deductible portion of your IRA contribution and to any earnings that have accumulated tax-deferred in your account. But you pay no penalty when you withdraw your nondeductible contributions.

And, as we will see later, if your IRAs are made up of nondeductible contributions and either deductible contributions or tax-deferred earnings or both, a *pro rata* portion of any withdrawals will be considered to come from deductible contributions and tax-deferred earnings, which will result in that portion of the withdrawal being subject to the 10 percent penalty.

Say, for example, that your account balance stands at $10,000. That amounts consists of $7,000 of deductible contributions, $2,000 of nondeductible contributions, and $1,000 in earnings on your investments. So, 80 percent of the amount withdrawn is subject to the 10 percent penalty: that is, $7,000 + $1,000 ÷ $10,000.

Of course, if you are almost that age already, early withdrawal probably will not be a problem. Go ahead and contribute to your IRA.

If you are young, say in your twenties, you should not underestimate the long-term value of tax-deferred earnings on an annual contribution of $2,000. So consider making nondeductible contributions to an IRA. (However, if your employer offers a 401(k) plan, contributions to it are usually a much better deal.)

Some people feel that investing in tax-free bonds is a reasonable alternative to making a nondeductible IRA contribution. And they have a point.

The earnings from these bonds are tax-free. And you do not have to pay a penalty if you want to get at your money. Moreover, you are not limited to investing $2,000, or $2,250 for you and your nonworking spouse. But the bonds come with two potential drawbacks.

You can get locked into the bonds. If interest rates rise, and the value of your bonds falls, you would have to take a loss to sell. So you are stuck with the bonds until maturity or until rates fall again.

The other potential problem with tax-free bonds is that, depending on the market, their yields are sometimes low compared to the after-tax yields of other securities. So they can be a poor investment.

Should you make a nondeductible IRA contribution? The answer depends on your circumstances. The key point is to take your personal situation into account. Lay out all the pros and cons each and every year before you make your decision.

But remember this: The option is time-limited.

After the deadline passes for making this year's contribution, deductible or not, there is no changing your mind. Once missed, the opportunity is gone forever.

WHAT YOU NEED TO KNOW ABOUT 401(K) PLANS

It is true that the name 401(k) does not tell you much. It refers to the part of the tax code that describes these attractive retirement plans. But do not let a name put you off. Taking advantage of an employer-sponsored 401(k) is easy—and the benefits are substantial.

Substantial benefits? Yes, two of them, actually.

First, the money contributed to a 401(k) and the earnings that accumulate in it are tax deferred. That means your savings grow more rapidly than they would otherwise.

How much faster?

Well, compare two investment plans, one tax deferred and one not. With both plans, you invest in the same mutual fund each year for 20 years. The fund earns 10 percent a year, and you reinvest these earnings, less any taxes due, in the account. Your marginal tax rate is 28 percent.

In order to compare apples to apples, let's say that in the taxable fund you invest $7,979 (the maximum the law allows in 1990 for tax-deferred plans) from your salary, less the $2,234 you owe Uncle Sam in taxes, or $5,745 each year. At the end of 20 years, this taxable fund has grown to more than $258,000. Not bad, you say, and you are right.

But the tax-deferred fund is larger still—more than $502,000—for two reasons. You have been able to invest a full $7,979, since money earmarked for a 401(k) is not taxed currently, and you have not had to pay federal income tax on the earnings as they accumulated.

Tax deferred, of course, does not mean tax-free.

It only means that you do not pay taxes on the money contributed to a 401(k) or the earnings that pile up until you withdraw the funds.

Let's go back to our example. The true value of the tax-deferred fund is not $502,000 but nearly $362,000; that is, $502,000 minus the $141,000 in income taxes you pay when you withdraw the money. Still, you come out nearly $104,000 ahead in your tax-deferred 401(k) fund.

But we said there were two substantial benefits to a 401(k). The second: The law allows your employer to help you build your 401(k) retirement fund. Many employers, in fact, contribute to employees' 401(k)s—up to a certain limit. It is almost like giving yourself a raise.

No doubt about it. A 401(k) retirement plan is an attractive arrangement. But, as you might expect, Congress has established limits to keep it from becoming too attractive.

So, to get the most out of your 401(k), you need to know the rules. There are not many, at least when it comes to joining a plan.

If your company sponsors a 401(k) plan, signing up is simple. You authorize your employer to create an account for you and regularly deduct an amount from your pay.

Let's say your salary adds up to $50,000 in 1991. You instruct your employer to subtract $400 a month from your pay and deposit it in a 401(k) plan.

When you get your W-2 form for the year, it will not show your entire $50,000 salary. Instead, it will report that you were paid $45,200: $50,000 less the $4,800 deducted for your 401(k). The $4,800 is treated as "deferred compensation" and is not reported as current income to you.

☞ **CAUTION** Although you do not currently have to pay federal income tax on the money that you contribute to your company-sponsored 401(k), this amount is still subject to Federal Social Security (FICA) tax in the year that you earn it.

Within Limits

Not surprisingly, there are limits to the amount of money that you and your employer may contribute annually to a 401(k) plan. But these limits seem rather generous when compared, for instance, to the $2,000 cap on IRA contributions.

The government sets two limits on 401(k)s.

One caps the amount that you may contribute to your own retirement plan. The other restricts the amount that you and your employer together may contribute. The federal government adjusts both of these figures annually for inflation.

If you play your cards right, you can ensure that your plan receives the maximum total contribution while minimizing your personal 401(k) expense.

In 1990, the maximum amount an employee may salt away annually, tax deferred, in a 401(k) is $7,979: $9,500 in the case of a tax-sheltered annuity.

What, you ask, is a tax-sheltered annuity?

It is a kind of tax-deferred account for teachers, church workers, and employees of other nonprofit groups or institutions. It is usually sold by life insurance companies in the form of a contract that guarantees a payment to you at some future date, usually at retirement.

The second ceiling limits the amount that you and your employer together may contribute to a 401(k) and all other defined-contribution plans. In 1990, the ceiling is $30,000 or 25 percent of your after-contribution salary, whichever is less.

Say, for instance, that your salary comes to $100,000 in 1990, and you contribute $7,979 to a 401(k). How much may your employer contribute?

Calculate 25 percent of your after-contribution salary. That amount adds up to $23,005 ($100,000 − $7,979 = $92,021 × 25 percent).

Since $23,005 is less than $30,000, $23,005 is the most that you and your employer together may contribute to all your defined-contribution retirement plans.

You have already put away $7,979, so your employer's maximum contribution is not $22,021, that is, the $30,000 ceiling minus your $7,979 contribution, but just $15,026 ($23,005 minus $7,979).

So maybe you would be better off reducing your own contribution? First, let's assume that your employer does not use a matching formula to tie its contribution to the amount you pay in. Instead, it contributes a certain percentage of your compensation.

Now, in the example above, if you were to reduce your contribution from $7,979 to $5,000, your after-contribution salary would total $95,000 ($100,000 minus $5,000).

And 25 percent of that amount comes to $23,750.

By reducing your contribution, you have raised the maximum ceiling on the total retirement contribution for the year by $745 (the difference between $23,750 and $23,005). And you have also allowed your employer to increase its contribution.

The company may now chip in as much as $18,750 ($23,750 minus your $5,000 contribution). Less sometimes can be more.

QUESTIONS AND ANSWERS

QUESTION: *Where should I invest my 401(k) funds?*

You really do not have much choice about where to invest your 401(k) plan dollars. Unlike an IRA, where you have control of how your funds are invested, you must choose from among the options your employer offers for your 401(k) plan.

Some 401(k) plans limit you to a single investment option. Others let you split your account among two or more choices.

QUESTION: *Does my participation in a 401(k) plan affect the level of other benefits I might receive?*

You will want to check with your employer to find out.

Why? The value of some benefits—life insurance, for instance, and contributions to profit-sharing plans—is often tied to your total earnings. And what you get in these other benefits may vary depending on how the company tallies up your compensation.

The key point is this: Does the company reduce your compensation by the amount you have contributed to your 401(k)? Or does it add that amount back to your pay before calculating the value of your other benefits? Employers are *not* required to do the latter.

Ask your company about what procedure it follows.

QUESTION: *What is the deadline for making a contribution to an IRA?*

For 1990, you may contribute to an IRA any time after January 1, 1990, but no later than April 15, 1991—the due date of your annual tax return.

QUESTION: *I have heard that there is a form that people who make nondeductible IRA contributions must fill out. Is my information correct?*

If you do make nondeductible IRA contributions, you must report the amount on Form 8606. Uncle Sam will use this form to keep track of the nontaxable part of an IRA. And you face a $50 penalty if you do not file it.

QUESTION: *I receive alimony, and it is my only income. Does alimony count as earned income, so I can make a tax deductible IRA contribution?*

The answer is yes. Alimony is considered earned income when it comes to calculating your IRA contribution.

23

Taking Money Out of Your Retirement Plan

It is when you want to take money out of your tax-deferred retirement plan, no matter which type of plan you have, that the tax consequences become acute. How and when you withdraw the funds can make a big difference in how much tax you will pay.

Whenever you begin to withdraw your funds, you really have just a few options. Depending on your retirement plan, you may pull money out of your plan at retirement or before retirement. And, you may pull it out in one *lump sum* or spread your withdrawals over time. Let's see how the tax law views each of these options.

First, we consider withdrawal at retirement—both in lump sum and in periodic payments. Then we look at the early withdrawal option.

One point some people may need to keep in mind regardless of how they decide to withdraw their funds is the potential penalty they may incur for excessive distributions.

Here is the general rule: If the total distribution you receive from all retirement plans, including IRAs, tops $150,000 in one year, you owe a 15 percent penalty on the excess. Special rules apply if the totally vested benefit in your retirement plan before August 1, 1986, was more than $562,500.

Also, the penalty is assessed separately if you get a lump sum distribution and elect to take advantage of special income averaging rules. The penalty is imposed only on the amount that exceeds $750,000.

TIP If you think your yearly retirement benefits will exceed the limit, you may want to take some distributions earlier. The best way to know: Run the numbers and consult your tax adviser.

CAUTION This penalty applies whether you are over or under 59½. But the IRS will not also assess the 10 percent early withdrawal penalty (see below) on the excess distribution.

LUMP SUM WITHDRAWAL

The obvious disadvantage to taking your accumulated savings out of a retirement plan in a single lump sum is that you incur a big tax liability in the year you do so. But the tax law allows you to mitigate that liability somewhat, except in the case of IRAs and SEPs, by using a device called *five-year averaging*.

Five-year averaging can reduce the tax rate levied on lump sum withdrawals. Here is why. Even though you pay your full tax in the year you receive your lump sum, you calculate the tax as if you received the money evenly over five years.

To figure your taxes on five-year averaging, first compute the tax on one-fifth of the lump sum distribution in the year that you are taking it. (You use the rates for single taxpayers, even if you are married, and do not take into account any other income.) Then multiply that number by five. This figure is the total tax you will owe. And the amount may be smaller than the tax you would pay if you included the whole amount in your income in one year.

Be aware, though, that you may use five-year averaging just once, and not until you have reached age 59½.

Also, Uncle Sam attaches conditions to lump sum distributions that are eligible for five-year averaging:

- The employee must have been a participant in the plan for five tax years before the tax year of the distribution (unless the distribution was paid out because the employee died).

- The distribution must total the full amount due the employee from all plans of the same type, for example, pension, profit-sharing, and stock bonus plans.

- The distribution must be paid in a single year.

- The distribution must be payable after the employee reaches age 59½, becomes disabled or dies, or terminates his or her employment.

Because the five-year averaging rules were enacted by Congress in 1986, the law still includes some special deals for individuals who were born on or before December 31, 1935. These folks have an additional option open to them in dealing with lump sum distributions.

They may use five-year averaging or, they may use *ten-year averaging* rules. If they take this latter course, however, they must apply the tax rates that were in effect in 1986.

Moreover, these individuals do not have to wait until age 59½ to enjoy the benefits of averaging. However, if they receive a distribution after age 50 and before age 59½, they have to receive it because of separation from service.

If you fall into this age category, the only way to know which option is the better tax choice is to do both calculations and compare the results.

Anyone eligible to use ten-year averaging under this transition rule, however, must also be aware that if you use it on a lump sum distribution you receive before you reach age 59½, you may not use the averaging device (either ten- or five-year averaging) ever again.

One last point: Uncle Sam may consider part of your distribution as a capital gain. If that is the case and you elect ten-year averaging, you may pay less tax. That is because the maximum 1986 capital gain rate of 20 percent was less than the highest 1986 ordinary rate of 50 percent. Our advice: If you find yourself in this situation, see your tax adviser *before* you withdraw your money.

PAYMENTS OVER TIME

Suppose you do not take your retirement plan benefits in a single lump. Your alternative is to withdraw the money in the form of an annuity—annual payments the size of which depends upon your life expectancy or, in some cases, the life expectancy of you and your spouse. (The IRS uses its Standard Annuity Tables to determine life expectancy.)

The payments are taxable unless you have made nondeductible contributions to the plan. If so—and this is true for many individuals—some part of each payment will be nontaxable. That part is based on the "exclusion ratio," and it reflects the proportion of nondeductible contributions you have made to the total value of your retirement plan.

You may only continue to exclude that portion of your regular benefit payments from taxable income, however, until you reach your actuarial life expectancy. At that point, as far as the law is concerned, you have pulled all your nondeductible contributions out of the plan. The payments that follow this statistical milestone will be fully taxable.

As a general rule, if you should die prior to your life expectancy and the annuity ceases, you're allowed a deduction for your unrecovered nondeductible contributions.

Early Withdrawals

Under certain circumstances, you may tap your retirement fund early, but you must comply with quite a number of restrictions to avoid paying expensive penalties on early withdrawals.

If, for instance, you leave a job before age 59½ and your employer requires you to take your pension benefits with you, you will incur a 10 percent early withdrawal penalty unless you roll the account over into an IRA or other qualified retirement plan within 60 days.

You may also avoid the penalty if:

- You use the distribution to pay for deductible medical expenses.

- You receive the benefits (after separation from service) in the form of an annuity spread over your life or the joint lives of you and your beneficiary. (Payments must be substantially equal and made at least annually.)

- You retire after reaching age 55 but before age 59½.

- You receive distributions from an Employee Stock Ownership Plan (ESOP) before January 1, 1990.

WITHDRAWING MONEY FROM YOUR IRA

You may take your money out of an IRA at any time.

But if you do not want to pay a penalty equal to 10 percent of the amount withdrawn which is taxable, you must wait until you reach the legal age of 59½. (Disabled individuals may make penalty-free withdrawals at any age.)

We talk about early withdrawals shortly, but first let us cover the normal route. Say you are older than 59½, and you want some or all of your IRA money.

How do you get at it? And does it matter?

Yes, it certainly does.

In general, there are two ways to withdraw money from any retirement fund. You may take it out bit by bit, as you need it, over a period of years. Or, you may withdraw it in one lump sum. There are perfectly good reasons why you might choose either option.

Maybe you just need a little money every year to augment your Social Security and company-paid retirement income. So gradual withdrawal makes sense for you. Or, maybe you need a large sum of cash to pay off the mortgage on your house. You want your IRA money all at once.

Hold on, though, because the lump sum alternative triggers an unfortunate tax consequence.

IRAs are different from all other tax-deferred retirement plans in one important respect. As a general rule, with other plans, you may, for tax purposes, spread a lump sum withdrawal after age 59½ over five years. You get the money all at once. But—even though you pay the tax all in one year—you are taxed as if you had spread the withdrawal over a five-year period.

Not so with IRAs. Your lump sum withdrawal is taxed at ordinary income rates in the year you make the withdrawal. This rule is not a bar to lump sum withdrawals, of course, but it is a consideration you ought to keep in mind before deciding to empty your IRA in a single shot.

However you decide to withdraw IRA funds, you are going to owe some tax. Remember, at least some of the money you contributed to the IRA over the years was untaxed income, and all the earnings from your IRA investments have been accumulating tax-free.

Now it is time to pay the piper. The principle that governs your tax liability at this point is simple enough: If the money you are withdrawing was taxed once, it is not taxed again. The way you apply this principle in figuring your taxes is pretty simple, too.

Let's say that you have had an IRA for ten years. Now you want to begin withdrawing from it. For the first eight years you made tax-deductible contributions of $2,000 each year. Your total deductible contributions: $16,000.

During the last two years you also contributed $2,000 annually, but those were nondeductible contributions. Your total nondeductible contributions: $4,000. And, you are pleased to learn, your savvy investment decisions have resulted in accumulated IRA earnings of $10,000.

So, all together you have $30,000 in your account.

What if you make a lump sum withdrawal? Easy. You owe tax on the $16,000 in deductible contributions and on the $10,000 in accumulated earnings, but not on the $4,000 in nondeductible contributions. You are taxed on $26,000 of your $30,000 withdrawal.

But what if you want to withdraw just part of it, say, $4,000 in the first year? May you withdraw just the $4,000 that represents the nondeductible contributions you made and thereby escape paying income tax? No, you may not.

In this case, $26,000 of the $30,000 in your IRA, or 87 percent, has been contributed or has accumulated tax-free. So, 87 percent of any withdrawal you make that first year will be subject to tax. (Of course this proportion will change slightly from year to year as earnings continue to accumulate tax-free in your IRA while you make periodic withdrawals.)

The same rule of proportion applies even if you have several separate IRAs, some with mostly deductible contributions and others with nondeductible contributions. For purposes of computing the taxable proportion of any withdrawal you make, the IRS considers them all one.

But, remember, each spouse's contributions are grouped separately when it comes to withdrawing these funds.

TIP Remember, once you reach age 59½ but before you reach age 70½, you may withdraw your IRA dollars any time you choose and in any amount without penalty. Plan accordingly.

One last point: As we noted previously, if you take an extremely large distribution from your IRA, you may be subject to a 15 percent excise tax on excess distributions.

As we have seen, if you want your IRA money before you reach age 59½ and you are not disabled, you will pay a penalty—10 percent of the "untaxed" funds you withdraw. The same rule of proportion applies here as applied in the example above.

If, say, 80 percent of the money in your IRA consists of deductible contributions and accumulated earnings, you pay a 10 percent penalty as well as regular income tax on 80 percent of any early withdrawal you make. But you can avoid the penalty. Just take your distribution in the form of lifetime annual payments.

The law demands that these payments be of approximately equal amounts. Also, the payments must be based on your life expectancy or joint lives or life expectancies of you and your beneficiaries as determined by IRS tables.

Say, for instance, that you are 50 with a life expectancy of 33 years, according to the IRS tables. Your IRA contains $50,000. You may purchase an annuity contract that lets you take annual distributions of $4,340 (assuming an 8 percent interest rate) from the account without incurring a penalty.

Just as it discourages early withdrawals, the law also takes a dim view of late IRA withdrawals. The law requires you to begin pulling your accumulated IRA funds out before April 1 of the year following the year you reach age 70½.

Exactly how much you must withdraw depends on your life expectancy or, if you choose, the joint life expectancies of you and your beneficiaries.

If you do not withdraw the required amount, the law says, you start paying a hefty penalty. It equals 50 percent of the difference between the amount you withdrew and the amount you were required to withdraw. Here is an example.

Say you are age 72. Based on your life expectancy, you must withdraw a minimum of $6,000 a year from your IRA. But, in 1989, you made a mistake.

You withdrew only $4,000.

What are the tax consequences? You pay a penalty that equals 50 percent of the difference between the amount you withdrew, $4,000, and the amount you were required to withdraw, $6,000. In this case, you fork over $1,000, that is, 50 percent times $2,000.

 TIP To get the maximum deferral from your IRA, consider naming your child or another younger person as beneficiary. That way your joint life expectancy will be quite long. And the amount you will have to take out of your IRA account will be much less than it would be otherwise.

TIP Here is another strategy to consider: Name your spouse as your beneficiary. A spouse—but not a child—can roll over an IRA he or she inherits from a deceased spouse. Now the spouse can avoid minimum withdrawal requirements until age 70½.

CAUTION Other individuals who inherit IRAs must withdraw the money within five years after the inheritance or must begin receiving annuity payments immediately; otherwise, they pay the 50% penalty.

WITHDRAWING MONEY FROM YOUR 401(K)

Two sets of rules govern withdrawals from 401(k)s.

One set is imposed by the federal government, the other by your employer, and you must abide by both when you make a withdrawal.

You should know that the rules imposed by your employer may never be more generous than those outlined by Uncle Sam; but your employer's rules may be *less* generous. So familiarize yourself with the provisions of your employer's 401(k).

The IRS rules governing access to funds in a 401(k) plan are similar to the restrictions that apply to other retirement plans.

You may receive your money, without penalty, when:

- You reach age 59½ regardless of whether you are working or not.

- You reach age 55 or older and retire early.

- You die or become disabled.

If, at any of these times, you choose to make your withdrawal in a lump sum, you can likely reduce your taxes if the withdrawal is eligible for five-year averaging.

Remember, too, that you may take your money out with no penalty to pay medical expenses that would ordinarily be deductible. (See Chapter 7 for more information on writing off medical expenses.)

And after you leave your job, you may receive your money in the form of an annuity, that is, periodic payments over your lifetime.

As for financial hardship, you may withdraw your money from your 401(k) if your employer's plan allows, but you still pay taxes and a 10 percent penalty.

And your company may distribute the cash in the plan to you when your employment ends, even if you have not yet reached age 59½.

In this case, Uncle Sam gives you just 60 days to roll the 401(k) funds over into an IRA or other approved retirement plan. Any amount that you do not roll over is taxed as ordinary income, and you pay a 10 percent penalty to boot if you are younger than age 59½.

If your employer's plan allows, you may withdraw your money from a 401(k) in the form of a loan. (That is generally not the case with other retirement plans, such as IRAs.)

But borrowing from your 401(k) plan, while possible, has restrictions attached to it. Your loan, together with any outstanding loans, is limited to the lesser of: $50,000 or the greater of $10,000 or one-half of your vested 401(k) account balance. Moreover, the $50,000 limit is reduced by the excess, if any, of:

- The highest outstanding loan balance during the one-year period before the date of the new or extended loan, over

- The outstanding loan balance on the date you take out the loan.

An example should make this rule clearer. Say on January 1, 1990, the amount you have vested in your 401(k) comes to $100,000, and outstanding loans from your plan total $40,000. Eight months later, on September 1, you want to borrow more money. You've already paid back $15,000 of your loan, so your outstanding loan balance now totals $25,000.

Now you need another loan and want to know how much more you can borrow. The answer is $10,000—$50,000 less the current balance of your outstanding existing loan ($25,000), less the difference between the highest outstanding loan balance during the previous year ($40,000) and the outstanding balance of your existing loan ($25,000), or $15,000. What happens if you pay off the $40,000 balance by September 1? It makes no difference.

There's a simpler way to state the answer: According to the rules, you may borrow $10,000—$50,000 less the highest amount that was outstanding during the previous year ($40,000).

Also, you must repay the loan within five years, unless you use the money to buy a principal residence. In that case, you may take as long as your plan allows, usually 15, 20, 25, or 30 years, the terms of typical mortgages.

However, the law requires that you repay your loan in equal payments, which you make at least quarterly over the term of the loan. The interest you pay on the loan must be "reasonable," which is to say that it may not be too low or too high.

But whatever it is, you usually may not deduct it, even if the deduction would otherwise be allowed, as mortgage interest, say. The reason for this rule: The legislators figured you should not be able to deduct interest that you are, in effect, paying to yourself.

You do get a break, though, if you took out a loan from your 401(k) plan before 1987. In this case, Uncle Sam allows you to deduct your interest under the interest tracing rules. For example, interest on a loan used to buy stock is classified as investment interest (see Chapter 5).

But if you took out a loan after 1986, you are out of luck. The interest is not deductible, no matter how you used the money.

And here is more bad news: When it comes time to cash out of your 401(k), you are taxed on the amount of interest that you paid in. It is treated in the same way as any other interest or dividends that accumulate on the amounts you have contributed.

☞ **CAUTION** Say you leave a job and still have a 401(k) loan outstanding. If your plan requires repayment at the time you stop being an active participant in the plan—which in fact most plans do—your failure to repay the loan when you leave is a default. The amount of any defaulted loan balance will be treated as a distribution at that time.

In that case, you pay taxes on the distribution.

And, what's worse, you'll pay the 10 percent early distribution penalty, unless you are one of the exceptions to the rule—you are age 59½, say.

QUESTIONS AND ANSWERS

QUESTION: *Is there any point at which I must begin withdrawing funds from my retirement account?*

No matter what kind of retirement plan you have and how you

decide to take the money out, the law requires that you begin withdrawing your benefits not later than April 1 of the year following the year you reach the age of 70½.

One exception: Employees who reached age 70½ by January 1, 1988, may generally defer the distributions until they actually retire.

And you fall under another special rule if you reached age 70½ during 1988 and did not retire. In this case, you can defer your first withdrawal until April 1, 1990. (This rule does not apply to IRAs, however.)

Failure to begin taking any of your benefits in time will subject you to a 50 percent penalty on the amount that is required to be distributed each year.

24

What You Need to Know About Your Children's Taxes

Children may once have brought joy and tax shelter to your happy home. Now, by and large, you have to settle for the joy. Since tax reform, more children than ever before will file tax returns. And the youngest of these youngsters will probably pay taxes at a higher rate, too.

In this chapter we cover when and how children file. We also show you how the new rules on children's taxes may change your own tax strategies as a parent. And we tell you how the rules governing trusts have changed.

Let's begin with who has to file. Keep in mind that the key point here is not how old your children are but how much they make.

FILING REQUIREMENTS ARE NOT AS EASY AS ABC

The requirements on filing are far from straightforward.

The rules say that dependent children with *unearned incomes* greater than $500, or with gross incomes greater than the standard deduction, must file returns. (There are, of course, exceptions to this rule, and we discuss them below.)

The standard deduction? That's the tricky part. In 1990, it's the greater of $500 or the amount of a child's earned income—up to a limit of $3,250 in 1990. Both these figures are subject to an annual adjustment for inflation.

As a consequence, a child with modest unearned income and less than $3,250 in gross income may still have to file a tax return.

Consider this example. Assume that Molly reports unearned income—from interest and dividends—of only $400 in 1990. That is less than the $500 filing limit.

But she also earns $1,000 working at a summer job. Her standard deduction, then, is limited to the amount of her earned income— $1,000. But her gross income is $1,400—higher than her standard deduction. Molly has to file. And she must also pay tax on $400 of her income.

When you or your tax adviser calculate Molly's tax liability, you subtract the standard deduction, which in her case equals her earned income of $1,000. The remainder is the amount subject to tax.

Molly, a dependent of her parents, may not use the personal exemption, $2,050 in 1990, to reduce her taxable income. Only Molly's parents may claim her and take the personal exemption.

Since Molly's parents are entitled to claim her as a dependent, Molly may not claim herself. There is no option here. If the parent may claim the child's personal exemption, the child may not. (For more information on the personal exemption, see Chapter 3.)

You may report your child's unearned income on *your* return to avoid the hassle of filing separately for your child. To do so you must file Form 8814, "Parent's Election to Report Child's Interest and Dividends," with your 1040.

You and your child must meet certain requirements, however. Your child must be under 14 years of age. Also, the child's gross income, which can consist only of interest and dividends (including Alaska Permanent Fund dividends), must come to more than $500 but less than $5,000.

So if your child has any earned income—from baby sitting, say, or running errands for the local drugstore—you may not report his or her income on your return.

Also, you may not make this election if your child has made estimated tax or withholding payments in his or her name and/or under his or her own Social Security number.

If you do make this election, Uncle Sam treats your child as if he or she had no gross income for the year. And your child will not have to file a return.

Instead, you add your child's gross unearned income of more than $1,000 to your—the parents'—gross income on your return.

Here is how the IRS taxes the total amount of your child's unearned income:

- You pay no tax at all on the first $500 of unearned income (thanks to the standard deduction).

- You pay a flat 15 percent on the second $500 of unearned income.

- Then you are taxed at your highest marginal rate on any remaining unearned income.

In addition, you must treat any of the child's interest that is a tax preference item for purposes of the alternative minimum tax (AMT) as if it belonged to you, the parent.

When you make this election, your investment income should increase by the amount of your child's unearned income (excluding Alaska Permanent Fund Dividends) for the purpose of determining your investment interest expense deduction. Why do we say "should"?

Congress enacted this new provision for your administrative convenience, not to give you a break on the investment interest expense write-off. But it is possible to read the statute's language as giving you this unintended break.

Two drawbacks: Including your child's income on your return will also increase your adjusted gross income for purposes of the medical and miscellaneous itemized deductions. And, it may subject that income to state income tax (or to a higher state income tax) than may have been the case had the child's income not been included in your return.

IT TAKES TWO

At this point it makes sense for us to separate children into two groups: those who have reached the age of 14 and those who have not.

Why? Because the tax law does. The distinction is a result of Congress's effort to significantly dilute tax benefits of a common tax-saving strategy known as income-shifting. Parents, using this popular tactic, would shift income to their children so that it would be taxed at the child's lower marginal rate.

Parents may still use this strategy with children who are 14 years of age or older but not for their younger offspring except for relatively modest amounts.

It does not matter when during the year your child turns 14. In other words, your child is taxed as a 14-year-old all year even if his or her birthday is not until December 31.

FIGURING YOUR CHILD'S TAXES

The net unearned income of children under 14—that is, the income that comes their way from investments, not from wages—is taxed at the higher of the parents' rate or the child's rate. (The parents' rate is almost always higher.)

This rule makes the calculation of the younger kids' taxes a bit difficult. The trick is to determine net unearned income.

First, you add together all of your child's unearned income from interest, dividends, capital gains, and so forth. Then you subtract $500, because the first $500 of unearned income is taxed at the child's rate no matter what the child's age.

Finally, you reduce the balance by the greater of the following: $500 of the standard deduction or, if the child itemizes deductions for the year, $500 of itemized deductions; or any amount of deductions that are directly connected with the production of the unearned income, such as investment adviser fees, as long as this amount is greater than $500 *after* you apply the two percent floor for most miscellaneous itemized deductions. (See Chapter 9 for more information on the two percent rule.)

Now what you have is "net" unearned income. Let's run through an example to see how your youngsters might fare.

Assume that the year is 1990 and you are in the 28 percent tax bracket. Your hardworking 13-year-old, Rachel, earned $800 babysitting and raking leaves this year, and she received $2,000 in unearned income—interest and dividends from stocks and bonds that you have given to her over the years.

Let's compute her net unearned income. Beginning with the $2,000 in interest and dividends, subtract $500. Why? The law says that the first $500 of Rachel's unearned income, no matter what her age, is taxed at Rachel's rate, not yours.

Now we reduce the remaining $1,500 in unearned income by the greater of the following: any deductible expenses—in excess, of course, of two percent of Rachel's adjusted gross income (AGI)—related to producing that income (in Rachel's case there were none); $500 from the standard deduction; or up to $500 in itemized deductions (again, none in Rachel's case).

So you take $500 from the standard deduction and subtract it from her remaining $1,500 of unearned income. The result?

Only $1,000 of Rachel's unearned income ($2,000 minus the $500 taxable at her marginal rate minus $500 from the standard deduction) is taxed at your marginal rate. The $1,000 is her net unearned income.

What about her wages? Any earned income—in this case, the $800 Rachel was paid for baby-sitting and raking leaves—is taxed at her rate. But Rachel pays tax on just $500 of her earned income.

Here's why: The law allows her to claim a standard deduction equal to the greater of $500 or her earned income (up to the $3,250 limit in 1990). So she is entitled to a standard deduction of $800—the amount she received for her work.

We know that she has already applied $500 of her standard deduction against her unearned income. That leaves $300 that she can use to reduce her earned income. Subtracting this $300 from $800 leaves $500, the amount of Rachel's earned income subject to tax.

Her tax liability on earned income comes to $75 (15 percent times $500). On her unearned income, however, she owes Uncle Sam a total of $355—$75 from the $500 taxable at her 15 percent marginal rate plus $280 from the $1,000 taxable at her parents' 28 percent marginal rate. Her total tax: $430.

Here is a simple way of figuring the tax on your child's net unearned income—that is, the unearned income that will be taxed at your rate. First, calculate the net unearned income. Add it to your taxable income. Then calculate your tax. Next calculate your tax bill without adding in your child's income. The difference between these two figures is the amount of tax due on your child's net unearned income.

☞ **CAUTION** If you are the parent of more than one child under the age of 14, the rules say you must add all of their net unearned incomes to your taxable income. Then you calculate your tax again. If the result is an increase in your tax bill, you then must allocate a pro rata portion of this increase to each of your children.

CHILDREN'S AMT

Children under the age of 14 may be subject to the alternative minimum tax (AMT) on their net unearned income in excess of $1,000 but only if their parents are. So if you have to pay AMT, here is how to figure your child's tax.

First, calculate the child's net unearned *minimum* taxable income. Basically, this calculation involves adding back certain preferences, such as miscellaneous deductions, and making certain AMT adjustments. (See Chapter 20 for detailed help in making these adjustments.)

Then, just as you did in figuring the child's regular tax, add his or her unearned minimum taxable income to your AMT income. If this increases your AMT liability, the amount of the increase is the amount your child owes in AMT. Do not forget: The child's AMT bill is in addition to his or her regular tax liability.

Children 14 and older will rarely be subject to AMT, but if you suspect that this might happen, consult your tax adviser to see how the child might avoid future AMT liabilities.

FURTHER CONSIDERATIONS

It bears repeating: Any dependent child with $500 or more in unearned income must file a return—even if he or she owes no tax. The only exception to this rule? If you elect to report your child's income on your return.

Furthermore, the source of the unearned income makes no difference. It might come, for instance, from dividends paid by stocks given by grandparents or purchased with the child's own money. And the stocks may have been given or purchased long before Congress adopted the 1986 tax law. Nonetheless, the same tax rules apply. The net unearned income generated by the stock is taxed at your rate or your child's rate, whichever is greater.

What if Rachel's parents are divorced? Then her net unearned income is taxed at the rate of the parent who has custody. If her parents have joint custody, her rate is the same as the parent with the higher rate—just as it would be if her parents were married but filed separate returns.

If both parents are deceased, a child pays taxes at his or her own rate.

A child who is 14, or who turns 14 during the tax year, pays tax almost like an adult. By that we mean that a 14-year-old's marginal tax rate on unearned income depends strictly on his or her income level, not on the income of his or her parents.

But older children are entitled to claim a standard deduction of only $500—or their earned income if this amount is greater, up to $3,250—and they may not reduce their taxable income by their own personal exemption. As we have seen, as long as they are dependents, their parents, not they, may claim that exemption.

WHY THE IRS WANTS YOUR KIDS' SOCIAL SECURITY NUMBERS

The law now requires you to list on your return the Social Security numbers of all of your children who are two years of age or older and for whom you claim a dependency exemption. It also requires that each of your children must note your Social Security number on their returns.

Why? The IRS plans to use these numbers to make sure that you do not claim deductions to which you are not entitled. For example, if you claim a personal exemption for your child, the IRS will check to see if your child is claiming one for himself or herself as well.

If you don't provide a Social Security number, the IRS may disallow the dependency exemption, which is worth a hefty $2,050. The IRS may also impose a penalty of $50 for each Social Security number that you failed to include on your return.

Getting a Social Security number for your child is a simple process. Start by asking your local Social Security office for a copy of Form SS-5. Then fill out the document and send it in.

When you mail the application, include proof of your child's age and citizenship. A public birth certificate is the best evidence. But a hospital record of birth or a religious record showing age or date of birth is also acceptable.

Since you are applying on behalf of your child, you must prove your identity. Acceptable evidence includes a driver's license, church membership or confirmation record, U.S. passport, voter's registration card, or military record.

☞ **CAUTION** The law also gives children under the age of 14 access to your tax return. Not a big deal, you say. But it might be for divorced parents.

If you and your ex-spouse have joint custody of a child under 14, then, as we mentioned earlier, the child pays the same rate on his or her net unearned income as the parent with the higher rate pays—just as he or she would if you were still married and filing separate returns.

So the only way the child will know which parent has the higher rate is if he or she—and your ex-spouse—have access to your return. As a practical matter, there is not much you can do to avoid disclosure.

INCOME SHIFTING

The tax treatment of younger kids means that the opportunities for income shifting—moving income from a family member with a higher marginal rate to one with a lower marginal rate—are more limited than in the past.

In fact, because the tax law draws a clear distinction between children who have reached the age of 14 and those who have not, we can separate income-shifting strategies that apply to children into two categories. Some are appropriate for the older group, some for the younger, and some for both.

Now we'll take you through a number of income-shifting devices. With just a little calculation, you can decide which will pay off for you.

FAREWELL TO CLIFFORD TRUSTS

Before we begin, a reminder that one of the most popular devices for shifting income, the Clifford trust, is defunct.

A Clifford trust allowed the person establishing the trust, the grantor, to get back the assets or cash he or she contributed at the end of the trust term, usually after a minimum of ten years.

While the trust was in effect, however, its income was taxed either to the beneficiary or to the trust. In both cases the rates were a good deal lower than the grantor's.

Today the game has changed. The rules require that the grantor, not the beneficiary, report and pay taxes on the trust income. So if you give assets to your child, you must make an outright and irrevocable gift if you want to have the income treated as your child's.

But there is one exception to this rule. If you established a Clifford trust before March 1, 1986, it remains valid. Income from the trust, however, is taxed according to the new rules. So if your child is under 14, the money will be taxed at your presumably higher rate. For children over 14, of course, the income remains taxable at their rate.

What if you, the grantor, make a new contribution to a Clifford trust that was established before March 1, 1986? Earnings generated by this contribution are reported as income to you, the grantor.

MAKING GIFTS TO CHILDREN 14 OR OLDER

Because the unearned income of children 14 years of age and older is taxed at the child's rate—which is usually lower than the parents'—shifting income to these senior offspring can produce tax savings. How large?

Say you invest $20,000 at 10 percent compounded annually for five years, and you are in the 28 percent bracket. You would have just $8,314 in after-tax earnings at the end of five years.

But let's say you and your spouse gave your 14-year-old son Liam the $20,000 and allowed him to make the same investment.

His earnings probably would be taxed at only 15 percent. So at the end of five years Liam would have after-tax earnings of $10,073— $1,759 more than your own.

Put another way, Liam's after-tax rate of return on the investment would be 8.5 percent compared to the 7.2 percent net rate of return that you were able to earn.

The bottom line: Giving the $20,000 to Liam increased the *family's* net income by $1,759 over five years.

What is the best way to shift income to your children?

Probably the most sensible and simplest method is through the Uniform Gifts to Minors Act (UGMA) or the newer Uniform Transfers to Minors Act (UTMA).

Under these acts, parents (or any person, for that matter) may give money to a child and keep those assets under a custodian's control.

You may select a member of your family, a legal guardian, or any adult you trust as the custodian. One word of warning, though: It usually is not a good idea for the donor—the person who gives the money—to serve as custodian.

Here is the reason. Say a favorite relative, Aunt Caitlin, is the donor, and she also acts as custodian. And say she dies before your child reaches the age of majority.

Under these circumstances the money she has given your child is subject to estate tax. The situation is not so bad, though, if her estate is small—less than $600,000.

You do not have to worry about legal fees in setting up an UGMA or UTMA account. Just go to a financial institution, such as a bank, and ask for the appropriate forms.

One last point about these accounts: The UTMA may make more sense if you want to make sure your child uses the account's assets for college.

With an UTMA account, the custodian does not have to distribute assets until your child reaches 21 or even 25 in some states.

With an UGMA account, however, the custodian must distribute the money when your child reaches majority, which is 18 in many states. Moreover, an UTMA account lets you invest in real estate. With an UGMA account you may transfer only money, securities, annuities, and insurance contracts. Transfers of other personal property and real estate are prohibited.

Not every state allows you to establish an UGMA or UTMA account. You'll have to check the law in your state.

It is easy to see that shifting capital to your older children is an effective way of reducing the family tax burden. There are just two caveats, though.

First, you and your spouse may not give a child more than $10,000 each (other than money you give for support) in any year without facing a possible gift tax problem.

What is the difference between a gift and support? The distinction is not always clear-cut. In Uncle Sam's eyes support items include food, clothing, lodging, medical expenses, baby-sitting costs, educational expenses, and so forth.

But what if you are an exceptionally generous soul and buy your 16-year-old daughter a $35,000 sports car? Does the IRS consider the car a gift or part of your child's support?

Chances are Uncle Sam will decide that the car is a gift. Although the courts have ruled that a child's transportation expenses count as support, the IRS would probably consider a $35,000 automobile excessive.

Second, as we have seen, once you have turned over your hard-earned cash to your child, it legally belongs to him or her—not to you. Legally, you cannot dictate how the money is spent.

If Liam decides to withdraw the $20,000 you gave him toward

college expenses and buy a used Porsche instead, legally he is free to do so. Sorry, Mom and Dad.

But giving gifts to children 14 years and older is still an attractive income-shifting device. As we will see, it is less effective for younger siblings.

You do, however, have alternatives when it comes to shifting income to younger children.

INCOME-SHIFTING TO THE YOUNGER SET

As long as a child is younger than 14, the government will tax most of the child's unearned income as if it were received by the parents.

But do not despair. This unfortunate rule does not mean that gift giving has lost all of its value as an income-shifting device to lower the family's overall tax burden.

As we have already discussed, the first $500 of the younger child's annual unearned income is not taxed at all, and the second $500 is still taxed at the child's lower rate.

Take advantage of these rules. It still makes sense to shift some income-producing assets to younger children, even if the tax savings are not dramatic.

Say you give your four-year-old son $3,000 and invest the money in a mutual fund that yields a 10 percent annual return. Your marginal tax bracket is 28 percent.

Since his annual interest is less than $1,000, he pays no tax on his first $500 of annual earnings and only 15 percent on the second $500. And at the end of ten years the $3,000 would have grown to $7,704.

What if you kept the $3,000, invested it in the same mutual fund, then gave the account to your child when he turned 14?

You would pay tax on your annual earnings at 28 percent, so the account would have grown to only $6,013. By taking advantage of this $1,000 break your family accumulated $1,691 more than it otherwise would.

Take a look at these other devices.

Savings Bonds

Ironically, one of the best income-shifting devices for younger children comes from the government itself.

If you redeem qualified U.S. savings bonds to pay educational expenses, Uncle Sam excludes the interest on the bonds from your gross income as long as you meet certain conditions:

- The bond must have been issued after December 31, 1989

- You must be 24 years old or older

- You must use the bond proceeds for qualified educational expenses incurred by you, your spouse, or dependents for higher education.

Qualified educational expenses include tuition and required fees that are over and above any scholarships, fellowships, employer-provided educational assistance, or other tuition-reduction amounts. Not eligible are expenses for any course or activity that involves sports, games, or hobbies unless the course is part of a degree program.

Also, the total proceeds of the redemption—that is, the principal and the interest—may not top the qualified educational expenses.

If they do, you must multiply the amount of interest by a fraction, using the qualified educational costs as the numerator and the aggregate redemption proceeds as the denominator. Then you may exclude the resulting sum from your income. You report the total amount received on your Schedule B of your 1040 and then attach Form 8815, "Exclusion of Interest from Series EE U.S. Savings Bonds Issued After 1989" to it to support the amount excluded.

One other caution: The law phases out the exclusion if your adjusted gross income falls within certain ranges—between $60,000 and $90,000 if you are married and file jointly and between $40,000 and $55,000 for single taxpayers. Beginning in 1991 these amounts will be adjusted annually for inflation.

You should also consider the traditional Series EE savings bonds. They mature in 12 years. But you can continue to hold onto them until 30 years after their date of issue and receive interest. (Bonds you bought between November 1982 and October 1986 mature in ten years, but you can hold onto them and receive interest until 30 years from their date of issue.)

Unless you elect to report it annually, the interest on these bonds is not taxed until the bonds mature and you cash them in. (If you cash them in before they mature, any interest you have accumulated to date is taxed at the time you redeem them.) And note that interest from Series EE bonds is not subject to state or local income taxes.

So you can give your child cash and allow him or her to buy EE bonds. Or you may buy the bonds in your child's name. The only requirement: Your child needs a Social Security number when you buy the bond or when you cash it in. If you put your number on the bond, Uncle Sam taxes the interest to you—unless you specify that the bond is a gift at the time you buy it.

Uncle Sam gives taxpayers two choices of when to report the interest income. He or she may report it annually—a good idea if the child's income is less than $1,000 and would be taxed at the child's rate or if the income from the bonds is less than $500 and would not be taxed at all. Or he or she may report the interest when the bonds are redeemed. So if your child reports the interest when the bonds are redeemed, and if at that time the child is 14 or older, the interest will be taxed at the child's lower rate, even though some of the interest was earned when the child was under 14.

If you choose to report the interest annually, but later decide that reporting it when you redeem the bond is better for you, you can switch only with the consent of the IRS.

In the past, you generally had to file Form 3115, "Application for Change in Accounting Method," within 180 days of the beginning of the tax year. That's no longer the case. Now you can file Form 3115, attached to your Form 1040, and file both forms by the due date of your return for the tax year of the change.

TIP Under this procedure, you can wait until you know your income for the year to decide whether to continue to recognize income annually or to defer the income until the bond matures or is redeemed.

☞ CAUTION Once you have used this procedure to switch to deferring income, you cannot use it again for the next 5 years.

You may purchase EE bonds for as little as $25 or as much as $5,000. (The face value equals twice the amount of the purchase price.)

The only catch: Uncle Sam imposes a cap on savings bond purchases of $15,000 (a face value of $30,000) per person per year. It does make more sense, however, to buy the smaller denominations. That way, you can cash your bonds in gradually.

You can buy EE bonds through banks and savings and loans, payroll deduction plans, the Federal Reserve, or the Bureau of the Public Debt (Parkersburg, WV 26106-1328).

There are no sales charges when you buy an EE bond. And if you keep the bond until it matures, you'll receive at the very least its full face value.

But you might actually receive more than the face value. Here is why. The interest rates on these bonds vary, but only upward. The government guarantees that at maturity you will get at least twice what you paid for them, even if interest rates have dropped precipitously. But if interest rates go up, you will collect more than the face value. And, with the extended maturity dates, the interest on these bonds continues to "pile up"—tax-deferred.

TIP There's another type of saving bonds: Series HH. In the past, you could exchange Series EE bonds that had matured for Series HH bonds. Although the interest you would earn from the HH bonds was taxed annually, you could defer the accrued interest from the Series EE bonds until the HH bonds matured.

With the extended maturity dates offered on EE bonds, it makes more sense to hold the EEs until their final maturity dates and continue to accrue tax-deferred interest.

You may buy HH bonds, which have an initial maturity of ten years, but which can be held, earning interest for 20 years after their issue dates, in multiples of $500. They give you semiannual interest on which you pay tax.

☞ CAUTION Don't list yourself as co-owner of your child's savings bonds. If you die, the bonds are included in your estate.

Growth Stocks

The same principle applies to buying growth stocks.

These are shares issued by relatively fast-growing companies that probably are paying low or no current dividends. And if there are low (less than $500) or no dividends, there is no tax to pay until your child sells the appreciated (one hopes) stock after he or she turns age 14.

Then the gain is taxed at the child's lower rate.

You could also buy the shares in your own name and transfer them to the child when he or she reaches age 14. That way you can make good use of capital losses if the stock goes down.

But remember: With growth stocks you always face the possibility that the stock prices will tumble, and you will lose some or all of your principal. So before buying these investments, you should carefully think through whether you want to take this risk with your child's education fund.

Appreciating Property

You may make a gift of any appreciating property to your child—land, collectibles, gold, coins, stamps, or art. He or she can then sell the property after turning 14, and the gain is taxed at his or her lower rate.

Tax-Exempt Municipal Bonds

Tax-exempt municipal bonds are issued by cities or states for local projects. They are free of federal income taxes. And if you buy municipal bonds issued in your own state, you usually do not pay state taxes either.

So purchasing one of these bonds for your child—or buying shares in a municipal bond fund—lets him or her avoid taxation altogether. (However, income on tax-exempt, so-called private activity bonds issued after August 7, 1986, is taxable for purposes of the alternative minimum tax.)

Remember: Buying municipal bonds or shares in a bond fund is not a way to shift income from one family member to another. It's a way to avoid taxation.

☞ **CAUTION** Any gain realized when you finally sell a tax-exempt municipal bond is subject to tax. Only the interest generated by the bond is tax-free.

So you may want to give your child money to purchase these bonds. (Remember, you and your spouse each may give a child up to $10,000 a year with no gift tax consequences.)

TIP Buy zero-coupon municipal bonds or bond funds in your child's name. Zero-coupon bonds are quite similar to U.S. Savings Bonds. They are sold at a deep discount from their face value and pay no current interest. When they mature, you receive the full face amount.

With corporate zero-coupon bonds, the IRS requires you or your child to include a portion of the discount (called original issue discount, or OID) in your or your child's gross income each year, even though you receive nothing until the bond matures. And as a result, you or your child may have to pay taxes on this amount.

But when you buy zero-coupon municipal bonds, you are home free. That is because the rules on reporting OID do not apply to tax-exempt bonds.

THE FAMILY BUSINESS

Say you own a business, and it is a sole proprietorship—that is, you report your business income on Schedule C of your Form 1040.

You have an opportunity to shift income right in your own backyard. Just put your child to work in your business, and you will reap a double tax benefit.

First, your child's wages are considered earned income, which is always taxed at the child's lower rate, regardless of his or her age.

Second, the wages that you pay your kids are legitimate business expenses. So they are tax-deductible.

And that is not all. Here are two other benefits.

Under a special provision in the tax law you do not have to pay Social Security taxes on your child's wages as long as he or she is under 18. (Neither does your child.)

What's more, your child may open an Individual Retirement Account (IRA) and shelter some or all of his or her earnings. Under the rules a child may sock away and divert the lesser of $2,000 or 100 percent of his or her earnings in an IRA, assuming, of course, that your child's AGI is less than $25,000.

The earnings of an IRA are tax deferred—that is, your child pays no taxes on the earnings that accumulate until the money is withdrawn, usually at retirement. (But keep in mind: An IRA is a long-range investment. If your child withdraws money before age 59½, he or she will have to pay income taxes and a 10 percent early withdrawal penalty to boot. We cover IRAs in Chapter 23.)

Say your child contributes $2,000 to an IRA in 1990 and deducts the full amount. Next he subtracts $3,250 for the 1990 standard deduction.

His deductions, then, add up to $5,250. So that means he could earn as much as $5,250 in wages in 1990 without paying federal income tax.

☞ CAUTION You have to be sure that the job is a legitimate one and that you can justify the salary that you pay. Abuse—paying 12-year-old Sally $10 an hour to sweep up—may attract Uncle Sam's attention and ire.

The business does not have to be a sole proprietorship, but if the family firm is a corporation or partnership (other than a family partnership), you will have to pay Social Security and unemployment compensation taxes on wages you pay your children. And your children will have to pay Social Security taxes on their wages. Obviously, doing so will eat up some of your income tax savings.

The exemption applies to partnerships only if the parent-and-child relationship exists between the child and each of the partners—for instance, a family partnership where the mother and father are the only partners.

CHILD CARE CREDIT

The child- or dependent-care credit was designed primarily to help parents defray the cost of child care. For the most part, the credit may be taken by single parents who work outside the home or by married couples if both husband and wife are employed outside the home.

To qualify you must meet a host of requirements. For one, the expenses you incur must be necessary for you to be employed or actively seek employment away from home.

Also, you must bear financial responsibility for maintaining your household, and you must spend money for the care of any of the following dependents while you are on the job:

- Youngsters under 13 who are dependents.

- Dependents who are physically or mentally incapable of caring for themselves—a person with Down's syndrome, for example.

The child-care credit ranges from a low of 20 percent to a high of 30 percent of expenses paid during the year. The percentage is based on your AGI. If your AGI comes to $10,000 or less, the 30 percent credit applies; if it tops $28,000, the 20 percent credit applies.

What if your income falls between $10,000 and $28,000? The 30 percent credit is reduced by 1 percent for each $2,000 of AGI in excess of $10,000. For instance, a person with an AGI of $14,000 would qualify for a 28 percent credit.

The credit applies only to employment-related expenses of up to $2,400 for one dependent and $4,800 for two or more dependents—so the maximum credit is $1,440 (30 percent times $4,800). The IRS defines employment-related expenses as the cost of hiring people to care for your dependent or to provide household services—cleaning, cooking, and so on.

☞ **CAUTION** You should know that in one case the Tax Court denied the child-care credit for children's airline expenses. During school holidays the parent paid airfare to send her children to stay with relatives, rather than hiring a baby-sitter.

The airfare did not qualify as an employment-related expense, the judge ruled, because it was not an expense for household services or for the care of a qualifying individual.

The IRS and the court rejected the parents's claim that the children were under the care of the cabin attendants. There was no evidence, the ruling said, that the attendants were under the direction of the children's parent.

☞ **CAUTION** If your child-care expenses top your earnings, watch out. Uncle Sam says the credit may be applied only to expenses that are equal to or less than your earned income. (If you are married, you must use the earned income of the spouse who makes the least amount of money.)

Say you earn $2,000 working part-time, and your spouse earns $25,000 working full-time. Also, you and your spouse collect $3,000 interest from your money market fund. So your joint AGI comes to $30,000. You pay someone $2,400 to care for your child while you are on the job.

Under the law you may claim only $2,000 worth of child-care expenses. And your credit totals $400 (20 percent times $2,000), not $480 (20 percent times $2,400).

TIP Say you are married and file a joint return. You work outside the home, and your spouse is a full-time student. Uncle Sam gives you a break. You are entitled to claim a child-care credit, even though your spouse is a student and not employed outside the home.

When it comes time to calculate your child-care credit, the rules assume that your "student spouse" earned $200 a month for each month he or she attended school full-time. If you claim a credit for more than one child, the amount jumps to $400 a month.

CAUTION If your employer provides a dependent-care assistance plan, you may have to pass up the child-care credit. Here is why.

The law says you must reduce the amount of expenses eligible for the credit dollar-for-dollar by the amount excluded from your gross income under the dependent-care assistance plan (up to a maximum of $5,000). Doing so may reduce or completely eliminate any expenses you have that would otherwise make you eligible for the child-care credit.

TIP How do you decide whether the child-care credit or the dependent-care assistance plan provides the greater tax benefit to you?

The answer is, you must run the numbers.

Usually, if you are in the 28 percent tax bracket, the dependent-care assistance plan provides a greater benefit because it reduces not only your taxable income but also your wage base for purpose of calculating Social Security taxes.

CAUTION The amount you set aside in a dependent-care assistance plan will be forfeited if not used for the payment of eligible expenses.

TIP To take advantage of either the child-care credit or an employer-provided dependent care assistance plan, you must provide your child care provider's Social Security number (or other taxpayer identification number) along with the person's correct name and address, in Part I of Form 2441, "Child and Dependent Care Expenses," which you file with your Form 1040.

Record the necessary information on Form W-10, "Dependent

Care Provider's Identification and Certification,'' which you don't file with your return, but keep for your records to substantiate the information you included on Form 2441.

QUESTIONS AND ANSWERS

QUESTION: *I own my own business, and I will report my earnings on Schedule C of my 1990 Form 1040. My net profit for 1990 should add up to $45,000. Should I hire my two kids, aged 12 and 13, to help with the filing and cleaning? Will this strategy save me taxes? And, if so, how much?*

Let's say you'll pay each of your kids $250 a month ($3,000 a year) for their efforts. And you'll deduct this amount—$6,000 in total—on your Schedule C.

This write-off will reduce your business profits of $45,000 by $6,000. So your total savings in income taxes should be $1,561. How do we arrive at this number? You receive a deduction of $6,000 for the salary you'll pay to your kids, leaving $39,000 in self-employment earnings. But, as a result of two new changes in the law for 1990, the computation gets a little tricky.

The first change in the law: This year, self-employeds may deduct a portion of their Social Security self-employment tax in determining their self-employment wage base. (For 1990, the self-employment tax rate is 15.3 percent on the first $51,300.) Here's how to do it.

Multiply net earnings (in this case, $39,000) by one-half the tax rate (7.65 percent). Subtract the product—$2,984—from net earnings of $39,000. Multiply this amount—$36,016—by the tax rate of 15.3 percent to get the self-employment tax owed—$5,510.

The second change in the law: Beginning in 1990, self-employeds will receive an income tax deduction for one-half of the self-employment tax paid. (You report this deduction on line 25, Deduction for self-employment tax, which will appear under Adjustments to Income on the 1990 Form 1040.)

So, you'll receive an additional deduction that reduces your adjusted gross income by $2,755 (or one-half of your self employment tax of $5,510). Should you not hire your kids, your deduction for the self-employment tax would be $3,179 (or one-half of $6,358, the self-employment tax on $45,000) or $424 more.

Thus, if you hire your kids, you'll have a net increase of deductions of $5,576 ($6,000 salary less the $424 deduction you lost by hiring your kids). Assuming you're in a 28 percent bracket, your total savings in income taxes is $1,561 ($5,576 multiplied by 28 percent).

You also save $848 in self-employment taxes—the difference between $6,358, the self-employment tax owed on your net earnings of $45,000 (that is, without your kids on the payroll), and $5,510, your net earnings of $39,000 (which takes into account the $6,000 you paid to your kids).

Your total tax savings add up to $2,409 ($1,561 in income tax plus $848 in Social Security tax). Meanwhile your kids will pay no federal taxes on the amount they receive because it is less than their 1990 standard deduction of $3,250 (assuming, of course, that they will report no other income). And neither you nor your children pay Social Security taxes on their wages. So by paying your kids to help you—rather than just giving them money—you'll slash your family tax bill by $2,409.

Not a bad deal, you say. But what if your earnings, after you deduct what you have paid your child will top the $51,300 self-employment tax cap?

If your earnings are greater than $51,300 but less than $55,550, you may still receive some self-employment tax benefit. Let's say that in the above example, you expect your earnings before you pay your kids to be $60,000. Your self-employment tax would be $7,849—you arrive at this figure by subtracting 7.65 percent of $60,000 ($4,590) from $60,000. Since this result—$55,410 or $60,000 minus $4,590—is greater than the cap of $51,300, you use $51,300 times 15.3 percent to arrive at your self-employment tax of $7,849.

By paying your kids $6,000, however, your anticipated 1990 income will be $54,000 (or $60,000 minus $6,000). To determine the amount of self-employment tax, subtract 7.65 percent of $54,000 (or $4,131) from $54,000. Since this result—$49,869—is less than $51,300, you would use $49,869 and your self-employment tax would be $7,630. So you would save $219 ($7,849 minus $7,630) in self-employment tax by having your kids on the payroll.

If your earnings after you have paid your child exceed $55,550, you save income taxes, but not self-employment tax, by having your kids on the payroll.

Still not a bad deal, you say, and you are right. One drawback:

The Social Security benefits you receive at retirement are based on the amount you pay in. So, potentially, you could receive less in Social Security when you retire.

QUESTION: *When it comes to a child's income, who is liable for any penalties and interest for failing to file a return or for paying the tax?*

The child is responsible. The law says that a child's parents are not responsible for paying penalties and interest or taxes simply because they are responsible for filing the return on their child's behalf.

25

Crash Course: Tax-Wise Ways to Finance Your Child's Education

As astronomical as college costs are today, they are going to climb even higher in years to come. In fact, they are expected to nearly triple by the year 2000.

This kind of price escalation is not a worry if you have won the state lottery. The rest of us, however, have to prepare for financing our children's future education, a process that includes tax planning.

So that is what we do in this chapter.

In the first section we suggest tax-efficient ways to put money aside for college expenses ahead of time. Then we show you how to get the most out of the cash you set aside for college costs, including minimizing the share that has to go to Uncle Sam.

PLANNING AHEAD

What is the best way, tax-wise, to finance your child's education? The answer, as you might expect if you have read Chapter 24, depends in large part on whether the child you are saving for has reached 14 years of age yet. That is because your opportunities to minimize the tax bite are far fewer before your child reaches 14.

So first let's look at the techniques that apply in the case of a younger child. Even with the harsher rules, you do have some options when it comes to cutting the tax bite on college savings.

PRE-14 STRATEGIES

Say you've set aside a few dollars for your child's education, and you want to put them in an investment that pays current income—dividends or interest, say.

Should you make the investment in your name? Or should you make it in your child's name? If your child is under age 14, it does not much matter taxwise.

Here's why. As we have seen, a child under age 14 pays taxes on his or her unearned income at the higher of the parents' rate or the child's rate. And the parents' rate is almost always higher.

The only significant difference is that younger children are not taxed on the first $500 of unearned income, and the next $500 is taxed at their lower 15 percent rate. Given a maximum 1990 tax rate of 28 percent, this small break could yield a tax saving of up to $205 each year.

But keep in mind: Because of a 5 percent surtax on income falling between certain levels, some higher-income taxpayers will find themselves paying tax at a 33 percent marginal rate. And for these people the tax savings could jump to $255 each year.

These savings help a little, of course, but not much.

So about the best tax strategy you can use when putting aside education money for younger children is one that involves tax deferral—delaying the tax until the child reaches 14. After that point, more tax saving is possible.

How can you defer taxes? Look again in Chapter 24 at the strategies we suggest for the under-14-year-old. As you recall they include buying

- Series EE U.S. savings bonds.

- Non-dividend-paying growth stocks.

- Appreciating property.

- Tax-exempt municipal bonds.

Another option you might consider for your pre-14 child is not exactly a tax-deferral device. The effect is much the same, however.

MINORS' TRUSTS

Minors' trusts allow you to make one or more gifts to a child—subject to the usual $10,000 per person per year limit, or, in tax lingo, the annual gift tax exclusion.

This rule means that you and your spouse can add up to $20,000 a year to each of your children's trusts without worrying about a federal gift tax. (Check with your tax adviser for the rules governing gift taxes levied by your state.)

The principal and earnings that accumulate remain in the trust until the trustee—who may be anyone you would like—distributes them.

The trust document, which creates the trust, must specify that the trustee has the discretionary power to distribute the property and income for the child's benefit until the child reaches age 21. Of course, you are free to specify how and when you want the assets distributed, but unless the trust document grants the trustee the authority to carry out your wishes, the gift tax exclusion does not apply.

Note: It is a good idea not to name yourself as trustee. If you do and if you die, the assets of the trust would be included in your taxable estate.

The income earned by the property in the trust is taxed each year but at a partially reduced rate as long as you allow earnings to accumulate within the trust.

The reason is that Uncle Sam taxes the trust, not the recipient. The first $5,450 of income in a minor's trust is taxed at only 15 percent in 1990, the rest at 28 percent. (The IRS phases out the 15 percent rate by applying a 33 percent rate on that part of a trust's taxable income that falls between $14,150 and $28,320.)

The potential annual tax savings is $709—that is, the difference between the first $5,450 of trust income being taxed to the trust at a rate of 15 percent versus being taxed at a potential rate of 28 percent to the individual recipient.

Income distributed from the trust, on the other hand, is taxed under the so-called kiddie tax rules.

Another tax advantage of a minor's trust is that the rules allow you to specify when a child is to receive the dollars in trust. If you want to ensure that a child spends his or her money on college, pick 18 or 21 as the age for distribution of the funds.

Another important point: When income and principal are eventually distributed to a child at age 18, say, there is no need to recalculate the tax on that income to account for the period of accumulation. With other types of trusts you might have to perform this complicated recalculation.

The minor's trust you establish does have to comply with two major conditions.

All of the assets in the trust must be distributed to the beneficiary by the time he or she reaches age 21. And should the child die before reaching age 21, the trust document must provide for the assets and accumulated income to be paid to his or her estate or be subject to the child's general power of appointment—legal talk that means the child must have the right to name the recipient of the balance in the trust in the event of his or her death.

Is a minor's trust worth the trouble—and the expense? Remember, you are going to have to pay administrative fees to a bank or other institution that acts as trustee. (These fees typically range from 0.5 to two percent of the trust's principal.) The answer is: Probably, if you have a lot of money—$10,000 a year or more, say—to put into it.

Say, for instance, that you and your spouse together give your child $20,000 each year for three years, beginning with the child's first birthday.

Assume that the trust funds earn income at a 10 percent annual rate and that taxes on the first $5,450 of annual income are paid at the 15 percent rate.

By the time the child reaches 18 and the tuition bills come due, the trust will have grown to $202,591. Had you simply saved the money and paid taxes at your normal 28 percent rate, the fund would have grown to only $182,796. You are $19,795 ahead by having set up the trust fund.

Don't forget, though, to offset this amount by the administrative costs of the trust. These charges vary from institution to institution (they are deductible if they exceed two percent of the trust's adjusted gross income). Ask your bank or trust company about the charges it imposes.

A word of caution: If the income from the trust is used to support your child, it is taxable to you. The laws defining legal support vary from state to state.

CRUMMEY TRUST

There's another type of trust that can also be useful. Called a Crummey Trust after the court decision that recognized it, this trust basically allows the distribution of principal and income at the trustee's discretion but does not require the mandatory termination of the trust when the child reaches 21. Instead, the trust document may allow distribution of the principal in stages.

The catch, however, is that the trustee must notify the beneficiary child annually of his or her right to withdraw over a reasonable period—usually 30 to 60 days—any gifts made to the trust each year.

Whether the child actually withdraws anything from the trust or not, he or she will be taxed each year on the amount of the trust that *could* have been withdrawn. Another drawback: Income that accumulates above this amount is subject to recalculation of income tax under the complex throwback rules.

Because Crummey Trusts are complicated, and because under some circumstances they may actually increase the overall tax liability of a child older than 14, you should consult your tax adviser before creating one.

Keep in mind, as well, one other idea—which we also covered in the preceding chapter—for your under-14-year-old child.

Parents who are business owners can shift some of their income to their younger tykes by putting the youngsters to work. (See Chapter 24 for more information on employing your child.)

BACCALAUREATE BONDS

Here is an idea worth considering. Why not purchase so-called baccalaureate bonds? These bonds are a special type of zero-coupon municipal bonds offered by some states.

These bonds are safer than many other types of municipal bonds because they are backed by the full faith and credit of your state.

And income from these bonds is exempt from federal tax. The same is true for state and local taxes as long as you continue to live in the state that issued them. Also, baccalaureate bonds are less likely than other municipal bonds to be called early.

POST-14 STRATEGIES

Just because your child has reached age 14 does not mean that it is too late to start saving for college expenses. It is true that you do not have as much time to accumulate assets when your child is this old.

On the other hand, it is only when the child reaches 14 that Uncle Sam truly becomes your partner in the savings effort. From this point on, the child's unearned income will be taxed at his or her rate, not yours.

So at this point you can begin to do some income-shifting—transferring income on which you would pay a high tax rate to your now less-taxed youngster.

How do you shift income? Usually by gifts.

Just give a child $10,000 or $20,000 with no strings attached? Not exactly. To make sure the kids do not blow their college money on something you would consider foolish, you will probably want to use the Uniform Gifts to Minors Act (UGMA) or the Uniform Transfers to Minors Act (UTMA). (See Chapter 24 for more on UGMA or UTMA accounts.)

WHAT TO DO WHEN SAVING TIME IS OVER

Your child is a high school senior and ready to choose a college. The time for long-range planning is over. Either you have earmarked money for covering college expenses, or you have not. In either case, now you have to come up with the cash. So what do you do?

You have three options, which you will probably want to use in some combination. You can tap your capital, including whatever assets, if any, you or your child have been accumulating against this day. You or the prospective freshman can borrow money. And you can always apply for financial aid from the government or from the school.

Let's run through the options to see what possibilities they offer and how you can coordinate them.

TAPPING CAPITAL

If you have specifically put aside some savings or assets as college money, you will have no reluctance to liquidate them when the bills come in.

But even if you have not had such foresight, you can nevertheless tap some of your assets and still get a bit of tax help from Uncle Sam.

Let's say that you own stocks or bonds that have appreciated in value. Naturally, you might think of selling some of them to raise college cash. But if you sell in 1990 you're going to be taxed on the gain that you realize at a 28 (or 33) percent tax rate.

Why not, instead, give the stocks or bonds to your college-bound daughter? (Remember, you and your spouse each may make up to $10,000 worth of gifts annually tax free. If you give more, your gift tax liability will typically be covered by the unified gift and estate tax credit.)

Your daughter will have to pay the taxes on the appreciated value of the securities.

But she'll pay taxes only at her 15 percent rate—as long as her gain plus her other taxable income doesn't top $19,450, which is the limit for single people paying at the 15 percent rate. By giving her the assets to sell, there is more after-tax money left to pay the college bills. How much more?

Assume that a stock you bought many years ago has appreciated in value by $15,000. If you sell it, you get the $15,000 appreciation minus $4,200 ($15,000 times 28 percent) in taxes. In other words, out of the $15,000 gain, you get to keep $10,800.

If you give the stock to your daughter, and she sells it, her tax bill will add up to just $2,250 ($15,000 times 15 percent). She gets to keep $12,750 of the $15,000 gain. So by giving the stock to your daughter, she winds up with $1,950 more than you would to put toward tuition bills.

Just bear in mind, though, that she does not have to sell the stock. Once you give it to her, you have lost legal control over what she does with it.

BORROWING POWER

If you have to borrow to finance a youngster's education, probably the best way is through a home-equity loan. Why? The interest is deductible.

As a result of tax reform, you may not fully write off the interest you pay on a student loan unless the loan is secured by your home. On any other sort of loan, interest is only 10 percent deductible in 1990 and not deductible at all thereafter.

On the other hand, you may deduct interest on a home equity loan of up to $100,000 no matter how you use the money. That fact makes home-equity loans very attractive for financing education costs.

☞ CAUTION   Your kids can always borrow some or all of the cash they need for college from you, provided you have got it to lend. But beware.

You must be careful to treat the transaction in a businesslike manner or Uncle Sam might consider the loan a gift. So make sure to write up a promissory note that states the amount your child borrowed, the interest rate, and the repayment schedule.

And note, too: Zero-interest loans to offspring do not impress Uncle Sam. He will impute (meaning attribute) interest income to you and interest expense to the borrower.

Furthermore, whether it is a zero-interest loan or one made at fair market rates, you actually incur a tax disadvantage when you lend money to your children. These loans result in greater income to you, the higher-bracket taxpayer. And they produce a limited deduction to your child, the lower-bracket taxpayer, because the interest is personal interest and limited to a 10 percent deduction in 1990.

So tax-wise, it is not a smart move.

SCHOLARSHIPS AND FELLOWSHIPS

Did you know that degree-seeking candidates who are awarded scholarships or fellowships may exclude from their income much of the money they receive? And it makes no difference whether they are in graduate or undergraduate school.

If your son, for instance, is in a degree-granting program, he may exclude from income amounts he uses for tuition and books, equipment, supplies, and other course fees. But amounts that are earmarked for room, board, or other living expenses are fully taxable.

And he must pay tax on wages he receives for research, teaching, or other services that the school may require as a condition of receiving the scholarship or fellowship.

☞ CAUTION   The IRS has issued proposed regulations that strictly define related course expenses. For example, say your child uses part of his or her scholarship to buy a word processor because a professor suggested it might be useful. The professor did not, however, require that your child use the word processor as part of the course. In this case, the amount your child spends is not considered part of the tax-free scholarship. Instead, it counts as taxable income.

TIP If your child receives a scholarship or fellowship, it is a good idea to keep records that prove that the money covered qualified expenses.

For example, he or she should hold onto copies of bills, receipts, canceled checks, or other documents that verify how scholarship proceeds were spent. In addition, the student should retain documents that list study aids—a calculator or personal computer, say—that are required for each course.

QUESTIONS AND ANSWERS

QUESTION: *I have heard a lot about prepaid tuition plans. What are these plans? And are they a good idea?*

Prepaid tuition plans actually come in two general types, each with some potential variations.

With the first type, you pay all four years of tuition when your child becomes a freshman. Because you pay at the first-year price, you are protected against future increases.

These plans may be a good idea under two conditions: You can afford the hefty up-front cost, and you are fairly certain your child will not want to transfer. In any case it makes sense to check whether your money is refundable if your son or daughter does switch schools.

The second, newer type of prepaid plan is a much dicier proposition. These plans, which have been established by some colleges and at least one state, let you pay four years' tuition at a steep discount when your son or daughter is a mere tot. When your child is old enough to enter college, his or her tuition is already paid, presumably at a price far below current levels.

One drawback is immediately obvious. Should your child decide against the college you have paid for, or should that institution close its doors, you may lose your money entirely. Or the college or state may refund only the amount you have paid in—with no allowance for many years' interest on your cash.

Granted, some schools are forming umbrella plans that allow

your scholar a choice of institutions. But there is no guarantee that any of these colleges will appeal to your youngster.

And the plans may have tax-related drawbacks. In one case the IRS found that the plan created by the Michigan legislature triggered three tax liabilities.

First, it triggered a gift tax to the parent when he or she purchased the contract. Furthermore, the IRS said, the $10,000 annual gift tax exclusion did not apply in the case of prepaid education programs.

Second, the plan created a tax liability for the trust in which the funds were deposited on the amount of the trust's earnings.

Third, the prepaid plan also triggered a tax liability for the child when he or she began school. The amount taxed is the difference between the annual tuition cost and one quarter of the cost of the tuition contract (assuming that the contract covered four years of tuition). This means that the income earned by the original purchase price of the contract is actually taxed twice—once when it is earned by the trust and then again when the child receives the education. (If you consider the fact that the original gift was probably made from after-tax dollars, the gift, in effect, has been subject to yet a third tax.)

The IRS ruling on the Michigan plan means that its only real savings (if any) to the individual who buys it is the difference between the future value of the current price paid and actual tuition charge when the child enters school. You will also want to determine whether the income earned by a prepayment trust in your state is subject to state as well as federal taxes. If it is, that is another reduction of savings overall.

But for many taxpayers these programs are one way to ensure that their children will not be denied college because of lack of funds.

QUESTION: *My parents have offered to pick up the tab for my daughter's schooling. Are there any tax angles I should know about?*

You are in luck.

Generous grandparents (or anyone else) may pay your child's educational expenses and still make other tax-free annual gifts of up to $10,000 each ($20,000 as a couple) per recipient.

The only qualification: They must pay the college or university directly. So make sure they write their check to the school—not to you or your daughter. Otherwise, the IRS will consider the amount of the payment as a gift to which the $10,000 annual exclusion will apply.

QUESTION: *My son was planning to live in a dorm. But friends tell me that it may pay off to buy a small condominium for him to live in instead. Do you agree?*

There certainly can be tax advantages to seeking alternative housing for your son.

Say you buy an off-campus apartment. You may, under the tax law, treat this unit as your second home and deduct mortgage interest and property taxes. (Uncle Sam allows you to deduct interest expense on your principal residence and one other house; property taxes are deductible on any home(s) you own.) Meanwhile, your son has a free place to live.

Or you could rent the apartment to your son and deduct—subject to the passive loss rules—mortgage interest, property taxes, maintenance, utilities, depreciation, and other expenses associated with maintaining rental property. If you end up with a loss, you may be able to use it to offset your regular income.

But the laws in this area are complex.

First, Uncle Sam requires that the house be your son's principal residence. Also, you must charge him and any of his friends a fair-market rent. And you must actively manage the property yourself—that is, you must participate in collecting rents, authorizing repair work and maintenance, and so on.

If your adjusted gross income (AGI) is $100,000 or less, you may deduct from your income up to $25,000 in losses from rental real estate in which you actively participate each year. But this cap is gradually phased out if your AGI falls between $100,000 and $150,000. So when your AGI reaches $150,000, you are entitled to use the losses you incur but only against other passive income.

When your child graduates, you can sell your property. You may now deduct any losses you were unable to take while you owned the property. And, with luck, your property will have appreciated in value.

There's also a tax bonus to setting your son up with a place he can share: You may hire him to manage the property.

Your son can earn up to $3,250 tax-free, provided he has no other income, and you can write that off against the rent his friends pay you. Just be sure that the amount you pay junior for this job is reasonable, or the IRS may challenge the arrangement.

QUESTION: *I plan to claim a dependency exemption for my son, who is 25 and a full-time student. May I?*

No, you may not claim a dependency exemption for a student who reaches the age of 24 before the end of the year.

Uncle Sam does carve out an exception to this rule for students whose gross incomes add up to less than the exemption amount—$2,050 in 1990.

TIP Even if you are unable to claim an exemption for your child on your tax return, your child may claim an exemption on his or her own return.

26

The Lowdown on Withholding and Estimated Taxes

April 15 may be tax day, but most of us pay taxes all year long. If you do not, you may face a rude shock when you do file your next tax return.

Uncle Sam penalizes people who underpay their taxes.

Most of us pay taxes the easy way—through *payroll withholding*. That way, we never see the money that our employers send to the IRS on our behalf.

On the other hand, those of us who are *self-employed* or who have substantial nonwage income—dividends, say—must make *estimated tax* payments four times a year.

But it makes no difference whether you make tax payments yourself or rely on the company paymaster to withhold them for you. Uncle Sam still holds you responsible for making sure that the taxes you pay are adequate according to the law.

In this chapter we cover the rules governing withholding and estimated taxes. We show you how to figure out what the law requires you to pay in estimated taxes. And we explain what happens if you do not make estimated payments or if your payments fall short.

Finally, we suggest some strategies for keeping your estimated tax liability, as well as any penalties, to a minimum.

WITHHOLDING TAXES

Most of us pay taxes on our earnings the painless way—through payroll withholding. Our employers deduct the money from our paychecks and forward it to Uncle Sam.

The amount of income tax our employers withhold from our paychecks depends on two factors: our earnings and the information we provide on our W-4 Forms.

When we begin a new job, we must fill out a Form W-4 and return it to our employers. What happens if you do not fill out a W-4? The law requires your employer to withhold taxes at the highest rate—that is, as a single taxpayer with no allowances for dependents.

If you found that you paid too little or too much in withholding taxes when you filed your 1989 return, you should fill out a new W-4 in 1990. That way, the amount withheld from your pay will more accurately reflect the tax you expect to owe Uncle Sam.

When you fill out the worksheet provided on page one of the W-4 to figure the number of allowances you may take, you must take into account not only your income but your spouse's income and any nonwage income, such as interest or dividends, that the two of you earn.

Don't make the mistake some taxpayers do of overlooking the value of certain fringe benefits that are subject to withholding.

If you paid too little in withholding taxes last year, you should consider reducing the number of allowances you take compared to the number you claimed previously. (No need to worry: The number of allowances you claim for withholding purposes does not affect the number of exemptions you may claim on your 1040.)

You should know that the sooner you revise your W-4, the more your withholding will approximate your actual tax liability for 1990. And this fact is important.

Why? As we will see, you must pay 90 percent of your current year's tax liability or 100 percent of last year's tax paid through withholding or estimated taxes to escape underpayment penalties on estimated taxes.

What happens if the number of withholding allowances you are entitled to decreases to fewer than the number you have previously claimed on your W-4?

In this case you must file a new W-4 within ten days of the event that led to the decrease in allowances—you and your spouse divorce, say, or you no longer furnish more than half of the support of a dependent you had previously claimed.

And here is another rule: If you claim more than ten withholding allowances, your employer must send copies of your W-4 to the IRS. And you may then be asked to verify your allowances.

The IRS wants to make sure you fill the W-4 form out correctly. So Uncle Sam may fine you $500 if he discovers you deliberately filed, with no reasonable basis, a Form W-4 that results in your having less tax withheld than you should.

But take heart: The IRS has stated that taxpayers who make honest mistakes in calculating their withholding are not the targets of the $500 penalty.

The law also imposes criminal penalties—of $1,000 or a year in jail or both—if you willfully supply false or fraudulent information or fail to supply information that might require an increase in your withholding.

TIP If both you and your spouse are employed, the IRS recommends that the spouse with the higher salary take all of the withholding allowances. That way, your withholding will more closely approximate your actual tax liability.

If you have more than one job, or if your spouse works, you may claim all of your allowances on one job or you may claim some on each job. However, you may not claim the same allowances on both jobs.

Say, for example, that you spend your days working for XYZ Corp. and your nights for ABC Co. You claim your four withholding allowances—for your four children—when you fill out your Form W-4 with XYZ. When you file a W-4 with ABC, you claim no withholding allowances for your children.

TIP As soon as you discover your employer has withheld too much tax, you should immediately file a new W-4 claiming as many exemptions as allowable.

Of course, this strategy makes sense only if you discover the overwithholding before the end of the year. So periodically review your pay stubs to make sure you aren't giving Uncle Sam a float—that is, an interest-free loan—on your overpaid tax dollars.

Also, make sure that you take into account a new marriage, a new child—whether by birth or adoption—or a new house. These changes may increase the number of withholding allowances you may be able to claim.

TIP Your children are completely exempt from withholding if they paid no income tax last year and expect to pay none this year. This rule is a plus for those youngsters who file returns just to collect a tax refund. But this exception applies only to income tax, not Social Security.

To claim this exemption, your children must give their employers a completed Form W-4. This exemption is good for only one year.

So if your children were exempt from withholding in 1990 and expect to be exempt in 1991, make sure they file a new Form W-4 by February 15, 1991. Otherwise, they will be subject to income-tax withholding on their wages for the entire year.

Also, if your children have no tax withheld this year but expect to pay income taxes next year, they must file new W-4s by December 1, 1990, for the 1991 tax year.

CAUTION If you claim your children as dependents on your return, they may not claim personal allowances for themselves on their W-4s.

And this rule translates into more kids having taxes withheld from their pay than ever before. Here is why. Since a child loses the personal exemption when the parents claim it, he or she can earn in 1990 only up to $3,250—the amount of the standard deduction that year—without paying income tax and without having to file a return.

But remember: If your child reports any combination of earned and *unearned income* greater than $500, he or she is not exempt from withholding and must file a return.

TIP If your child works only part-time or summers, his or her employer may overwithhold because the amount of withholding is based on the assumption that a worker's pay continues for the entire year.

So your child should request that the employer use the part-year method to withhold taxes. The result: Your child will not end up making an interest-free loan to Uncle Sam in the form of extra withholding. Rather, he or she will pocket more after-tax dollars in each paycheck.

To qualify for this method, your child must meet two requirements. First, he or she must be a calendar-year taxpayer—that is, he or she must pay taxes on a 12-month year that runs from January 1 to December 31. (Almost every child meets this requirement.)

Second, your youngster must expect to remain employed fewer than 245 days during the year, and that includes weekends, vacation days, and sick days. The clock starts running the first day your child starts to work and stops on his or her last day of employment.

The next step is to request in writing that your child's employer use the part-time method of withholding. This request must state that your child passes the two tests. And if your child worked for another employer during the calendar year, he or she must include the date of his or her last day on the job.

YOUR QUARTERLY ESTIMATED TAX PAYMENTS

If you are self-employed or you report income beyond wages and salaries, you must make your tax payments in the form of estimated taxes.

The IRS expects to get your estimated tax payments once a quarter. For calendar-year taxpayers, the due dates are April 15, June 15, September 15, and January 15.

If the due date falls on a Saturday, Sunday, or legal holiday, your payment is considered on time if you make it on the next business day.

You should know that the IRS considers the postmark on the envelope the date of payment—as long as the envelope is postmarked by the U.S. Postal Service and not by a private postage meter. If you are uneasy about the reliability of the U.S. mails, you might want to send your payment by registered or certified mail. That way you will have proof positive—via your receipt—that you mailed your estimated tax on time.

TIP Uncle Sam says you may skip your January estimated tax payment if you file your return and pay your tax bill in full on or before January 31st.

TIP People who make their living farming or fishing get special treatment under the tax law. They need to make only a single estimated tax payment of two-thirds of their estimated current year's liability. And that payment is not due until January 15 of the following year.

What's more, they need to make no estimated payments at all if they file their tax returns and pay their full tax bills by March 1.

Also exempted from the quarterly payment requirement are individuals whose estimated current-year tax liability—after credit for taxes that are withheld by their employers—is less than $500. Teenagers often fall into this category.

Excluded, too, are people who owed no tax last year. (These individuals must be U.S. citizens or they must have been U.S. residents for the entire previous 12-month period.)

FIGURING YOUR PAYMENT

How much, exactly, must you pay by the due dates? The tax law requires that your four quarterly payments total either

- 100 percent of the tax you paid during the previous year—that is, the amount of tax shown on your previous return, assuming you had a 12-month taxable year, or

- 90 percent of the tax that you will owe in the current year—that is, the amount listed on the tax return you file for the current year.

So the IRS gives you an option, which you may use to your advantage. How? Consider this example. Assume that last year your tax liability came to $35,000.

This year, you estimate, it will total $40,000. The question is, how much should you fork over to the IRS in quarterly payments during the current year?

You may send Uncle Sam either $35,000—the amount of last year's tax—or $36,000—90 percent of the $40,000 you estimate you will owe this year.

Naturally, you choose the $35,000 option.

So far, we have talked just about the total of your quarterly estimated payments for the year. What about each individual payment? The government requires that each of your quarterly payments equal or exceed 25 percent of either:

- 100 percent of last year's tax liability, or

- 90 percent of the current year's tax liability.

TIP The law provides an alternative method—the so-called *annualization method*—that you may use for determining what you owe.

This method is used primarily by self-employed people with seasonal or fluctuating incomes. With this method, you may pay installments that actually reflect the income you earn in the period immediately before the installment is due.

If your annualized tax installment is less than you would pay under the minimums we just described, you may safely pay it without being underpaid in your estimated taxes. But you must attach Form 2210, "Underpayment of Estimated Taxes by Individuals," to your Form 1040 to show that you are not subject to the penalty.

To help you annualize your income and figure your adjusted self-employment income for each quarter, the IRS provides worksheets in IRS Publication 505, "Tax Withholding and Estimated Tax," and in the instructions to Form 2210.

THE TAB FOR UNDERPAYMENT

If you come up short on your quarterly estimated tax payments, the IRS will impose a penalty on the amount of the shortfall.

The percentage amount used to calculate the penalty varies—it rises or falls with current interest rates (11 percent as of the fourth quarter of 1990). Moreover, unlike the practice in past years, if you borrow money to pay your estimated income taxes, the interest you pay on the loan is not fully deductible.

This interest is classified as personal interest, which is only 10 percent deductible in 1990 (see Chapter 5).

So should you borrow to avoid the penalty?

The answer is probably no, given the fact that it is hard in today's market to borrow money at a rate less than the 11 percent used to determine the underpayment penalty.

TIP If you must borrow to pay your estimated taxes, use a portion of a home-equity loan. That way, the interest on this loan is fully deductible. (Uncle Sam imposes a few restrictions on the deductibility of interest on home-equity loans. We cover these rules in Chapter 5.)

Employ this same strategy to pay an underpayment penalty. The penalty is nondeductible, but you could write off the interest on the money that you borrow to pay it.

Clearly, the tax law supplies some sound reasons for making sure that you satisfy the IRS's quarterly payment requirements.

But the specifics of those payments are a bit tricky sometimes, and the unwary taxpayer may find that he or she has quite unwittingly underpaid the estimated taxes due.

Then there's the alternative minimum tax (AMT) to consider. (See Chapter 20 for more on the AMT.)

The amount of AMT you might owe counts when it comes to determining the percentage of estimated tax you must pay in order to avoid a penalty. So does the amount of Social Security self-employment tax that you may owe on, say, fees you receive as a freelance consultant.

When any single quarterly payment falls short—even if you make up the shortfall in a subsequent payment—the IRS maintains you underpaid and will impose a penalty. And this rule holds true even if you eventually receive a tax refund when you file your 1990 return.

Say, for example, that your tax last year added up to $40,000 and that this year it will total $80,000. Your quarterly payments are either $10,000 (one quarter of $40,000) or $18,000 (one quarter of $72,000, which is 90 percent of $80,000).

No fool, you pay $10,000 for each of the four quarterly installments. If you make those payments on time, you will not be guilty of underpaying, even though your estimated payments amount to only half of your current year's tax liability. Of course, you will have to come up with the $40,000 unpaid balance when you file your tax return.

On the other hand, assume that money is tight and that you pay only $4,000 in each of the first three installments. Although you have underpaid each installment by $6,000 ($10,000 less $4,000), the IRS will first apply your estimated tax payment to any underpayment in the order in which such installments were required to be paid. The IRS starts the penalty clock on each underpayment on the date the installment was due.

TIP You can limit the penalty or perhaps even eliminate it. Here is how. If on the fourth installment you hand over $28,000 to the IRS (the $10,000 due on the fourth installment plus the $18,000 you underpaid on the first three installments), the penalty clock stops running.

You still owe a penalty, the size of which depends on current interest rates, but you have put a cap on the time period of its accrual.

TIP Or you could eliminate the penalty altogether—provided you are drawing a salary that is subject to tax withholding.

You see, unlike the estimated payments, which are credited to your account when you make them, the IRS simply totals all your payroll withholding of income tax at the end of the year. Then it credits one-fourth of the total to each of your four quarterly installments.

So you may ask your employer to increase the amount of your tax withholding at the end of the year by simply filing a new Form W-4, "Employee's Withholding Allowance Certificate," and claiming fewer or even zero allowances and requesting that an additional amount be withheld. That way, you can make up the shortfall from any earlier underpayment of estimated quarterly payments.

To see how this strategy works, just take the last example, and assume that you made those three quarterly estimated tax payments on income that you earn from freelance consulting. You are also employed as an executive of a large oil company, and you usually receive a holiday bonus. You claim no withholding allowances on your W-4. And even though you claimed no withholding allowances on your W-4, you calculate that you are still underpaid by $18,000 for the first three quarters.

To eliminate the underpayment penalty you have incurred on your freelance income, you simply have your company withhold an extra $28,000 ($18,000 in underpayments plus the final $10,000 installment) from your year-end bonus check. As long as the extra payroll withholding is done before the end of the tax year, you are off the penalty hook.

But now suppose the situation is different. Suppose you do not want the IRS to credit your withholding equally to all four quarterly installments. Instead, you want Uncle Sam to credit the amount withheld in the quarter in which the withholding actually happened.

Why? Well, it could be useful in minimizing the penalty. Let's say that you quit your job on April 1. For the first three months of the year, your income from salary and bonuses is subject to withholding that totals $24,000.

Based on your investment income, you calculate you will owe the

IRS $10,000 a quarter in estimated taxes. Because cash is short, you do not make the quarterly payments.

Later you come into some money, and you want to stop the underpayment penalty that has been accruing. So you make one estimated tax payment of $16,000 on January 15. If the IRS prorates your withholding as it normally would, it would credit $6,000 ($24,000 divided by four) to each quarterly installment. And you'd then be penalized for being underpaid during the first three quarters.

But what if you could claim credit for the $24,000 withheld from your salary and bonus on the dates it was actually withheld?

In that case the IRS would consider your first two $10,000 installments paid in full. You would have underpaid the third installment by just $6,000—that is, the $10,000 due minus $4,000 remaining from your withholding. Since you made up for this underpayment with the $16,000 that you sent the IRS in the fourth installment, you have minimized your penalty.

To claim credit for the amounts you had withheld on the actual dates of the withholding, all you have to do is retain proof—such as copies of paycheck stubs—of the dates of the actual withholding. Attach these copies to Form 2210, show the amounts of withholding on Form 2210 according to the dates actually withheld, and include the completed Form 2210 with your 1040.

MAKING AMENDS

If your tax picture changes during the year—your income goes up, say, or your expenses decrease—you should consider amending your estimated tax payments. The only exception that may apply is if you base your installments on 100 percent of the tax shown on your previous year's return.

Let's say your income increases. In this case, you should total up your tax liability for the year, then subtract the tax payments you have already made. Now divide the result by the number of quarters remaining in the year—three, say—and pay the extra tax in three equal installments.

Your first installment may still fall short if you pay only estimated taxes and do not have tax withheld from your wages. For example, assume your tax liability last year came to a whopping $70,000. This year, you estimate that you will owe a more modest $40,000.

So you base your estimated tax installments on 90 percent of

$40,000, or $36,000. And each of your quarterly payments comes to $9,000.

On September 15, however, you revise your tax liability for the current year to $60,000. So you must change the estimated tax you owe to $54,000 ($60,000 times 90 percent).

Since you have already made $18,000 in estimated payments on April 15 and June 15, your remaining estimated tax comes to $36,000, which you will pay in two installments on September 15 and January 15.

Because your first two payments fall short, Uncle Sam might penalize you, unless your withholding is enough to cover the shortfall or you satisfy the IRS that you are entitled to a waiver—a subject we get to shortly.

TIP To minimize the penalty you should consider a September 15 payment of $22,500 and a January payment of $13,500. In this way, the penalty for the first and second quarters would be cut off as of September 15.

TIP If you are able to apply the annualization method, you might be able to minimize or eliminate the penalty for the first two installments.

And if your income decreases? Again, add up your tax liability and subtract the tax payments you have already made. You may find you have already paid the required amount. One drawback, though: If you are entitled to a refund, you must wait until you file your current return to receive it. In that case, file your return as early as possible to get your refund and minimize your interest-free loan to the IRS.

SOME DISCRETION

Although the underpayment penalty is mandatory in most cases, the IRS may—but is not required to—waive it in three situations where it would be unfair.

There is one condition, though: You must file Form 2210 with your return and attach an explanation of the circumstances entitling you to a waiver. The three situations:

- Your underpayment is due to a disaster or a casualty.

- It is the result of "unusual circumstances"—a phrase, alas, that the IRS to date has not defined.

- You retired after reaching age 62 or became disabled in the current or previous tax year, and your underpayment is due to reasonable cause, not willful neglect.

APPLYING OVERPAYMENTS

If you overpay your taxes in one year, should you apply the overpayment to your estimated tax bill for the following year?

It depends. If your overpayment is approximately the same as you will owe on your first installment, it is usually a good idea. After all, your first installment is due April 15, and there is little sense in writing a check to cover an amount that the IRS already has in its hands.

But what if the overpayment substantially exceeds the amounts you owe in the first and second quarters? Pay your first and second quarter installments from the overpayment, then ask for a refund of the remainder. Of course, if you anticipate a significant drop in income for the year, and you expect to pay little or no estimated tax, request a refund for the full amount of the overpayment when you file your return. Why? Once you request that an overpayment be applied to your estimated tax, you cannot change your mind.

TIP Here is a way to speed receipt of your tax refund. Ask your tax preparer to file your return electronically—that is, via computer.

The IRS says it will forward refunds from these electronically filed returns within 18 to 21 days. The agency normally requires four to eight weeks to process refunds from traditional paper returns. (See Chapter 29 for more information on electronic filing.)

BACKUP WITHHOLDING

Before we finish, a few more words about withholding.

Under certain conditions, you may be subject to so-called backup withholding on some types of income on which taxes are not ordinarily withheld.

That is because Uncle Sam wants to collect all of the tax that is due him. Income that falls into this category includes interest and dividends, rents, profits and other gains, commissions and fees earned by independent contractors, payments by brokers, and royalties.

A business, bank, or other institution must withhold as income tax a flat 20 percent of the amount you are paid if any of the following applies:

- You do not provide the payer with your Social Security number (or other taxpayer identification number, or TIN).

- The IRS notifies the payer that the number you provided is incorrect.

- You do not certify that you are not subject to backup withholding, even though you are required to.

- The IRS notifies the payer to begin backup withholding because you have underreported interest or dividends on your 1040. (Before taking this action the IRS will have mailed you four notices over a 120-day period.)

☞ CAUTION   Make sure you provide a correct Social Security number to payers to avoid backup withholding.

Be especially careful when you open bank accounts for children who have not yet applied for or received their Social Security numbers. You will be asked to sign a certificate stating that backup withholding does not apply to your children because you are waiting to receive their numbers. Then you have 60 days to report the numbers. If you do not, the payer will begin withholding taxes on your children's earnings.

💵 TIP   To stop backup withholding once it starts, provide any payers with your Social Security number or other taxpayer identification number and certify that it is correct. The IRS will not automatically pay you back the amount already withheld. You will have to file a return to claim it.

You need to do more, however, if the withholding was triggered by your underreporting income. In this case you must request a determination from the IRS to stop the withholding. And you must establish one of the following:

- No underreporting occurred.

- You have a bona fide dispute with the IRS as to whether or not you actually did underreport.

- Backup withholding will cause or is causing you undue hardship, and you are unlikely to underreport interest and dividends in the future.

- If you had not previously filed a return, you corrected the underreporting by doing so and by paying all taxes, penalties, and interest you owed for any underreported interest or dividend payments.

Then, if Uncle Sam agrees with you, he will notify the payer to stop withholding tax.

☞ **CAUTION** You can get hit with a $500 civil penalty if you give false information to avoid backup withholding. The IRS can also impose a $1,000 fine or up to one year of imprisonment or both.

QUESTIONS AND ANSWERS

QUESTION: *Which return does the IRS use to determine how much estimated tax I owe and if I must pay an underpayment penalty?*

Uncle Sam uses the return you mail on or before the due date for filing for that tax year. Say you file an amended return before the due date for filing your original return (including extensions). In this case Uncle Sam considers the amended return your return for the taxable year.

What is more, he uses the amount of tax you owe on this amended return to calculate any underpayment of estimated tax.

TIP You may be able to sidestep the underpayment penalty by carefully timing when you file an amended return.

Say you file your return on April 1. On April 10 you receive a corrected K-1 statement that shows your partnership income was much greater than you had originally reported.

Now, say you file an amended return by April 15, 1991.

The IRS will use your increased tax liability shown on your amended return to determine if you have underpaid your estimated taxes. But if you wait one day after the due date to file your amended return, Uncle Sam uses your April 1 return to calculate whether you owe the underpayment penalty.

☞ **CAUTION** Do not make the mistake some taxpayers do, of waiting too long after the original due date to file your amended return. Granted, you avoid the underpayment penalty, but you will still pay interest on the amount by which you underpaid your tax.

The interest rate on underpayments and the rate charged as the underpayment penalty is the same—three points over the federal short-term rate, adjusted quarterly. And the interest begins to add up starting with the original due date of the return.

Also, if you understated the tax on your April 1 return by more than $5,000 or 10 percent, whichever is greater, you could face a penalty of 20 percent of the amount by which you underpaid.

The law also makes an exception to the rules on amended returns for some married people filing jointly.

Say you are married and file an amended joint return after the filing due date to replace separate returns that you filed before the due date.

In this case the IRS uses the tax shown on the amended joint return to compute whether or not you underpaid your estimated tax, even if the amended return is filed after the original filing due date. The reason is that Uncle Sam wanted to help married taxpayers minimize their liability.

💰 **TIP** In analyzing the tax savings of filing jointly or separately, don't overlook underpayment penalties. And keep in mind that once you file jointly, you cannot subsequently amend your return after the due date to file separately.

QUESTION: *If I make a joint payment of estimated taxes with my spouse, must I file a joint return?*

Making joint estimated tax payments with your spouse does not mean that the two of you must file a joint return. You may still file separately, and you and your spouse may divide up the estimated payments any way you want.

QUESTION: *If my spouse and I make separate estimated payments, can we file a joint return?*

The answer is yes. However, you and your spouse may not file jointly if either of you is a nonresident alien, legally separated under a decree of divorce or separate maintenance, or have different tax years.

Also, you and your spouse can file jointly even if you are not living together—if you have a "commuter marriage," for example.

☞ **CAUTION** If you and your spouse file separate estimated tax payments and separate returns, you cannot use an overpayment by your spouse to offset your underpayment, or vice versa.

However, the rules are different if you file separate returns and live in the community property states of Arizona, California, Idaho, Louisiana, Nevada, New Mexico, Texas, Washington, or Wisconsin.

In this case you and your spouse must each report half of the income from all of your community property in addition to reporting your own separate income. And each of you takes credit for half of all taxes withheld on your community income.

What happens if you are divorced during the year? Usually, each of you reports half of the community income and half of the withholding on that income for the portion of the year before the divorce took effect.

And if you made joint estimated tax payments and were later divorced in the same year? Either you or your ex-spouse may claim all or part of the joint payments. If one of you does so, you must provide the other person's Social Security number in the block provided on the front of your 1040.

And never fear, the IRS thinks of all possible circumstances. Should you remarry in the year you got divorced, you write your current spouse's Social Security number on the front of your 1040. But under the heading "Payment" on page 2 of Form 1040, you write your ex-spouse's Social Security number, followed by "DIV."

QUESTION: *I plan to request an extension to file my tax return for 1990. Does that mean I can also extend the time to make my first 1991 estimated tax payment, which is due on the same day as my 1990 return?*

The answer is no. Regardless of the reason for extending the date of your return—whether, for example, you requested and received an automatic four-month extension or you got an extension because you were living abroad—your first estimated payment for 1990 is due on April 15, 1991.

There are some exceptions to this rule, however: You don't have to pay estimated tax on April 15 if you're a farmer or a fisherman or a fiscal-year taxpayer or if you meet the requirements to pay estimated taxes after certain dates.

If you fall into this last category, you must make your first estimated tax payment by June 15 if you meet the requirement after March 31 and before June 1, by September 15 if you meet the requirement after May 31 and before September 1, and by January 15 if you meet the requirement after August 31.

27

Ouch! Avoiding IRS Penalties

The IRS is fairly generous on one count: handing out penalties to people who don't live up to the letter of the law.

Carelessness or misunderstanding is no excuse. If you are late with your taxes or don't pay all that you owe, you'll get hit with a fine. And these fines can add up quickly, especially when coupled with the interest that you'll also owe on the balance of taxes due.

As part of 1989's budget reconciliation legislation, Congress passed significant penalty reform measures. The objective of the new penalty provisions was to provide fairness and simplification in the penalty structure. In this chapter, we incorporate the new provisions that most commonly affect individuals.

If you do find yourself in a situation where you are likely to face a penalty, there are some ways you can at least keep it from growing any larger than it is.

Here we explain how the IRS applies its discipline.

INTEREST OWED AND OWING

Penalties aside, if you owe the government money, you must pay interest on the amount due—from the very day that it's due. Filing extensions doesn't change the fact that interest on any unpaid amount that you owe begins to accrue on April 15.

Likewise, you may collect interest from the IRS on overpayments.

The rate will be lower than the one you would pay if you owed the IRS money.

The rules say the IRS must fork over your refund within 45 days from April 15 or the date you file your return, whichever is later.

What if the IRS fails to meet this deadline?

It must pay you interest on your refund.

What's more, it must calculate the interest due you from April 15 if you file a timely return (including extensions) or the date on which you file your return if it's a late filed return.

Both rates—what the IRS pays and what you pay—are compounded daily and are adjusted quarterly based on the *federal short-term rate*. This rate is the average market yield of Treasury bills and other U. S. obligations with terms of three years or less.

When the IRS owes you, it pays the short-term rate plus 2 percent. If you owe the IRS, however, you pay the short-term rate plus *3* percent. (In case you are curious, these rates recently have hovered near 10 percent and 11 percent, respectively.)

Any interest the IRS pays you is taxable as income. But any interest you pay the IRS is considered personal interest, and it's only partially deductible through 1990. After 1990 you may not deduct any of it. (See Chapter 5 for more information on interest deductions.)

WHAT HAPPENS WHEN YOU FILE OR PAY LATE?

Late filers and late payers are both subject to their respective penalties. And if you're a late filer and a late payer, you're subject to both. The penalties are in addition to interest that's due on the unpaid amounts. Let's take late filing first.

If your return isn't filed by the date it's due (or by the next business day if the deadline falls on a Saturday, Sunday, or holiday), the IRS imposes a stiff penalty: 5 percent of the total tax due for each month or fraction of a month that you're late. Before 1989's penalty reform legislation, late filers could also be subject to negligence penalties in addition to the late filing penalty.

There's a cap on this late-filing penalty, though. The penalty may not add up to more than 25 percent of the tax you owe. If, however, the IRS proves that your failure to file was fraudulent or intentional, the penalty increases to 15 percent and the cap is increased to 75 percent.

What happens if you're just one day late filing your income tax return? You pay the full 5 percent for the first month. If you think the penalty will be small because you owe little or no tax and you file your return more than 60 days late, the minimum penalty you'll have to pay is the lesser of $100 or 100 percent of the tax due.

Further, even if your return is mailed to Uncle Sam on time, the IRS may consider it late if it's either unsigned or lacks enough information to compute the tax.

What determines whether your return is late is the postmark on the envelope you mail it in. If you've addressed it correctly, affixed the right postage, and gotten an official postmark that beats the deadline—and if the return makes it to the IRS—it's not late.

If the return never arrives, however, the burden is on you to prove that you mailed it—a difficult task unless you have the receipt from a certified or registered mailing.

☞ **CAUTION** In the eyes of the IRS a postmark from an office postage meter is not official. So think twice before you use your company's meter.

If you don't owe any tax—say, for instance, your payroll withholding more than covered your tax liability for the year—you don't owe a penalty for late filing.

What happens if you file on time but just don't pay the total tax due? More fines, of course, but late payers' penalties work a bit differently, and are assessed at a lower rate.

Initially, the agency assesses you 0.5 percent of the tax not paid for each month or fraction of a month that the tax remains due.

Say you file your tax return on April 15, and it shows you owe $1,000 to Uncle Sam. And you don't pay that amount until three months after you file. You owe a penalty of $15—that is, 0.5 percent times $1,000 times three months.

And if you still don't pay up?

Usually the IRS then sends you four or five notices demanding payment. These letters are mailed to you over a period of six months or so. Then, 30 days before it does so, the agency lets you know through a levy notice that it intends to file a lien against your assets.

Beginning with the month following the date which is 10 days after the levy notice is given, the penalty rate doubles. From then on, it's 1 percent of the unpaid tax for each additional month the tax remains unpaid. No matter how late you are in paying, though, the penalty may not exceed 25 percent of the taxes due.

If the late filing and late payment penalties both apply for the first five months, the IRS reduces the late-filing penalty by the amount of the late-payment penalty.

In other words, you aren't subject to more than a 5 percent combined penalty in any one month—a maximum of 25 percent during the first five months.

TIP There's only one proven way to avoid the late filing penalty: File your return on time. Even if you owe Uncle Sam money and cannot pay it when you file your return, go ahead and file your return by April 15. Then make arrangements with the IRS to pay the amount due.

The agency may waive the late payment penalty if you show reasonable cause for not paying on time—serious illness or financial hardship, for example.

REASONS FOR UNDERPAYMENT

Now let's say that you have filed your return on time and paid all of the taxes you claim to owe. So there are no late-filing penalties due.

But what if it turns out you owe more tax than you claimed on your return? The IRS may generally assess three kinds of penalties: those related to honest mistakes, the so-called accuracy-related penalty, and fraud penalties.

What is the difference? An honest mistake is, well, just that. You added five and three on your return and got four. If you make an honest mistake, the IRS will give you ten days from the day it notifies you of the underpayment to pay up.

If you don't pay within ten days, the penalty is 0.5 percent per month of the amount you have not paid. This penalty may not exceed 25 percent of the underpayment.

The accuracy-related penalty is a product of the 1989 legislation. Congress combined the old penalties for negligence, substantial understatements of income tax, substantial valuation overstatement, substantial overstatement of pension liabilities, and substantial estate or gift tax valuation understatement.

If any one of the above applies to you, you could be hit with a penalty equal to 20 percent of the underpayment. However, if you get caught in more than one arm of the accuracy-related penalty, you are still subject to only one 20-percent penalty.

Negligence includes acts of ommission and commission. The most common is keeping inaccurate or inadequate books or records. No longer will you automatically be considered negligent if you fail to include on your return an amount that was shown on a Form W-2 or 1099, but Uncle Sam will usually consider it negligence if you fail to do so. Other examples include taking clearly improper deductions, making substantial errors in reporting income, continuing to deduct items that were held to be nondeductible in previous years, or failing to offer any explanation for understatements of income.

Whether something constitutes negligence may depend on a taxpayer's circumstances. For example, whether your books are adequate depends on the size and complexity of your business. The IRS generally holds a highly educated person to a stricter standard than one who is less educated.

If you rely on a tax professional for advice or preparation of your return, you probably will not be found negligent—unless, of course, you negligently failed to supply your accountant or tax preparer with adequate records.

The agency's finding of negligence is presumed true.

In other words, in the case of an error that results in an underpayment, the burden falls on you to prove that you were not negligent.

A substantial understatement is not so subjective. You're guilty of substantial understatement when the amount of tax shown on your return falls short of the tax you should have listed by $5,000 or by 10 percent of the correct tax, whichever is greater.

Here's how a substantial understatement could happen. Assume that you're a talent agent who spends lavishly on lunches and dinners in search of contracts for your clients. The tax return you filed showed a total tax of $15,000.

The IRS, in an audit, disallows many of your entertainment expenses. Consequently, you owe Uncle Sam an additional $6,000 in taxes. On top of that, you owe a $1,200 ($6,000 times 20 percent) accuracy-related penalty because the shortfall is considered a substantial understatement since it exceeds $5,000 (which is greater than 10 percent of the correct tax of $21,000—$15,000 original tax plus $6,000 assessment).

There's a way to avoid both the negligence and substantial-understatement arms of the accuracy-related penalty. Say you take a position in your return that is not clear under the tax law—you deduct as investment interest all the interest on money you borrowed to fund your IRA, say, instead of deducting only 10 percent as personal interest.

As long as you disclose in your return all the facts of a nonfrivolous position, the IRS will not impose the accuracy-related penalty for that position on the grounds that it was negligent or that it created a substantial understatement.

However, you can not bury away a proper disclosure in an obscure place on your return. The IRS insists that you highlight the disclosure by marking in the upper left corner of page one of your Form 1040, the following statement: "DISCLOSURE MADE UNDER SECTION 6662. SEE LINES XX-XX OF SCHEDULE XX."

Or you may use Form 8275, which the IRS devised just for this purpose.

In other words, you don't have to be right. You only have to be honest and alert the IRS to controversial (but not frivolous) positions in your return.

The other three arms of the accuracy-related penalty are less common for most individual taxpayers.

A substantial valuation overstatement is an overstatement of more than 200 percent, but less than 400 percent of an asset's value that causes an understatement in tax of at least $5,000.

A substantial valuation overstatement might occur, for example, when you make a charitable contribution of property. Since a deduction for contributed property is equal to the fair market value of the property, an overstatement of the fair market value would give you a greater deduction and therefore cause a tax underpayment.

A substantial overstatement of pension liabilities applies only when you have a pension plan, and the pension deduction is based on actuarial determinations, which is usually the case with defined benefit plans (see Chapter 22).

A substantial overstatement of pension liabilities is an overstatement of more than 200 percent, but less than 400 percent, of the amount determined to be correct that causes an understatement in your tax of at least $1,000.

A substantial estate or gift tax valuation understatement exists when the value of an asset you claim on an estate or gift tax return is less than 50 percent, but more than 25 percent, of the asset's correct value and the claim causes an understatement in your tax of at least $5,000.

In the case of any substantial valuation overstatement or substantial overstatement of pension liabilities that is 400 percent or more of the correct value, or a substantial estate or gift tax valuation understatement that is less than 25 percent of the correct value, the accuracy-related penalty is increased from 20 percent to 40 percent of the understatement of tax caused by the valuation.

In short, you should use the services of your tax adviser and a competent appraiser or actuary in these three situations:

- You have a deduction in your income tax return that is based upon the value of an asset

- You're filing an estate or gift tax return where the value of the estate or gift is based upon an asset valuation

- You have a defined benefit plan

If the accuracy-related penalty is assessed, the IRS's finding is presumed true. In other words, if you make an error that results in an understatement and do not properly disclose that error, the burden falls on you to prove that you were not negligent or that you had reasonable cause and acted in good faith.

If, on the other hand, the IRS wants to assess the third kind of penalty for underpayment, a fraud penalty, the burden is on the IRS to prove with clear and convincing evidence that the underpayment resulted from fraud. Fraud is a deliberate attempt to evade the tax law. If the IRS succeeds in proving that any part of an underpayment is due to fraud, you may be liable for a penalty of 75 percent of the entire underpayment.

Maybe the underpayment is only partially due to fraud. The other part was a simple error. But if the IRS concludes that only part of the underpayment is due to fraud, it's then up to you to prove that it was not all due to fraud.

If you're successful, the fraud penalty applies only to that portion of the underpayment attributable to fraud. But Uncle Sam may still conclude that the accuracy-related penalty applies to the remaining underpayment.

However, the fraud and the accuracy-related penalties may not both be applied to the same portion of an underpayment.

Also, the new law says that you must have filed a return before the IRS may assess the fraud or accuracy-related penalties. So when you fail to file a return, the IRS can assess only the late payment, late filing, and/or fraudulent failure to file penalties.

Here's an example of how the IRS levies accuracy-related and fraud penalties. The agency audits your return and finds a $1,000 underpayment. Part of it, $100, was due to a math error. Another part, $200, was the result of negligence.

You mixed personal expenses with your business travel and entertainment deductions. But $700 of the underpayment, the agency decides, was fraudulent. You deliberately omitted income from your return. You reluctantly agree. How do the penalties apply?

The 75 percent fraud penalty ($525) applies to the $700 omission—that part of the underpayment attributable to fraud.

Assume that you can show that the remaining underpayment was not due to fraud. In this case, the accuracy-related penalty applies only to that portion related to negligence—the $200—for a penalty of $40 (20 percent of $200). Before the passage of the 1989 law, the negligence penalty would have applied to the math error as well, regardless of whether you proved that it was an honest mistake.

If you paid the $100 underpayment stemming from the math error within 10 days from the time the IRS asked for payment, you would pay no penalty.

To further encourage voluntary compliance, the IRS charges interest on the late filing, accuracy-related, and fraud penalties from the due date of the return rather than from the date the penalty is assessed.

FRIVOLOUS RETURNS

The IRS is a collection agency, not a debating society. It does not want to read about your antiwar sentiments, say, on one of its 1040 forms.

People who deliberately use their tax returns to register a protest or make a point about public policy may find their social activism rewarded with a $500 penalty for filing a frivolous return. The IRS may impose the penalty if the person filing the return makes a claim that delays or impedes the processing of the return or the payment of tax that is plainly, and legally, due.

What is frivolous? A position is not frivolous simply because it is novel. Rather, a frivolous claim is one that has been repeatedly rejected as utterly meritless.

Examples include claiming clearly unallowable deductions, such as a discount because the United States is no longer on the gold standard or claiming a deduction for the proportion of taxes that would have gone to support the Defense Department.

The burden of proving your return is frivolous falls on the government, but the $500 fine is based on the irregular return, not on any tax underpayment. So the penalty may apply even if you actually paid the correct amount of tax.

Now we are not suggesting that you should not stand up and be counted. We are only pointing out that there may be a cost involved if you use your tax return as a soap box.

TAX SHELTER PENALTIES

Promoters and investors who play loose with the laws that apply to tax shelters face substantial penalties.

For promoters, failure to register a tax shelter carries a minimum fine of $500. And the fine can go as high as 1 percent of the total amount invested. Failure to register a tax shelter partnership that raises $3 million, for instance, can cost the organizer $30,000.

Neglect to maintain a list of those who invest in the tax shelter you have promoted, and the IRS may fine you $50 per name omitted—up to a maximum of $100,000.

And as an investor, forgetting to report a tax shelter identification number on your return may net you a $250 wrist slap from the IRS, which takes its tax shelter rules very seriously.

FILING FORMS

The agency is also serious about getting the information it needs to track taxpayers' taxable income. Employers who do not file information returns—Form 1099s—with the IRS or who fail to supply a copy of the form to taxpayers face stiff fines.

If you file a correct information return late but within 30 days of the prescribed filing date, you're subject to a penalty of $15 per return, with a maximum penalty of $75,000 per calendar year.

After 30 days, but before August 2 of the calendar year, the penalty increases to $30 per return, with a maximum penalty of $150,000 per calendar year.

Finally, if you fail to comply by August 1, the penalty increases to $50 per return, with a maxmum penalty of $250,000 per calendar year.

However a *de minimis* exception to these rules applies if you file corrected information returns before August 2 of the calendar year. In this case, the IRS treats the original return as if it were filed with all the correct information. The number of information returns that will qualify for this *de minimis* exception is limited to the greater of 10 returns or one-half of one percent of the total number of information returns required to be filed.

Small businesses (defined as companies having less than $5 million in average annual gross receipts for the most recent three tax years) are subject to lower maximum levels for this penalty. The maximum penalty for small businesses is $25,000 (instead of $75,000) for failure to comply within 30 days; $50,000 (instead of $150,000) if the failure to comply is corrected before August 2, and $100,000 (instead of $250,000) for failure to comply before August 2.

As with the previous law, any person who fails to timely furnish a correct information statement to a payee is subject to a penalty of $50 per statement, with a maximum penalty of $100,000. However, if the failure is due to intentional disregard of the requirement, the new law provides a penalty of $100 per statement, or, if greater, 10 percent of the amount required to be shown on the statement, without limitation.

And as a business owner or taxpayer you will be dealing with more Form 1099s than ever before. The law requires 1099s to be filed for real estate transactions and for royalty payments amounting to more than $10 in any calendar year.

In the case of real estate transactions, the person responsible for closing the transaction—usually the settlement agent, buyer's attorney, seller's attorney, or title company representative—must file the form. If those people are not present, then the primary mortgage lender, the buyer's broker, the seller's broker, or the buyer, in that order, must furnish copies of the 1099 to the buyer, seller, and IRS.

In the case of royalty payments, the person or organization that pays the royalties must fill out the required 1099s.

As should be clear by now, Uncle Sam is serious when it comes to income taxes. And he backs up his beliefs with hefty penalties if you transgress.

The only way to ensure that you do not get slapped with penalties is to educate yourself about the workings of the tax law. Then check to be sure that you have filed a completely accurate return and paid the full amount of taxes due.

QUESTIONS AND ANSWERS

QUESTION: *I was due a refund of $300. But the IRS sent me $3,000 instead. I deposited the full amount in my checking account. Soon afterward I sent the IRS a check for $2,700 to cover the error. They say I owe interest for the time the money was in my account. Do I have to pay it?*

Uncle Sam must reduce your interest liability in the event of an erroneous refund attributable to an IRS administrative error.

If Uncle Sam should overpay you by $50,000 or less—send you a refund of $3,000 instead of $300—interest will not start to accrue on the overpayment until the IRS officially notifies you that you owe them the $2,700.

Another rule may work in your favor.

In an audit, for instance, you might concede that a deduction was a bit aggressive and agree to pay the additional tax. But if it takes the IRS a year to get around to mailing you the bill, the agency now may abate the interest attributable to the one-year delay that was its fault.

TIP These interest abatement rules apply retroactively to 1979, so if you have paid interest to Uncle Sam any time since then, you may be due a refund. Check it out. You should know, though, that this rule does not apply to returns on which the statute of limitations has expired.

QUESTION: *My return was late. But I had a good excuse. I was in the hospital in a coma when April 15 rolled around. Do I still have to pay a penalty?*

The IRS does accept some excuses. And yours probably qualifies. If you can show that your return was late not out of willful neglect but due to reasonable cause, you may escape the penalty.

Being too busy is not considered reasonable cause. If, however, you are seriously ill or if your tax records are destroyed by fire, you may qualify as having a reasonable cause. But it is up to you to convince the IRS that what is reasonable to you should also be reasonable to them.

QUESTION: *I received a notice from the IRS that I failed to report $100 in interest income. I failed to report that amount because I never received a 1099 from my bank. I do not think I should have to pay a penalty to the IRS. Do I have any recourse?*

You certainly do. You can ask the IRS to waive the penalty. In 1989 the IRS assessed some $11.8 billion in penalties but forgave $4.7 billion.

Explain your situation to the IRS in a letter. Include a copy of the notice that the agency sent you, plus a check for any taxes and interest you owe. Do not pay the penalty until you receive a reply from the IRS.

28

What to Do When the IRS Says Prove It

You filed your tax forms, mailed them off with your payment, and the canceled check has come back from the bank. Now you can breathe easy. Right? Wrong.

The fact that the IRS cashes your check, or sends you the refund you claim as your due, means that your return wasn't lost in the mail, the IRS computers aren't on the fritz, and you didn't make any obvious math errors on the return.

But it doesn't mean that the IRS is necessarily happy with your return or that it won't be asking questions. It doesn't mean, in other words, that you escaped an audit.

If your pulse races at the very thought of an audit, you aren't alone. The unhappy fact is that the IRS may audit your return at any time.

You do get one break, though—a statute of limitations. Uncle Sam is prohibited by law from assessing any additional income tax after three years have passed from April 15 or the date you filed your return, whichever is later.

But the law does carve out exceptions to this rule. For example, the statute of limitations doesn't apply if you didn't file a return or you filed a fraudulent return. Also, if you failed to report more than

25 percent of your income, the statute of limitations is extended to six years.

Never been audited before? You're lucky. Chances are that you'll face an IRS auditor at least once in your lifetime.

So, given that eventuality, we're going to suggest ways that will help you get through this unpleasantness when your turn comes. Provided you haven't deliberately tried to shortchange Uncle Sam, an audit need not be any worse than unpleasant.

And look on the bright side: If you did make an honest mistake, it may have been in the government's favor. You could get money back as a result of the audit.

Here's something else we think you should know: Taxpayers now have a new weapon on their side—a so-called *taxpayer bill of rights*.

Adopted by Congress in 1988, this law requires the IRS to disclose its obligations and your rights *before* it conducts an audit or takes any other action against you.

The agency must explain to you how to appeal an adverse decision, how to make a refund claim, how to file a complaint against the agency, and the procedures that the IRS itself will follow if it decides to assess and collect additional funds.

The law also excuses you from penalties when you act on erroneous written advice provided by the IRS.

The new law also establishes an Office of the Ombudsman. So, if you're about to undergo a significant hardship at the hands of Uncle Sam, such as having the doors of your business padlocked, you now have someone to whom you can turn for redress.

You can take some comfort that this new law exists, but don't flaunt these rules under the false assumption that you'll now be safe from the long reach of the IRS.

AUDITING FOR GOOD CAUSE

Why does the IRS audit tax returns? Although our system of taxation presumes that every citizen will voluntarily pay the amount of tax he or she owes, the government thinks that it sometimes gets shortchanged.

Some disagreements over whether or not a taxpayer paid all he or she should stem from different interpretations of the law—yours and the IRS's.

Others stem from lack of knowledge on the part of taxpayers. And every now and then, some individuals deliberately fail to report their income or overstate their deductions so they can pay less tax than they rightfully owe.

An audit gives Uncle Sam the tool he needs to make sure taxpayers are indeed paying the correct amounts. In an audit, the IRS gets to scrutinize individual tax returns for errors of omission or commission. Moreover, the fear that our returns may come in for similar scrutiny tends to make us all a little more scrupulous when we fill out our tax forms.

All told, the government audited about 1 million of the 107 million tax returns filed in 1988. That means the odds of being picked for an audit are about 0.9 percent.

But you're much more likely to face an audit if you fall into one of the taxpayer categories that the IRS watches closely or if your return upsets IRS computers.

You're also more likely to be audited if you live in certain states. For example, the least frequently audited taxpayers live in the Middle Atlantic region, while the most frequently audited taxpayers live in 19 states west of the Mississippi.

What, specifically, triggers IRS scrutiny?

When you mail your completed Form 1040 to one of the agency's regional service centers, a clerk enters the numbers from your return into a computer. The computer compares your numbers (your deductions, for instance) with the average deductions claimed by other taxpayers.

The computer then assigns a score to your return based on how much greater your write-offs are than the average. And the IRS selects returns for audit on the basis of these scores—that is, it selects all returns above a certain score.

At that point, a human takes over again. An IRS employee looks over your return and decides whether an audit might be worth the agency's time and expense.

How far off the average do your claims have to be before the computer picks out your return for this special attention? Not surprisingly, the IRS won't say. But our experience tells us that you can gauge the likelihood of an audit from your answers to the following questions.

How much income did you report? The odds of your being audited go up with your earnings. In 1988, for instance, the IRS examined 0.59 percent of returns with gross income of less than $25,000 but 1.81 percent of returns with gross income of $50,000 or more.

Did you itemize deductions? People who itemize are more likely to be audited than those who claim the standard deduction.

Are you self-employed? Individuals in business for themselves are audited far more frequently than those collecting a salary from someone else. That's because the IRS frequently finds abusers among this group.

Are your travel and entertainment deductions significant? The IRS scrutinizes these write-offs because it has found that taxpayers frequently inflate or claim improper travel and entertainment deductions.

Do you pay or receive alimony? The IRS has found that not all taxpayers report alimony payments as income. As a result, a number of the agency's offices now match deductions for alimony payments by one former spouse with the alimony income reported by the other.

Are you an investor in a tax shelter? If so, your chances of being audited increase dramatically. Often, the IRS earmarks tax shelter investors for audit after it has examined the return of the tax shelter itself or has found recurring problems with the promoter that sold the investment.

You should also know that the IRS is under pressure from a deficit-haunted Congress to audit a higher percentage of returns and collect more taxes.

But the fact is, your chances of being audited keep going down. In 1964, your chance of being audited was 5.1 percent; in 1988, it was 0.9 percent.

Of course, during this time, Uncle Sam has gotten better at selecting returns for audit that will result in additional taxes being collected.

Of all the individual returns audited during 1988, only 13 percent resulted in no change, and 4 percent produced refunds. Put another way, a little more than 83 percent of all audits ended with taxpayers paying additional tax.

WHEN YOU RECEIVE A LETTER FROM THE IRS

Not every letter from the IRS is cause for panic. The notice of an audit may be, but there's another letter the IRS mails.

It simply says the agency thinks that you've made a mistake and asks that you send it more money. Don't send the money—at least not right away.

But don't ignore the letter, either. If you wait too long before responding, the IRS may pull your return for an overall audit. So pull your return out of the file and go over it or have your tax preparer go over it for you.

Did you make a mistake?

The data-entry clerk at the IRS may have typed a number incorrectly. Or maybe you just forgot to file an obscure form.

In any case, don't assume that IRS is right. Check the letter out. If you do owe the money that the agency claims that you do, send it along.

But if after checking, you find that you don't owe, or that you still don't understand the agency's claim, write the IRS a letter. Explain why you disagree.

To be helpful, enclose a copy of the correspondence the agency sent you. That way, the IRS employee who gets your letter doesn't have to search through the agency files, and he or she has a better chance of matching your response with your IRS file.

TIP There's no need to panic if you receive a second notice from the IRS on the same issue. The IRS usually issues five notices, one every five weeks. A second notice is sometimes mailed before you have time to respond to the first one.

What if you receive a third notice? Write the Problem Resolution office of your IRS District, and contact your tax preparer.

TIP Send any correspondence to the IRS by certified mail, return receipt requested. That way, if you're called upon to prove that you responded to the IRS in a timely fashion, you can do so.

CAUTION You say you overlooked an item of income? Don't wait for the IRS to find you. If you pay the tax before the IRS contacts you, you reduce your interest payments and possibly avoid penalty assessments.

PREPARING FOR THE AUDIT

The IRS doesn't actually use the word "audit" when it writes to tell you that your return is going to be audited. It's much more polite.

The letter just says that the agency wants to verify the accuracy of your return, and it asks for a meeting.

Never ignore such a letter. The two most common types of audits, other than audits conducted exclusively through the mail, are *office audits* and *field audits*. If you must be audited, you'd prefer the office audit. It's often less detailed.

In an office audit, the IRS asks you to meet with its auditor at a specific time and place. The letter you get will specify the areas of your return that the IRS is questioning. And it will ask you to bring records to back up deductions or credits you've claimed, income you've reported, or any other item that has a bearing on the tax you have computed.

The letter also usually asks you to bring along a copy of your tax return for the year in question, plus a copy of your prior year's return.

For the more formidable field audit, however, the agency will announce that it's sending its representative to you. That's probably because the auditor will want to see more records than you can conveniently bring to him or her. The field audit isn't a minor affair.

If the date and time the IRS sets for either a field or an office audit is inconvenient, immediately call the agency's office and ask for a change. Chances are, the agent will accommodate you.

Now, start getting ready. Preparation and organization are the keys to getting through the audit as painlessly as possible.

You should have the answers to all questions about which the IRS has indicated an interest, and the records to substantiate your answers.

In either an office or field audit, let yourself be guided by this general rule: Provide only the information that is requested and answer only the questions that are asked. Don't raise issues that the auditor hasn't raised. Otherwise, the audit may extend into areas that you aren't prepared to discuss.

WHO GOES TO THE AUDIT?

The issue of who actually goes to the audit is left, by and large, up to you. If your return is a joint one, you or your spouse or both of you may go. But neither of you has to attend. You may send your accountant to represent you.

In fact, almost anyone who has your authorization (use IRS Form

2848D) or your power of attorney (use IRS Form 2848) may represent you at an audit.

Theoretically, you can go to the audit with your accountant, your attorney, and an army of advisers in tow. But it isn't a good idea.

Too many troops gives the impression that you're worried and have a lot to hide. And all those reinforcements are charging you for their time. Also, most audits are routine, so you don't need to roll out your heavy artillery.

If the matter seems simple, you may—with the right preparation and backup documents—be able to handle the audit yourself. If it's complicated, ask your adviser to be there with you. In any case, discuss the matter with your tax adviser before you decide who should go.

THE BIG DAY

The day of the audit is at hand. How should you behave? To begin with, be prompt. When the audit begins, pay attention to what's going on.

If the person you meet says anything to indicate that the examination of your return is anything but routine—or if he or she is introduced as a ''special'' IRS agent—stop the proceedings right there and seek legal help. Special agents work for the IRS criminal division, and they don't participate in audits unless you're suspected of serious wrongdoing.

By law, a special agent is supposed to inform you before the audit begins that this is something more than a routine check.

But listen carefully for the warning. You don't want to miss it. If in doubt, you can always request to see the person's IRS identification card. And you can copy down his or her name and any other information printed on it.

But, assuming that your audit is routine, how do you behave? Pleasantly, of course, but don't be lulled into letting your guard down. Speak when you're spoken to. Answer the questions you're asked.

Above all, don't become abusive, railing against the unfairness of the tax system. Keep your politics to yourself. If you know of a neighbor who's getting away with tax murder, this isn't the time to call attention to him or her. It won't distract the auditor's attention from you.

Listen carefully to the auditor's questions, and consider your answer before making it. IRS employees are skilled. They may probe a bit in hopes of identifying additional problem areas on your return.

In short, stay calm. Don't get flustered. Be patient. It will all be over in time.

STAGES OF APPEAL

When it's over, however, you may not agree with the auditor's finding. What can you do about it? There are several stages of appeal, beginning with the IRS itself and eventually, if it comes to that, the courts.

Step 1 is to ask for a meeting with your auditor's supervisor. Perhaps you can persuade him or her of the correctness of your position. Or you may receive a more satisfactory explanation for the finding than the auditor gave.

If you're still not happy, though, ask for a meeting with a representative of the Office of the Regional Director of Appeals. Your tax adviser should get involved if you decide to go this route. Filing a protest is a formal procedure that you shouldn't attempt on your own.

IRS statistics show that about 85 percent of cases that go to the Regional Director are settled at that level. Settlement often involves compromise by both the government and the taxpayers. It may be worth your while to go through this process if you've taken a supportable though not necessarily 100 percent correct position on your tax return.

If the appeals process doesn't work, there are always the courts. In fact, you can take your appeal to the courts at any time.

You don't have to exhaust the IRS internal appeal steps. But here's a word of caution about court appeals. They are expensive and time consuming.

If the attorney's fees are going to be greater than the IRS claims, you may want to swallow your pride and principles and pay the government what it wants. It could be cheaper in the long run. If you think you want to try an appeal, though, seek qualified counsel.

QUESTIONS AND ANSWERS

QUESTION: *Does the IRS ever do random audits?*
Most IRS audits aren't entirely random events—but some, in

fact, are. Every three years the IRS chooses 50,000 individual returns completely at random for audit in connection with its Taxpayer Compliance Measurement Program (TCMP).

The unfortunate souls who filed these targeted returns must justify every entry, line by line. The government isn't picking on them out of any specific suspicion. It just wants to see, by sampling, what proportion of taxpayers aren't complying with the laws and how they aren't complying.

And if, by the way, just knowing that one might have to endure such an audit helps keep us honest, the IRS considers that a very useful secondary effect.

So hold your breath. From now until April 1991, the IRS is selecting the 1988 tax returns that will be part of the current TCMP audit.

These random audits are also done on partnership tax returns and on information returns filed by businesses. For example, the IRS may check the accuracy of returns that report the payment of interest income, and these audits may indirectly influence your individual return.

QUESTION: *Any advice on how to avoid an audit?*

Perhaps the best advice we can give you is to fill out your returns as honestly and completely as you can. That way, if an audit does come your way, you know your heart—and your Form 1040— are pure. And that knowledge will help you more than anything else in breezing through IRS scrutiny.

29

How to Get Ready for Your Tax Preparer

Plenty of people find that the hardest part of their tax year is pulling everything together in preparation for filing. What *did* I do with those receipts?

You can fill out the tax forms yourself or pay someone to do it for you. Either way, the IRS holds you responsible for the accuracy of the information reported. And you're the one the agency will look to for documentary proof of the deductions you claim.

In this chapter we tell you how to get yourself and your records ready for filing time. But we want to offer this piece of preliminary advice.

Whether you enlist the help of a tax preparer or not, the time to start preparing for tax filing is at the beginning of the tax year. It's too late to make plans, devise a tax-savings strategy, or even start accumulating your records and supporting documentation, on April 14.

And if you do use a tax professional to prepare your forms, don't think of him or her just once a year. Work with your tax adviser before the year starts.

Chances are you'll end it on a happier fiscal note.

GET ORGANIZED

One of the keys to sound tax planning is good organization. And the sooner you tackle your organizing chores, the better. As we've seen, to reap benefits from year-end tax planning, you have to act during the year, not after the tax year ends.

The bottom line: It's never too soon for you and your adviser to start developing tax-savings strategies for the current year.

GOOD RECORDS SAVE TIME AND EXPENSE

Finally, it's time to assemble the correct data for Uncle Sam. Remember, all of the careful tax planning you've done will count for naught if you can't produce the records and the facts that you need at tax-filing time.

Keep in mind, too: A tax adviser's main function is to help you make the most of the tax law so that you can save money. You don't want to waste your adviser's time—and your cash—sorting through, organizing, and interpreting numerous slips of paper.

Here's another incentive to early preparation. Many tax preparers will be able to file your 1990 return electronically. Uncle Sam says that if your preparer files by computer, you'll receive any refund you have coming to you in as little as 18 to 21 days, not the now-common four to eight weeks. So if your tax data is ready, you could be that much closer to a refund check.

In the following pages we've compiled a checklist of the records and information that you'll want to pull together before you or your tax preparer begins work on your return. So get started. A tidy sum in tax savings might well be your reward.

Note: Many tax preparers send their clients forms listing income and deductions for the previous year and asking for data for the current year.

If your preparer sends such a form, use it in addition to our checklist. It may well jog your memory for deductions you might otherwise forget.

RECORDS DETAILING INCOME

Let's start with the records you need to gather to account for your income—whatever the source. Keep in mind that your employer, bank, broker, or a dividend-paying corporation in which you own stock is required by law to mail W-2s or 1099s by January 31. So if you haven't received the information by, say, February 10 (a date that allows for mail delays) start making inquiries.

1. Wages. Bring copies of all W-2 forms.

2. Dividends. Bring all copies of your 1099s.

3. Interest. Again, bring all copies of your 1099s, and if you have made loans to friends or relatives, make sure you have information on those loans too.

4. Self-employment income. Bring along any 1099s you've received from customers or clients, your checkbooks for the year, any other books you have kept, and your bank statements. Summarize all your receipts and expenses by category on a piece of paper, or, if you use a computer to keep track of these items, a copy of your computer printout. Also, don't forget to collect all your travel, meal, entertainment, and automobile records, including your charge card slips.

5. Capital gains and losses. Bring the purchase and sell transaction slips for any securities that you may have sold. You can save some steps if you make sure the sell slips agree with the Form 1099-B that you received from your broker. (The 1099-B may also remind you of what you sold during the year.)

Did you sell your personal residence or any other real estate? Bring along your closing statement and receipts for your fixing-up expenses. If you purchased a replacement residence, also bring along the closing statement for it.

6. Partnerships, estates, trusts, S corporations. Be sure that you have the Form K-1s that you should have received from any of these entities. The form lists your share of income or deductions.

Also, for partnerships and S corporations, know the date you made your investment and be ready to explain to your tax preparer whether your involvement is active or passive. (See Chapter 19 for more information.)

And if the funds you invested were borrowed, keep in mind that the tax law has specific rules governing interest deductions.

7. Real estate rental activities. Gather your receipts and expenses (with bank statements and canceled checks or invoices) for the year, and summarize them by category on a piece of paper or computer printout. If you bought the property this year, bring your closing statement.

You'll also want a list of any improvements made to the property this year. And if you or any family members used the property during the year, be sure that you know how many days of personal and rental use were involved.

8. Other income. Bring along all the other slips of paper starting with a "W" or "1099" that organizations have been sending you, and list them on a sheet of paper. For instance, you may have received:

- State tax refunds.

- Fully taxable pensions.

- Taxable Social Security benefits.

- Unemployment insurance.

- Alimony.

- Gambling winnings.

9. Supplemental gains and losses. If you disposed of or sold a car or other equipment that you used in self-employment or for work as an employee, bring any information you have relating to those transactions. You'll also need records of when you bought the car or equipment and its original cost.

RECORDS DETAILING EXPENSES

Up to this point the records you've been collecting will help you account for your income from whatever sources. Now you want to be sure that you also have the records you'll need to justify the deductions you have coming to you, deductions that will help you offset some of this income for tax purposes.

1. IRAs and Keoghs. Under certain conditions your IRA contribution is fully or partially deductible from your gross income. And you may deduct the money you've socked away in a Keogh. So have on hand your records of these investments including the current year contributions. (See Chapter 22 for more information about retirement plans.).

2. Alimony. You may deduct "above the line"—that is, directly from your income—any alimony you pay. And you should have your canceled checks as proof of your payments.

3. Interest you forfeit. You may not know it, but interest you forfeit is also deductible above the line. When might you have forfeited interest?

Say you take out a two-year CD at 8.5 percent. A year later interest rates rise to 10 percent. You cash in your CD prematurely and buy a new one with a higher payout.

When you do, your bank probably imposes a penalty; you lose, say, three months of interest you have already earned. The good news: You may write the amount off.

Keep the bank's statement handy.

4. *Employee expenses*. If your employer provides you with a car and reports the value of your usage of the auto on your W-2, bring your mileage log and any other documents that pertain to the car. (See Chapter 13.)

Also, if your employer pays you a per diem for your travel and entertainment expenses, bring your records documenting your expenses and the amounts you received. (For more information, see Chapters 10, 11 and 12.)

5. *Medical expenses*. Do you think your medical expenses will top the 7.5 percent floor? If so, collect all of your receipts from doctors, dentists, hospitals, pharmacies, and labs—anything related to your good health and well-being.

If you had to modify your house for medical reasons, bring the signed statement from the doctor and the receipt for the improvement.

Don't forget to include information about insurance reimbursements you might have received during the year. You are also entitled to a deduction for medical mileage. (Chapter 7 provides more information about medical expenses.)

6. *Taxes*. Although sales tax isn't deductible, other taxes such as state and local income taxes, real property taxes on all residences, and personal property taxes are. You should have the canceled checks or validated tax bills to substantiate your claim.

Gather your payroll withholding statements. Also, bring the canceled checks for current or previous years' state or local income taxes you paid, including amended state or local return payments. If you paid property taxes on a vacation home, bring the canceled check or the bill. (See Chapter 8 for more information about taxes.)

7. *Contributions*. Bring along canceled checks or the receipts you received for the current year's charitable contributions. If you gave old clothes or secondhand goods to a church drive, say, or Goodwill, bring the list you made or the receipt you received.

And note: If you donated more than $500 worth of used goods

during the year, the IRS wants to know how much these goods originally cost you, when you bought them, and how you determined their value when you gave them away.

If you donated stock to your favorite charity, note the day you made the donation, the average high and low selling price on that day (if publicly traded) and the price you originally paid for the securities.

If you donated a highly valued piece of jewelry or other property, you should have an appraisal and an acknowledgment (Form 8283) from the organization to which you made the donation. (See Chapter 6 for more information about charitable contributions.)

8. Interest. Under the reformed tax laws, interest deductions can be very complicated. In fact, interest deductibility depends on how you use the borrowed money, not on where you borrowed it. In any case, you should be able to relate each loan to its specific use.

To assist yourself or your tax preparer, separate your interest expenses into the following categories:

- Principal residence interest.

- Second residence interest.

- All other residence interest.

- Mortgage points.

- Credit card interest.

- Investment interest.

- Other personal loan interest.

- Passive investment activity interest.

Investment interest includes interest on money you borrowed to buy, say, stocks or bonds—margin accounts, for example.

Because not all mortgage interest may be deductible, you should be able to answer these questions for your tax preparer: Have you ever refinanced your original mortgage? If so, when did you refinance? What was the amount of your original mortgage? Its balance when you refinanced? Your refinanced mortgage amount? (You'll find more information about interest deductions in Chapter 5.)

Also, if you've sold your house, have in hand the records you need to substantiate the amount you paid for your home plus the cost of any improvements.

If you have more than two residences, be sure to talk with your tax preparer about which one you want to consider your second residence to maximize your deduction.

9. Miscellaneous deductions. Here's where you should list your out-of-pocket employee expenses and investment advisory expenses. If you used your car as an employee and the actual expenses topped the amount you were reimbursed, bring those records.

If you used your club for business entertainment, have those records handy. You'll also need receipts for your unreimbursed business meals. (See Chapter 9 for a complete list of these miscellaneous deductions.)

WHY IT'S BETTER TO BE PREPARED

Why is it so important to gather together all of this information? The answer is simple: The more organized your data, the easier it is for your tax adviser to efficiently prepare your return and save you tax dollars.

And keep in mind that the earlier you start your planning, the better the tax-savings opportunities. In fact, the best plan is to keep your records organized on an ongoing basis.

And stay in touch with your adviser as your financial circumstances change—you get married, say, you sell your home, or you make a killing in the stock market. Remember, you must invest your time today if you're to save tax dollars tomorrow.

30

What to Do When You Need an Extension

Oh no. Filing time is nigh, and you aren't ready. Worse, you're not going to be ready to file by April 15.

Relax. Getting a filing extension is easy.

If you pay attention to the extension rules, you won't incur a penalty charge, and you can keep interest charges, if any, to a minimum.

In this chapter we tell you how to get more time.

HOW TO GET AN EXTENSION

Anyone can get a four-month, no-questions-asked extension for filing his or her Form 1040. That gives you until August 15 to get your records together and get your tax forms filled out. Don't make the mistake some taxpayers do, though.

The extension applies to filing your tax forms. It doesn't apply to the payment of the balance due of your taxes. Uncle Sam expects you to pay taxes by April 15, 1991—no matter what.

If you want to ask for a payment extension, that's a different matter. We cover payment extensions later in this chapter.

How do you ask for a filing extension? Just fill out and file Form

4868, Application for Automatic Extension of Time to File U.S. Individual Income Tax Return, by April 15, 1991. The extension is automatically granted.

AVOIDING PENALTIES AND MINIMIZING INTEREST

You won't incur a late payment or late filing penalty after you receive an extension—provided you've paid at least 90 percent of the taxes finally due for 1990 by April 15 and pay the remaining 10 percent when you file your Form 1040.

If your payroll withholding and quarterly estimated payments aren't sufficient to meet this 90 percent requirement, you must include a check for the balance with your Form 4868.

But, you say, how can I know what my final tax bill will be? If I had all my records and all the time I needed to figure out my liability, then I wouldn't be asking for an extension.

Sorry, but the responsibility is yours to make a proper estimate and to be sure that you've paid enough tax by April 15 to meet the 90 percent requirement.

What, you ask, is a proper estimate?

You must make a bona fide and reasonable attempt to locate, gather, and make use of all of the information that will enable you to estimate your tax liability.

The IRS doesn't expect you to calculate your final tax bill to the penny, but the number should be as close to your final bill as possible.

What happens if the IRS decides that you didn't properly estimate your tax liability? It may deny your request for an extension.

Also, if the IRS grants you an extension and later discovers that you didn't make a proper estimate, it may treat your extension as void.

If the IRS treats your extension as void, or if you fail to file your extension request or return on time, you may be slapped with a late-filing penalty of 5 percent of the tax not paid by the regular due date of the return for each month or part of the month the return is late. The penalty is capped at 25 percent.

If your return is more than 60 days late, the penalty may not be less than the smaller of $100 or 100 percent of the tax shown on your return.

If, however, you can show that such failure has reasonable cause and is not due to willful neglect, then you will escape the penalty.

And the IRS doesn't accept an automatic extension that it voids as reasonable cause for your failure to file your return in a timely manner, if you fail to properly estimate your tax liability on your request for an extension.

You'll still pay interest on any balance due when you finally get around to filing. The rate is determined quarterly. The interest charge begins to accrue on the unpaid tax from the original due date of your return (April 15) and ends on the day you file your return and pay the balance.

What if you pay the IRS more tax before you actually file your return? Then the interest charge continues to accrue on the amount of tax that remains unpaid.

TIP One way to minimize the interest charges on your underpayment is to send the IRS as much of the tax you owe as possible. Also, be sure to indicate the tax year you want the payment to apply to, and file your return as soon as you can.

Now, back to penalties. If it turns out that you didn't pay 90 percent of your full tax liability by April 15, in addition to interest on the balance due and a late-payment penalty, you may also owe the IRS a late-filing penalty.

What if you're subject to both late-filing and late-payment penalties? Your late-filing penalties may be reduced by your late-payment penalties.

The penalty is 0.5 percent per month (or portion thereof) on the total balance due. Like interest, the penalty charge begins accruing on April 15 and ends the day you file your return and make your final payment.

The interest charge is considered personal interest, and it's 10 percent deductible on your 1990 tax return and not deductible at all on your 1991 return. However, the penalty charge, comes entirely out of your pocket. It isn't deductible at all.

(For more information on penalties, see Chapter 27.)

ASKING FOR EVEN MORE TIME

A four-month extension may not be long enough for you. If not, you may ask for two more months. The IRS has a form for this, too—Form 2688, Application for Additional Extension of Time to File U.S. Individual Income Tax Return.

Or you may send the agency a letter detailing your needs. You must mail either the form or the letter no later than the end of the original four-month extension.

In the form or letter you should explain why you're requesting the extension. You should also specify the tax year for which the extension applies, the length of time needed for the extension, and whether another extension of time to file was already granted for the tax year.

If the IRS approves your request, you then have until October 15, 1991, to complete and file your 1990 Form 1040.

Approval of this additional two-month extension isn't automatic, however. If the IRS doesn't think your reasons are good enough, it will deny the extension.

You'll receive a letter to this effect, and the IRS will give you a ten-day grace period—from the date of the letter or from the end of the four-month filing extension, whichever is later—in which to file your return.

LIVING OVERSEAS?

If on April 15, 1991, you're living somewhere besides the United States or Puerto Rico or if you're on assigned military duty outside the United States or Puerto Rico, you don't have to ask for a filing extension. You automatically have two extra months, until June 17, to file your return.

Furthermore, taxpayers on military assignment outside the United States or Puerto Rico (but not other taxpayers living overseas) also get an automatic payment extension. You don't have to pay your taxes until you file your return, although you must pay interest on the balance due from April 15, 1991.

When you do file, simply attach to your 1990 Form 1040 a note explaining why you qualify for this two-month extension—that your home and your primary place of business were outside the United States or Puerto Rico on the due date of your return.

To obtain two additional months in which to file, send the IRS a Form 4868 by June 17, 1991, and write across the top of it: "TAX-PAYER ABROAD."

This procedure will give you another filing extension—until August 15, 1991—but not a payment extension. You must send in 90 percent of your expected taxes along with the Form 4868. If you don't, you will incur a late-payment penalty of 0.5 percent per month of any balance due.

WHAT IF YOU DON'T FILE, DON'T ASK, AND DON'T PAY

If you don't file your tax return by its due date and you don't ask for an extension, the IRS becomes very upset.

How upset? So upset that it will impose a late-filing penalty of 5 percent per month (or portion thereof) of any tax due (the ceiling on this penalty is 25 percent).

So even if you can't pay your taxes when they're due, don't let that stop you from filing your return or seeking a filing extension.

By doing so, you avoid the late-filing penalty.

You're obliged, as we pointed out earlier, to pay 90 percent of your expected taxes at the time you ask for the filing extension. But if you can't, the IRS has a form for that, too. Ask for a payment extension by sending the agency a completed Form 1127, Application for Extension of Time for Payment of Tax.

Be aware, though, that the IRS doesn't grant payment extensions easily. The government expects its money, even if you have to sell assets to raise the cash. Sometimes the IRS will work out an installment payment schedule for you, but don't count on it.

QUESTIONS AND ANSWERS

QUESTION: *I requested an extension to file my tax return but was unable to pay the balance due on my taxes. Will the IRS bill me for the balance due?*

Uncle Sam will bill you for the amount you owe—plus interest from the date your return was due. Our advice: If you can't afford to pay the entire balance at once, pay as much as you can as often as you can. That way, you'll minimize the interest charges.

Also, attach to your extension request a letter detailing your proposed payment plan. And make your payments as specified in your letter.

What if you're without the funds to pay?

As we noted above, you file Form 1127.

QUESTION: *I requested an extension to file my Form 1040. Does that request also extend the time for filing my state and local tax returns?*

Not necessarily. State and local laws vary, so see your tax adviser. He or she will know the rules for your state or municipality.

A·B·C

Glossary

Accelerated depreciation–allows you to claim larger depreciation deductions in the early years of ownership. The 150-percent-declining-balance method and the double-declining balance method are examples of accelerated depreciation.

Acquisition debt–debt you incur to purchase, build, or substantially improve your principal residence or a second home. The debt must be secured by the property.

Active participation–means you're significantly involved in the management of a rental activity. You must own at least a 10 percent interest in the activity to be considered an active participant. Limited partners never qualify as active participants.

Adjusted selling price–the sales price of your home minus any selling costs and fixing-up expenses.

Alternative minimum tax (AMT)–a completely separate tax system that guarantees that everyone pay his or her fair share of tax. The AMT rate is 21 percent.

Amended return–corrected tax return.

Annualization method–way to minimize estimated tax payments if your annual income fluctuates. The annualization method allows you to reflect in each installment the income you earn in the period immediately before the installment is due.

Asset depreciation range (ADR) system–depreciation system that was used prior to 1981 and lists useful lives of business assets, such as equipment. These useful lives are the basis for determining recovery periods under the current depreciation rules.

Associated meals and entertainment–meals and entertainment that precedes or follows a bona fide business discussion.

Bargain element–the difference between the price at which you buy stock under an option and the fair market value at the time of exercise.

Basis–amount you use to calculate your gain or loss when you sell an asset. In most cases your basis is the same as your cost (less any depreciation, if applicable).

Beneficiaries–people you designate as your heirs.

Borderline business trips–trips that, when reviewed by IRS auditors, appear to be primarily personal rather than primarily business.

Business interest–interest on loans you take out to operate or buy assets for a business in which you materially participate.

Business meal–a meal that is directly related or associated with the active conduct of your trade or business. To qualify, you must actually discuss business before, after, or during the meal.

Business use (of an automobile)–the miles you drive your car between two business locations or the miles you drive between your home and a place where you're temporarily working.

Charitable contribution–a contribution or gift to, or for the use of, a qualified organization.

Charitable sporting event–one in which all of the proceeds go to charity and practically all of the labor is voluntary.

Collateral–asset pledged to a lender until a loan is repaid.

Commuting–trips to and from your home and your regular place of business.

Co-op–short for cooperative apartment.

Credit–direct, dollar-for-dollar reduction in your tax liability.

De minimis fringe benefit–one too small to really matter. In other words, it costs more for a company to keep tabs on the benefit than it costs to provide the benefit. For example, providing employees with free coffee in the morning is an example of a de minimis fringe.

De minimis loans–defined by Uncle Sam as loans of $10,000 or less.

Defined-benefit plan–retirement plan that allows you or your employer to contribute annually whatever amount is required to fund a specified retirement payout. The payout is fixed, and the contribution is based on actuarial tables for your life expectancy.

Defined-contribution plan–retirement plan that allows you or your employer to contribute some fixed percentage of your earnings to the plan each year.

Dependent–individual who satisfies the support and gross income criteria and for whom you may claim a personal exemption.

Depreciation–tax deduction you claim for the effects on business assets of decay, corrosion, wear and tear, and obsolescence.

Direct business expenses–expenses directly attributable to your business, which you would incur even if you did not have a home office, such as wages for secretarial help, photocopying, postage, office supplies, and so on.

Directly related meals and entertainment–any meals and entertainment during which you "actively" discuss or conduct business. Also, your primary purpose must be to transact business. That is, you must expect to gain some benefit from your entertainment other than goodwill.

Disqualifying disposition–disposal of stock purchased under an incentive stock option before the holding period requirement has been met.

Documentary evidence–any kind of receipt that is corroborated by a third party (a canceled check, say).

Double-declining-balance method–also known as 200-percent-declining-balance method. This method of depreciation yields depreciation deductions in the first year that are twice the amount you would get using straight-line depreciation.

Effective tax rate–overall rate at which your income is taxed. You calculate your effective tax rate by dividing your tax liability by your taxable income.

Employment-related education–training that enables you to maintain or improve your present work skills.

Equity–fair market value of an asset minus any debt secured by that asset.

Escrow–money or property placed in the hands of a third party, such as a bank.

Estimated tax–amount of tax that you expect to pay over the coming year aside from that amount withheld by your employer. Payment of estimated tax is made in quarterly installments.

Exercise–means to purchase stock under a stock option. *Date of exercise* is the date you purchase stock under a stock option.

Fair market value–the price at which property would change hands between a willing buyer and a willing seller, neither being under any compulsion to buy or sell and both having reasonable knowledge of relevant facts.

Federal short-term rate–the average market yield of Treasury bills and other U.S. obligations with terms of three years or less.

Field audit–IRS audit conducted at your home or place of business. A field audit is more detailed than an office audit.

Five-year averaging–allows you to reduce the tax rate levied on qualified lump sum withdrawals from retirement accounts. Even though you pay your full tax in the year you receive your lump sum, you calculate the tax as if you received the money evenly over five years.

Fixing-up expenses–maintenance and repair expenses you incur no more than 90 days prior to selling your home and that you pay within 30 days after the sale.

Form 1041 K-1, "Beneficiary's Share of Income, Deductions, Credits"–reports your share of trust or estate income and expenses.

Form 1065 K-1, "Partner's Share of Income, Credits, Deductions"–reports your share of partnership income and expenses.

Form 1099-B, "Statement for Recipients of Proceeds from Broker and Barter Exchange Transactions"–reports sales or redemptions of securities, futures transactions, commodities, and barter exchange transactions.

Form 1099-DIV, "Statement for Recipients of Dividends and Distributions"–reports distributions, such as dividends, capital gain distributions, or nontaxable distributions, that were paid on stock, and distributions in cases of liquidations.

Form 1099-G, "Statement for Recipients of Certain Government Payments"–reports unemployment compensation, state and local income tax refunds, agricultural payments, and taxable grants.

Form 1099-INT, "Statement for Recipients of Interest Income"–reports interest payments.

Form 1099-MISC, "Statement for Recipients of Miscellaneous Income"–reports miscellaneous income, such as non-employee compensation, rent or royalty payments and prizes and awards that are not for services, such as winnings on television game shows.

Form 1099-OID, "Statement for Recipients of Original Issue Discount"–reports by bond issuers to purchasers of bonds issued at less than face value.

Form 1099-R, "Statement for Recipients of Total Distributions from Profit Sharing, Retirement Plans, Individual Retirement Accounts, Insurance Contracts"–reports total distributions from retirement or profit-sharing plans, IRAs, SEPs, or insurance contracts.

Form 1099-S, "Statement for Recipients of Proceeds from Real Estate Transactions"–reports gross proceeds from the sale or exchange of most real estate transactions.

Form 1120S K-1, "Shareholder's Share of Income, Credits, Deductions"–reports your share of S corporation income and expenses.

Form 2439, "Notice to Shareholder's of Undistributed Long-Term Capital Gains"–reports gains realized by a regulated investment company but not paid out to you and the related tax credit.

Form SSA-1099, "Social Security Benefit Statement"–Reports Social Security benefits you receive.

401(k) plan–retirement plan created and administered by your employer. With a 401(k), you put away a portion of your salary or wages and pay only Social Security, or no income taxes on that amount, or any earnings that accumulate, until the money is withdrawn, usually at retirement.

Fraud–a deliberate attempt to evade the tax law.

Half-year convention–assumes that property is depreciable for just half the taxable year in which you place it in service. The deduction you may take this first year is one-half the amount that you would take for a full year of depreciation.

Hobby loss–loss from an activity not engaged in for profit. You may deduct hobby losses only to the extent of your hobby income.

Home-equity debt–debt other than acquisition debt you incur that is secured by your home. You may deduct interest on only your first $100,000 of home-equity debt.

Home-equity loan–loan secured by your home and in addition to your first mortgage.

Home office–an office that you maintain at home and use regularly and exclusively for business.

Home office expenses–expenses attributable to your home office, not including direct business expenses.

Incentive stock option–a type of stock option created by the Economic Recovery Tax Act of 1981. There is no regular tax due on an incentive stock option until you eventually sell or exchange the stock and then only if you sell or exchange it at a profit.

Individual Retirement Account (IRA)–retirement plan that you contribute to and create. Contributions to an IRA are deductible only if neither you nor your spouse is covered by a tax-deferred retirement plan or your adjusted gross income (AGI) falls below a certain level.

Insider–an officer or a director of a public company.

Investment interest–interest you incur when you borrow to make investments, for example, interest on a stock margin account.

Itemize–means you opt to list your deductions on Schedule A of your Form 1040, rather than claim the standard deduction.

Keogh–retirement plan for self-employed people.

Lease–a legal agreement that allows you to use an item—for example, a car—for a specified period of time in exchange for monthly rental charges.

Limited partnership–partnership that limits the liabilities of the partners to the amount they have invested or promised to invest.

Loan origination fees–same as points.

Log–a diary where you record all of your business engagements.

Long-term capital gain or loss–profit or loss from capital assets you hold for more than one year.

Lump sum–withdrawal of total amount from a retirement account.

Margin account–see *stock margin account*.

Marginal tax rate–tax rate on your last dollar of earnings.

Market price–last reported price at which an asset is sold.

Material participation–participation by a taxpayer in a trade or business that meets one of the tests classifying the activity as not a passive activity.

Medical expense–amounts you pay for the diagnosis, treatment, or prevention of disease or for treatment affecting any part or function of the body.

Mid-month convention–depreciation rule under which real estate is depreciated from the midpoint of the month the property is placed in service.

Mid-quarter convention–assumes that you placed your assets in service halfway through the quarter in which you actually put them into use. You must use the mid-quarter convention if the assets you place in service during the last quarter of the year top 40 percent of the cost of all assets placed in service during the year. With the mid-quarter convention, you may end up in the first year with fewer total depreciation deductions than under the half-year convention.

Minimum tax credit (MTC)–credit that recognizes that the AMT can result in prepayment of tax because of when you recognize income, not to the excessive use of tax exclusion preference items. The MTC credits you with the prepayment of these taxes.

Money-purchase plan–a type of defined-contribution retirement plan that requires an annual contribution of a fixed percentage of income.

Mortgage–a loan that is secured by real property and requires periodic payments.

Mortgage interest–interest on loans used to purchase your home(s), part or all of which may be deductible as acquisition or home-equity debt.

Negligence–a term that includes acts of omission and commission. Keeping inaccurate or inadequate books or records qualifies as negligence. So does failing to include on your return an amount that was shown on a Form W-2 or 1099. Other examples include taking clearly improper deductions, making substantial errors in reporting income, continuing to deduct items that were held to be nondeductible in previous years, or failing to offer any explanation for understatements of income.

Nonqualified stock option–a type of stock option. With NQOs you pay taxes when you exercise the option as well as when you sell the stock at a profit.

Office audit–IRS audit conducted at the office of an IRS agent. An office audit is less detailed than a field audit.

150-percent-declining-balance method–depreciation method that yields deductions in the first year that are 1½ times the amount you would get using the straight-line method.

Option price–price you pay for the stock under a stock option.

Original issue discount–the difference between the price paid for a bond on issue and the amount you receive for the bond at maturity.

Original issue discount bond–a type of bond that is sold to the first buyer at discount.

Paper profit–profit calculated by comparing the current market price of an asset with the purchase price.

Partnership–two or more people who agree to do business with each other. Profits and losses of the partnership are reported on the personal income tax returns of the partners. Partnerships pay no separate federal income tax.

Passive activity–a trade or business in which you do not materially participate or a rental activity where you do not provide significant services.

Passive activity interest–interest you incur by investing in a business in which you do not materially participate.

Passive income–income generated from a trade or business or rental activity that is deemed a passive activity.

Passive investment–a trade or business in which you don't materially participate in management.

Passive loss–loss incurred by you from a trade or business or rental activity that is deemed a passive activity.

Payroll withholding–income taxes deducted from your pay by your employer.

Per diem arrangements–a flat allowance paid by an employer to an employee. This method is used instead of reimbursing employees for actual expenses.

Personal exemption–amount you claim for yourself (as long as you are not listed as a dependent on someone else's return) and your dependents.

Personal interest–interest on a loan you take out to finance personal items, such as an automobile or a vacation.

Personal property–assets other than real estate. Personal property includes furniture, machinery, and equipment.

Points–the additional amount you pay when a mortgage loan is closed. One point is 1 percent of the amount of your loan.

Portfolio income–income from investments that generate income in the nature of interest, dividends, and royalties. Portfolio income also includes gains from the disposition of assets that generate interest, dividends, and royalties.

Principal residence–your primary home. But the fact that you own a house does not make that house your principal residence. You must actually live in the house for it to qualify as your principal residence.

Private-activity bonds–bonds issued by state and local governments to raise money for private enterprises.

Profit-sharing plan–a type of defined-contribution retirement plan which allows flexibility in the annual level of contribution.

Qualified organization–a nonprofit charitable, religious, or educational group that meets government guidelines.

Real property–IRS jargon for real estate. Buildings are depreciable; land is not.

Recovery periods–period of time over which you claim depreciation deductions. That is, the length of time it takes to recover the money you paid for depreciable assets. Different recovery periods apply to different types of assets.

Related entity–a member of your family or any entity that is controlled directly or indirectly by family members.

S corporation–a type of corporation. Owners pay taxes in the same way as sole proprietors and partners—that is, profits and losses are reported on the personal tax returns of the owners, and, with a few minor exceptions, there are no separate federal business income taxes to pay.

Second mortgage–a mortgage that allows you to borrow against the equity in your home. A second mortgage is similar to a home-equity loan.

Self-employed–people who work for themselves and file a Schedule C with their individual or joint tax returns. (Some partners are also considered self-employed.)

Selling costs–the costs of selling your home, such as sales commissions, advertising, attorney fees, and points.

Short-term capital gain or loss–profit or loss from capital assets you hold for a year or less.

Simplified Employee Pension (SEP)–similar to an IRA. An employer, rather than maintaining its own pension fund, makes contributions to the IRAs of its employees.

Single sum expenditure–a flat charge that includes all expenses—meals, lodging, gratuities, and so on.

Small business stock–stock of a corporation purchased at the time the corporation is formed. The original capital of the corporation is less than $1 million.

Standard deduction–amount you may claim on your tax return in lieu of itemizing your deductions on Schedule A of your Form 1040.

Standard rate–a flat amount determined by the IRS and allowed for each business mile you drive.

Stock appreciation rights–right to participate in the appreciation of a company's stock without actually purchasing the stock.

Stock margin account–brokerage account that allows you to buy securities with money borrowed from the brokerage firm.

Stock option–the right to buy a specific number of shares of a company's stock at a specific price within a specific period of time.

Straight-line method–depreciation method that produces the same write-offs from year to year except in the first and last year of depreciation.

Substantial understatement–the amount of tax shown on your return falls short of the tax you should have listed by $5,000 or by 10 percent, whichever is greater.

Surtax–a tax in addition to the regular tax that is imposed on taxpayers in certain income ranges that has the effect of eliminating either favorable rates or deductions.

Taxable income–amount of income on which your income tax is calculated. You determine taxable income by subtracting your allowable deductions from your income from all sources.

Taxpayer Bill of Rights–legislation adopted by Congress in 1988 that requires the IRS to disclose its obligations and your rights before it conducts an audit.

Taxpayer Compliance Measurement Program–program to choose at random tax returns for a detailed audit.

Ten-year averaging–allows you to reduce the tax rate levied on qualified lump sum withdrawals from retirement accounts. Even though you pay your full tax in the year you receive your lump sum, you calculate the tax as if you received the money evenly over ten years.

Unearned income–income from sources other than wages, salaries, tips, and other employee compensation (for example, dividends, interest, and rent).

W-2, "Wage and Tax Statement"–reports wages, tips, bonuses, the value of taxable fringe benefits, withheld income, and FICA taxes.

W-2G, "Statement for Recipients of Certain Gambling Winnings"–reports gambling winnings.

W-2P, "Statement for Recipients of Annuities, Pensions, Retired Pay, or IRA Payments"–reports annual payouts from retirement plans.

Wash sale–sale of stock either 30 days before or after your purchase of the same stock.

Zero-coupon bond–a type of original issue discount bond sold at a deep discount from face value and does not pay interest currently. Zero-coupon bonds are issued by the U.S. Treasury, government agencies, municipalities, and corporations. The tax consequences of these bonds depends on the issuer.

Appendix

1. ANNUAL LEASE VALUE TABLE*

Fair Market Value	Annual Lease Value
$ 0 to 999	$ 600
1,000 to 1,999	850
2,000 to 2,999	1,100
3,000 to 3,999	1,350
4,000 to 4,999	1,600
5,000 to 5,999	1,850
6,000 to 6,999	2,100
7,000 to 7,999	2,350
8,000 to 8,999	2,600
9,000 to 9,999	2,850
10,000 to 10,999	3,100
11,000 to 11,999	3,350
12,000 to 12,999	3,600
13,000 to 13,999	3,850
14,000 to 14,999	4,100
15,000 to 15,999	4,350
16,000 to 16,999	4,600
17,000 to 17,999	4,850
18,000 to 18,999	5,100
19,000 to 19,999	5,350
20,000 to 20,999	5,600
21,000 to 21,999	5,850

Fair Market Value	Annual Lease Value
22,000 to 22,999	6,100
23,000 to 23,999	6,350
24,000 to 24,999	6,600
25,000 to 25,999	6,850
26,000 to 27,999	7,250
28,000 to 29,999	7,750
30,000 to 31,999	8,250
32,000 to 33,999	8,750
34,000 to 35,999	9,250
36,000 to 37,999	9,750
38,000 to 39,999	10,250
40,000 to 41,999	10,750
42,000 to 43,999	11,250
44,000 to 45,999	11,750
46,000 to 47,999	12,250
48,000 to 49,999	12,750
50,000 to 51,999	13,250
52,000 to 53,999	13,750
54,000 to 55,999	14,250
56,000 to 57,999	14,750
58,000 to 59,999	15,250

For vehicles having a fair market value in excess of $59,999, the Annual Lease Value is equal to: (0.25 times the fair market value of the automobile) plus $500.

*IRS table used to determine the amount of annual compensation to include as income, based upon the original fair market value of the automobile provided. Original fair market value consists of all amounts attributable to the purchase of an automobile, including sales tax and title fees as well as the purchase price. Special rules apply in determining fair market value for leased automobiles. So, consult with your tax adviser on these rules.

2. BUSINESS MILEAGE LOG

MONTH OF: _____

DATE	DESTINATION & PURPOSE	BUSINESS MILES	PERSONAL MILES	COMMUTE MILES	BUSINESS TOLLS/ PARKING
TOTAL					

ODOMETER READING—BEGINNING OF MONTH _____

ODOMETER READING—END OF MONTH _____

TOTAL MONTHLY MILES _____

3. INDIVIDUAL AMT SYSTEM AT A GLANCE

Regular Taxable Income
+/− Post-1986 depreciation
+/− Sale of depreciable assets
\+ Passive losses allowed by phase-in
\+ Research and development expenses
\+ Itemized deductions denied:

> State & local income taxes
> Real estate taxes
> Medical expenses not in excess of 10% of AGI
> Miscellaneous deductions
> Personal interest expense
> Excess home mortgage interest expense
> Excess investment interest expense
> or
> Standard deduction

\+ Preferences:

> Percentage depletion
> Intangible drilling costs
> Incentive stock options
> Net "private activity" bond interest
> Appreciated property contributions
> Pre-1987 depreciation on real property

− AMT net operating loss deduction

Alternative Minimum Taxable Income (AMTI)
\+ Personal exemption deduction
− AMT exemption deduction

AMTI Subject to AMT
× 21 percent

Tentative Minimum Tax Before Credits
− Foreign tax credits

Tentative Minimum Tax (TMT)
− Regular tax after foreign tax credits

Alternative Minimum Tax (AMT)

Tentative Minimum Tax Before Credits
- Foreign tax credits

Tentative Minimum Tax (TMT)
- Regular tax after foreign tax credits

Alternative Minimum Tax (AMT)

4. FORMULA FOR DETERMINING THE DOLLAR LIMITS OF DEDUCTIBLE IRA CONTRIBUTIONS*

Upper phase-out limit:

    Married filing jointly $50,000

    Married filing separately   10,000   _____

    Other returns   35,000

Less: Adjusted gross income before IRA

    deduction   (_____)

Equals: Amount under the upper phase-

    out limit (if zero or less, stop, no

    amount is deductible)   _____

Divide by $10,000

Equals: Percentage of the maximum

    contribution that can be deducted (not

    more than 100%)   _____%

Times $2,000 ($2,250 spousal)

Equals: Deductible limit before rounding

    and minimum limit   _____

(If the deductible limit is not an even

    multiple of $10, round up to the next

    $10)   _____

(If the deductible limit is less than $200,

    increase the amount to the minimum

    limit of $200)   _____

*The formula is used to determine deductible IRA contributions when a taxpayer (or spouse) is an active participant in a qualified retirement plan.

Index